Literature of the 1990s

The Edinburgh History of Twentieth-Century Literature in Britain
General Editor: Randall Stevenson

Published:
Vol. 1   *Literature of the 1900s: The Great Edwardian Emporium*
         Jonathan Wild
Vol. 3   *Literature of the 1920s: Writers Among the Ruins*
         Chris Baldick
Vol. 5   *Literature of the 1940s: War, Postwar and 'Peace'*
         Gill Plain
Vol. 6   *Literature of the 1950s: Good, Brave Causes*
         Alice Ferrebe
Vol. 9   *Literature of the 1980s: After the Watershed*
         Joseph Brooker
Vol. 10 *Literature of the 1990s: Endings and Beginnings*
         Peter Marks

Forthcoming:
Vol. 4   *Literature of the 1930s: Border Country*
         Rod Mengham
Vol. 8   *Literature of the 1970s: Things Fall Apart, Again*
         Simon Malpas

www.edinburghuniversitypress.com/series/tclb

Literature of the 1990s

Endings and Beginnings

Peter Marks

EDINBURGH
University Press

Edinburgh University Press is one of the leading university presses in the UK. We publish academic books and journals in our selected subject areas across the humanities and social sciences, combining cutting-edge scholarship with high editorial and production values to produce academic works of lasting importance. For more information visit our website: edinburghuniversitypress.com

© Peter Marks, 2018

Edinburgh University Press Ltd
The Tun – Holyrood Road, 12(2f) Jackson's Entry, Edinburgh EH8 8PJ

Typeset in 10.5/13 Adobe Sabon by
Servis Filmsetting Ltd, Stockport, Cheshire

A CIP record for this book is available from the British Library

ISBN 978 1 4744 1159 2 (hardback)
ISBN 978 1 4744 1160 8 (webready PDF)
ISBN 978 1 4744 1161 5 (epub)
ISBN 978 1 4744 5250 2 (paperback)

The right of Peter Marks to be identified as the author of this work has been asserted in accordance with the Copyright, Designs and Patents Act 1988, and the Copyright and Related Rights Regulations 2003 (SI No. 2498).

Contents

Acknowledgements		vi
General Editor's Preface		vii
	Introduction: Beginnings and Endings	1
1	United Kingdom?	21
2	New Ethnicities	46
3	Love in the Nineties	71
4	Class Resilience	95
5	Celebrity Culture	123
6	Rewriting the Past	150
7	Fantasiecle	174
	Conclusion: Endings and Beginnings	197
Bibliography		204
Index		211

Acknowledgements

I would like to thank Fiona Yardley for research assistance that suggested possibilities I would not otherwise have recognised.

General Editor's Preface

One decade is covered by each of the ten volumes in The Edinburgh History of Twentieth-Century Literature in Britain series. Individual volumes may argue that theirs is *the* decade of the century. The series as a whole considers the twentieth century as *the* century of decades. All eras are changeful, but the pace of change has itself steadily accelerated throughout modern history, and never more swiftly than under the pressures of political crises and of new technologies and media in the twentieth century. Ideas, styles and outlooks came into dominance, and were then displaced, in more and more rapid succession, characterising ever-briefer periods, sharply separated from predecessors and successors.

Time-spans appropriate to literary or cultural history shortened correspondingly, and on account not only of change itself, but its effect on perception. How distant, for example, that tranquil, sunlit, Edwardian decade already seemed, even ten years later, after the First World War, at the start of the twenties. And how essential, too, to the self-definition of that restless decade, and later ones, that the years 1900–1910 *should* seem tranquil and sunlit – as a convenient contrast, not necessarily based altogether firmly on ways the Edwardians may have thought of themselves. A need to secure the past in this way – for clarity and definition, in changeful times – encourages views of earlier decades almost as a hand of familiar, well-differentiated cards, dealt out, one by one, by prior times to the present one. These no longer offer pictures of kings and queens: King Edward VII, at the start of the century, or, briefly, George V, were the last monarchs to give their names to an age. Instead, the cards are marked all the more clearly by image and number, as 'the Twenties', 'the Thirties', 'the Forties' and so on. History itself often seems to join in the game, with so many epochal dates – 1918, 1929, 1939, 1968, 1979, 1989, 2001 – approximating to the end of decades.

By the end of the century, decade divisions had at any rate become a firmly established habit, even a necessity, for cultural understanding and analysis. They offer much virtue, and opportunity, to the present series. Concentration within firm temporal boundaries gives each volume further scope to range geographically – to explore the literary production and shifting mutual influences of nations, regions and minorities within a less and less surely 'United' Kingdom. Attention to film and broadcasting allows individual volumes to reflect another key aspect of literature's rapidly changing role throughout the century. In its early years, writing and publishing remained almost the only media for imagination, but by the end of the century, they were hugely challenged by competition from new technologies. Changes of this kind were accompanied by wide divergences in ways that the literary was conceived and studied. The shifting emphases of literary criticism, at various stages of the century, are also considered throughout the series.

Above all, though, the series' decade-divisions promote productive, sharply focused literary-historical analysis. Ezra Pound's celebrated definition of literature, as 'news that stays news', helps emphasise the advantages. It is easy enough to work with the second part of Pound's equation: to explain the continuing appeal of literature from the past. It is harder to recover what made a literary work news in the first place, or, crucially for literary history, to establish just how it related *to* the news of its day – how it digested, evaded or sublimated pressures bearing on its author's imagination at the time. Concentration on individual decades facilitates attention to this 'news'. It helps recover the brisk, chill feel of the day, as authors stepped out to buy their morning newspapers – the immediate, actual climate of their time, as well as the tranquillity, sunshine or cloud ascribed to it in later commentary. Close concentration on individual periods can also renew attention to writing that did *not* stay news – to works that, significantly, pleased contemporary readers and reviewers, and might repay careful re-reading by later critics.

In its later years, critics of twentieth-century writing sometimes concentrated more on characterising than periodising the literature they surveyed, usually under the rubrics of modernism or postmodernism. No decade is an island, entire of itself, and volumes in the series consider, where appropriate, broader movements and influences of this kind, stretching beyond their allotted periods. Each volume also offers, of course, a fuller picture of the writing of its times than necessarily selective studies of modernism and postmodernism can provide. Modernism and postmodernism, moreover, are thoroughly specific in their historical origins and development, and the nature of each can be usefully illumined by the close, detailed analyses the series provides. Changeful, tumultuous and challenging, history in the twentieth century perhaps pressed harder and more variously on literary imagination than ever before, requiring a literary history correspondingly meticulous, flexible and multifocal. This is what The Edinburgh History of Twentieth-Century Literature in Britain provides.

The idea for the series originated with Jackie Jones in Edinburgh University Press, and all involved are grateful for her vision and guidance, and for support from the Press, at every stage throughout.

Randall Stevenson
University of Edinburgh

This book is dedicated to Jo Watson and to Ella Marks, for reminding me about the important things.

Introduction: Beginnings and Endings

Geoffrey Howe was an unlikely political assassin. Portly and avuncular, his hair combed painstakingly into place, Howe had risen to serious political heights as Chancellor of the Exchequer (1979–83), Secretary of State for Foreign and Commonwealth Affairs (1983–9) and Deputy Prime Minister of Britain (1989–90). Over that long and highly successful journey he had acquired two qualities useful for any regicide: proximity to power and toxic resentment of his leader. Howe was not alone in harbouring these attributes, but his trusted place within the Conservative Party meant that few others had the lethal combination of access and motive. Even so, when he rose in Parliament on 1 November 1990, to deliver his resignation speech, few could have predicted the consequences. Howe began modestly and moderately, feigning 'astonishment that a quarter of a century has passed since I last spoke from one of the Back Benches'. Warming slowly to his task, he explained that he had decided to resign on matters of substance, the central element being Britain's economic relationship with Europe through the Exchange Rate Mechanism. From early on, though, the focus of his attack was manifest: Prime Minister Margaret Thatcher, doughty defender of British 'sovereignty'. Howe proposed that 'we commit a serious error if we think always in terms of surrendering "sovereignty" and seek to stand pat for all time on a given deal – by proclaiming, as my Right Honourable Friend the Prime Minster did two weeks ago, that we have "surrendered enough"'. In happier times, Howe had likened Thatcher to Joan of Arc, playing perhaps on the combination of her gender and her fighting spirit against formidable foe. Here, though, he presented an analogy with a markedly different gender inflection. Thatcher's recurring dismissal of economic integration with Europe, while Britain's Chancellor of the Exchequer (John Major) and Governor of the Bank of England (Sir Bernard King) were trying to bring about that very thing, was, Howe thought, 'rather like sending out your opening batsmen to the crease only for them to find, the moment the first balls are bowled, that their bats have been broken before the game by the team captain'.[1] It was ironic that Howe should employ a strikingly un-European sporting analogy to make his point about the need for closer ties with Europe. Odd, too, that it gestured back to the nineteenth-century world of Henry Newbolt's poem 'Vitaï Lampada', with its haunting, manly cry of 'play up, play up and play the game'. Listening stony-faced to this consciously personalised attack, Thatcher could not know that, partly as a result of Howe's speech, the most electorally successful British prime minister of the twentieth century would herself be making a resignation speech three weeks later. Indeed, on 21 November, when asked about her position after a leadership challenge, she had confidently vowed 'to fight on and fight to win'. In consulting her parliamentary colleagues, though, she found that she lacked sufficient support to continue as their leader. 'Thatcherism' lost its titular head and its most powerful spokesperson. While the 1990s would in many ways maintain and even build upon aspects of Thatcher's legacy, it would be in substantial ways a post-Thatcher decade.

John Major was an unlikely political victor. For several reasons: born into working class anonymity in South London, and without the Oxford degree characteristic of all post-Second World War prime ministers bar James Callaghan, Major seemed on first and on second sight not to have the political drive, connections, charisma or ruthlessness to claim the highest political office. True, Thatcher herself had in many ways been a marginal figure for the Conservatives at the outset, partly for being a woman in a party dominated by patriarchs, partly because her father was a Grantham grocer in a party historically dominated by so-called 'grandees'. She had, though, graduated from Oxford with a science degree, before marrying Dennis Thatcher, a millionaire businessman who funded her subsequent training as a barrister. These facts made her at least acceptable to the Tory establishment. For all that, her success in winning leadership of the Conservative Party in 1975 from Edward Heath caught many Conservative men, and perhaps some of the six other Conservative women then in the Commons, by surprise. Major represented a very different type of Conservative outsider, though, his father a former music hall performer with the memorably carnivalesque name of Thomas Major-Ball. Major-Ball had also sold garden ornaments. John Major left school at sixteen, working initially as a clerk, before taking a correspondence course in banking, an unlikely apprenticeship for a potential Conservative Party leader. Indeed, a Conservative poster for the 1992 election made much of Major's peculiar rise to eminence. Above a beaming photograph of Major ran a question in bold font:

'WHAT DOES THE CONSERVATIVE PARTY OFFER A WORKING CLASS KID FROM BRIXTON?' The answer was given beneath, in smaller font: 'THEY MADE HIM PRIME MINISTER'. And in far smaller font below that ran: 'No wonder John Major believes everyone should have an equal opportunity'. In fact, a rapid and unforeseen series of events propelled Major into office. Michael Heseltine, the extremely self-confident and nakedly ambitious former Secretary of State for Defence, had challenged Thatcher for the leadership, and polled well enough in the first ballot to force a second vote. This prompted a shocked and bitter Thatcher to withdraw, once sufficient colleagues had indicated their lack of support for her. Less than three hours after Thatcher announced her decision to resign, Home Secretary Douglas Hurd and Chancellor of the Exchequer John Major added their names to the list. Hurd, an Old Etonian and former Home Secretary, was seen as a 'safe pair of hands', a Conservative figure cut from traditional cloth. Major's candidacy, by contrast, was something of a surprise, as was his far better than expected second round victory against more credentialed rivals. Major polled so well in the second ballot that, although he did not secure an absolute majority, Hurd and Heseltine accepted they could not muster enough support, and so withdrew. Kenneth Baker's autobiography records Major's response to his rise from a new Cabinet member in 1987 to prime minister in 1990. Major began his first Cabinet meeting with the loaded rhetorical question: 'Well, who'd have thought it?' (Baker 1993: 427). Only a week earlier, the answer would have been: not many.

Tony Blair was both a likely political assassin and a political victor, although not necessarily within the Labour Party. His father, Leo, once a young communist who later supported the Conservatives, even considered running for parliament on the Tory ticket. Leo's son, Anthony (later the more casual Tony), boarded at Fettes College, the prestigious Edinburgh independent school, and studied law at Oxford, before joining the Labour Party and winning the safe northern England seat of Sedgefield at just thirty. Within five years Blair was in Neil Kinnock's Shadow Cabinet. After Labour's catastrophic showing in the 1992 elections, Kinnock's successor, John Smith, made him Shadow Home Secretary. When Smith himself died unexpectedly in May 1994, Blair's political ambition and strategic brain allowed him to outwit his main political rival, the fiercely intelligent and formidably aspiring Gordon Brown. Blair promised that if Brown would temper his own ambition and act as Chancellor of the Exchequer in a future Labour government, Blair would step aside after two elections in favour of Brown. Or so Brown and his supporters allege. Blair would always argue that no such deal was done, a vicious point of dispute that would create a tortured working relationship, which bled beyond the 1990s. Still, the rebranding of the party as New Labour, with a political manifesto titled *New Labour, New Life for Britain* in 1996, the relative youth and energy of its leadership team, and voter fatigue at a Conservative Party in office for more than a decade and a half, created the conditions for a Labour victory in 1997. Blair became the youngest prime minister in nearly two centuries. He would lead the party to two more victories, in 2001 and 2005, becoming its most successful electoral leader. He, like Thatcher, ultimately was brought down from within, though in this case by the most obvious assassin, Gordon Brown. Blair's demise would take place beyond the historical parameters of this study, which extend to 31 December 1999. On that last day of the 1990s, Blair was a robust, popular and politically impregnable figure. The decade of the nineties, one that started with political turmoil for the Conservatives, ended in political triumph for Blair and New Labour.

Assassination is a hyperbolic way of describing the toppling of political leaders in a parliamentary democracy. Perversely, through the 1990s, the person in Britain most vulnerable to actual assassination was a writer: Salman Rushdie. His novel *The Satanic Verses* had been published in 1988 to critical acclaim (winning the Whitbread Best Novel prize) and almost instant attack from sections of the Muslim community in Britain and beyond. *The Satanic Verses* was banned in India and South Africa, and burned publicly in Bradford in the late 1980s. Some Muslims regarded the book as a slur on Mohammed specifically and on their religion more generally. Because Islam is a global religion, the fury unleashed spread around the Muslim world, culminating in Iran's Ayatollah Khomeini issuing a fatwah, or formal opinion, in February 1989, calling on devout Muslims to kill Rushdie. Rushdie and his then-wife, the author Marianne Wiggins, immediately went into hiding. Rushdie adopted the pseudonym Joseph Anton, taking inspiration from Joseph Conrad and Anton Chekhov (Rushdie 2012). The worlds of literature and politics fused, Douglas Hurd announcing in February 1989 that the British government would not change blasphemy laws in response to Muslim demands. Geoffrey Howe observed in the *Daily Mail* that the death sentence 'illustrates the extreme difficulty establishing the right kind of relationship with the manifestly revolutionary regime with ideas that are very much its own' (Appignanesi and Maitland 1990: 78). The novel quickly become an international cause célèbre, a point of painful and, at times, literally deadly dispute. Repeatedly in the 1990s it tested British commitment to religious tolerance, multiculturalism and freedom of expression. A work that Rushdie saw as presenting a 'migrant's eye view of the world', that he felt sure 'celebrate[d] hybridity, impurity, intermingling, the transformation that comes of the new and unexpected combinations of human beings, culture, ideas, politics, movies, song' (Rushdie 1991: 394) was interpreted by millions around the world as naïvely insensitive at best and consciously provocative and blasphemous at worst.

The Rushdie Affair, as it became known, was in many ways unique, unrepresentative of the tenor of 1990s literature that this study examines critically. For one thing, *The Satanic Verses* was published in 1988, and so the interpretation of the novel rightly belongs to a study of 1980s literature; it receives just that treatment in one of the companion pieces to the current work, Joseph Brooker's *Literature of the 1980s: After the Watershed* (Brooker 2010: 168–71 especially). But the Rushdie Affair took several unexpected turns in the 1990s, not least when Rushdie published the declaration, 'Why I Have Embraced Islam', in 1990 (Rushdie 1991: 430–32). Rushdie later publicly uncoupled that embrace. A larger point obtains, that pressure waves initiated in the 1980s and earlier continued to influence the 1990s. The most obvious example is the fall of the Berlin Wall in November 1989, a precursor to the precipitous and surprising collapse of the Communist Party in Eastern Europe. For some, the 1990s began after the end of history itself. Francis Fukuyama's 1989 article 'The End of History?', published in *The National Interest*, an American magazine established by the neoconservative Irving Kristol, suggested the dawn of a transformative new era. 'What we are witnessing', Fukuyama observed,

> is not just the end of the Cold War, or the passing of a particular period of postwar history, but the end of history as such: that is, the endpoint of mankind's ideological evolution and the universalisation of liberal democracy as the final form of human government. (Fukuyama 1989: 4)

Fukuyama developed this thesis at length in his best-selling book *The End of History and the Last Man* (1992), by which time the question mark from the original article had disappeared. Time, however, has proven reports of the end of history to be greatly exaggerated.

Fukuyama's confidently presented argument offers a useful warning about interpreting historical periods. As the case of Salman Rushdie and *The Satanic Verses* proves, the literature produced in a particular decade cannot be ring-fenced from what comes before and after it. Still, focusing on a specific decade helps discern important trends and developments in a manageable time frame, to appreciate – borrowing loosely from Raymond Williams' terminology – dominant, residual and emergent forces. In a 1993 speech to the Conservative Group for Europe, for example, John Major argued that Britain's future belonged with that continent, rejecting the general thrust of Thatcher's opposition, while conjuring up a nostalgic Little Britain that he hoped would endure. As Christopher Hitchens noted, in a speech 'to reassure a Conservative audience in April 1993' Major reiterated a commitment to the theory and practice of the 'European', before insisting that

> Fifty years from now Britain will still be the country of long shadows on county grounds, warm beer, invincible green suburbs, dog lovers and pool fillers, and – as George Orwell said – 'old maids bicycling to Holy Communion through the morning mist' and – if we get our way – Shakespeare still read in schools. Britain will survive unamendable in all essentials.
>
> Mr Major thought well enough of this trope to include it in his autobiography. (Hitchens 2002: 117)

Against this nostalgic, regressive vision, a few years later the new Labour leader Tony Blair would proclaim a New Labour party, freed from the shackles of its own history and forging confidently into the future. In 1995, Labour revised Clause IV in its constitution, a clause that since 1918 had called for the party to secure for workers the means of production, distribution and exchange. Blair was not alone in wanting such a change, Tudor Jones noting that, 'by 1994 [Neil Kinnock] was prepared to admit that he no longer believed "that Clause IV is an adequate definition of modern democratic socialism"' (Jones 1996: 134). Brown also quotes Blair's October 1994 address to the Labour Party Conference in Blackpool, where Blair 'Without directly mentioning Clause IV ... promised that he and [Deputy Leader John] Prescott would shortly present a clear, up-to-date statement of the objects and objectives of our Party' (139). New writing was on the wall, Blair taking Labour away from reversing the privatisation of industries that many Labour voters felt was among the worst aspects of Thatcherism.

Yet New Labour was instrumental in the devolution of political power, so that by the end of the 1990s there were independent national assemblies in Scotland, Wales and Northern Ireland. At the beginning of 1990, when Margaret Thatcher was still prime minister, such changes would have seemed impossibly radical. Devolution reflected the release of new energies that characterised the 1990s socially, politically and culturally. The decade saw the rise to ascendancy of Young British Artists, figures such as Damian Hirst, Rachel Whiteread and Tracey Emin; the grubby exuberance of Britpop and the tailored Girl Power of the Spice Girls; and, in popular literature, the creation of 'Chick Lit' with Bridget Jones and the revival of children's fantasy through the Harry Potter series. The 1990s was also the decade of Irvine Welsh's *Trainspotting* and In-Yer-Face Theatre, a consciously provocative drama that took some of its impetus from the aesthetics of avant-garde European theatre, exploring what some saw as a post-emotional state of being created by the political and ethical emptiness of neoliberal and neoconservative times. In-Yer-Face Theatre subjected audiences to the confrontational themes and approaches of young playwrights such as Sarah Kane (*Blasted*) and Mark Ravenhill (*Shopping and Fucking*). The title of Ravenhill's play provoked controversy in itself, while the *Daily Mail* called *Blasted* 'This disgusting piece of filth' (quoted in Urban 2011: 65). That the work of Welsh, Kane and Ravenhill (and they were not alone) was first produced while John Major was still prime minister reveals how the literature of the 1990s not merely reflected changing values and circumstances, but at times predated or initiated them. Britain projected a new cultural confidence in the 1990s, a vitality and variety at odds with Major's lament for an irretrievable past.

While Fukuyama professed to divine the end of history, Britain in the 1990s was home to a range of invigorating beginnings. Some developed in ways that transformed the cultural habitat; others, more artificial or superficial, would fade away. The Poetry Society, for example, foregrounded the work of twenty young poets in 1994 in its journal *The Poetry Review*, labelling them the 'New Generation Poets'. In some ways this was a branding exercise smacking of a consumerist mentality, poetry's response to the literary journal *Granta*'s successful 'Best Young British Novelists' campaign a year earlier. That in itself was a follow-up to *Granta*'s 1983 list of such novelists, one that had publicised young figures such as Martin Amis and Salman Rushdie who soon would command the heights of British literature. The 'New Generation Poets' included figures less well known to the public, not surprising given poetry's lower profile, but the likes of Carol Ann Duffy (later Poet Laureate) and Simon Armitage (later Oxford Professor of Poetry) were given the oxygen of publicity by the promotion. While the *Vogue* photo shoot the poets endured was indicative of a certain weakness for glamour that characterised the 1990s, the writers themselves were lauded for their demotic language, their regional backgrounds, their concern with ordinary existence, and the fact that most of them had not gone to the traditional academies for aspiring British poets, Oxford and Cambridge. But if the 'New Generation Poets' campaign itself did not generate quite the sustained group awareness aimed for, it did for a brief while foreground individuals who would later establish themselves in the nation's imaginative cortex. Another manifestation of 1990s newness, one stemming from a perceived crisis in heterosexual masculinity, was the roughly simultaneous rise of the 'New Lad' and the 'New

Man'. The former was a negative reaction to the feminist challenge, a negativity embodied in soft-core porn magazines such as *Loaded* (first published in 1994) and *Maxim* (1995) that celebrated a juvenile mix of football, lager and misogyny. The older 'New Man', by contrast, was responsive to feminism, actively reconfiguring his attitudes and actions to evolving social norms and situations. Both of these positions were still works-in-progress at the decade's end, revealing slower-paced negotiations over gender relationships. New Labour sought to present itself as agile and progressive, open-minded and forward thinking, and it says much for its success that the 1990s is often remembered as the Tony Blair decade. In reality, John Major remained prime minister from 1990 to June 1997. Hindsight would also read Blair through the lenses of his twenty-first-century failings over the Iraq War, and the prolonged and disastrous handover of power to Gordon Brown, among other negatives. While Blair is now seen as a tarnished and much-diminished figure, it is worth remembering that in the 1990s he was generally thought of, nationally and internationally, as the youthful embodiment of a revived and confident Britain.

This study considers the literary output of the decade through seven thematically oriented chapters that aim to deal with changing notions of nationhood; ethnicity; sexuality and gender; class; celebrity culture; history; and speculative fiction. Interpreting fiction, drama and poetry – with occasional detours into representative films and music – it concentrates on emerging writers who give the decade much of its distinctive colour and flavour. But where pertinent it also situates those writers and their output in relation to established artists, movements and trends. The chapters aim to work interactively and cumulatively to present the 1990s as a decade in which new relations of cultural and political power were fashioned. These changes are examined within an environment when both political and cultural power devolved away from the traditional centres, London most obviously, even as economic power was pulled inexorably towards the nation's capital. London still remained an artistic powerhouse and a magnet for aspiring writers and artists, but areas, and indeed nations, that had formerly been seen as marginal or had been marginalised increasingly produced important cultural artefacts that did not require London's or, at the national level, England's imprimatur. The renaissance in Scottish literature that had begun in the 1980s, for example, continued and was enhanced substantially in the following decade. Established figures such as James Kelman, whose novel *How Late It Was, How Late*, won the Booker Prize in 1994, shared the stage with exciting newcomers such as A. L. Kennedy and Irvine Welsh. Wales established 'The Wales Book of the Year' award in

1992 to celebrate the best Welsh and English language works in fiction and literary criticism by Welsh or Welsh interest authors, a signal of Welsh cultural confidence and of the amount of quality literature being produced. Northern Ireland also experienced something of a literary revival as the massive weight of the Troubles was lifted, or at least lightened. Writing from what had been seen as peripheral places or groups was increasingly understood as reflecting nations in the process of positive transformation. While these changes slowly took effect over the decade, and while the Britain of 1999 was dramatically different from that of 1990, they were never systematic or inevitable, taking place in an environment where culturally and politically conservative forces continued to operate. By dealing with key themes that concerned and animated writers of the decade, this book aims to provide a synoptic account of that overall change. Naturally, no single-volume account can hope to be comprehensive, but the vivid assortment of literature interpreted in each chapter has been chosen to display the energised diversity characterising the 1990s.

The question mark in the title of Chapter 1, 'United Kingdom?', suggests the changing and often contested sense of Britain that marked the decade as a whole, politically instantiated in the three new national assemblies operating by 1999. While not quite the dismantling of Britain prophesied from the 1970s by Tom Nairn, initially in *The Break-up of Britain: Crisis and Neo-nationalism* (Nairn 1977), these developments registered a consequential political shakeup that would have seemed improbable while John Major was in power. The possibility of devolution set out in Labour's 1992 manifesto helped to reactivate nationalist passion in parliamentary terms (especially in Scotland), leading to broader contestations throughout the decade of what 'British' and 'Britain' meant, and, consequently, what it might mean to be that peculiar, antiquated term, a 'Briton', to which so few swore allegiance. These questions were not peculiar to the 1990s. They were, however, asked within a shifting world where John Major's comforting idyll of a 1940s England taken from George Orwell seemed hopelessly outdated. Questions were asked about the relevance of the monarchy itself. Simultaneously, phenomena such as the Young British Artists, Britpop and Cool Britannia, while often more mesmerised by alluring surfaces and catchy labels than with substance, seemed to reflect a revitalised cultural scene attuned to national labels. The question was: which nation? For as well as mandated political devolution, an informal but undeniable cultural devolution took place in the 1990s. In a similar manner to the dispersal of power away from London, cultural power also moved actively away from the centre. This process had already begun in Scotland in the 1980s, with the work of writers such as Agnes Owen, James Kelman and Alasdair Gray, whose 1982 novel *Lanark: A Book in Four Lives* 'broke' Scottish literature on the international stage. But the 1990s saw a noticeable acceleration of this process, the result of a critical mass of literary talent and a confidence derived from internal support mechanisms and external validation through publishing houses, sales, reviews and literary prizes.

The older generation continued to produce work of genuine quality, Kelman's *How Late It Was, How Late* a real (if, admittedly, controversial) talisman. But younger writers such as A.L. Kennedy, Irvine Welsh, Alan Warner and Iain M. Banks, writers who explored new, contemporary territory, gave literary voice and representation to young Scots and to others – in some of Banks's novels, to aliens. In doing so they challenged the traditional dominance of English models and representations. The developments were not so sustained or widespread in Wales or in Northern Ireland, but Chapter 1 examines how writers such as the poet Gwyneth Lewis in Wales and the novelist Robert McLiam Wilson in Northern Ireland dealt with and represented realities of life in parts of Britain far from the centrifugal power centre of London. One tangible marker of change was the ways in which forms of language other than Standard English increasingly were understood as valid and (nearly as importantly) commercially viable. Again, in Scotland, writers such as Owen, Gray and Kelman had paved the way in the 1980s, but the new generation, epitomised by Irvine Welsh, substantially expanded the range of Scottish voices 'heard' in literature. Not, it should be noted, that all Scottish writers invoked the demotic, one of the signal aspects of 1990s literature being multiplicity. Gwyneth Lewis, who published in Welsh and in English, actively investigated in her poetry the complex intersections, pressures and distinctions between the languages in a decade where the Welsh Language Act was passed (in 1993) and in which prizes for the Wales Book of the Year were established. These 'local' innovations demonstrate a degree of independence and assurance, and while it is important not to overplay the degree of change that took place in the 1990s, it is also critical to register what was achieved.

The quotation at the start of Chapter 1 indicates the complexities and contradictions built into the notion of the United Kingdom. It comes from Welsh's *Trainspotting* (1993), where the central character, Mark Renton, laments that the Scots are 'wretched, servile, pathetic trash' who are 'colonised by wankers' (78). This firmly held view openly rebuts the romantically appealing if reductive notion that Scotland (and, one might think, by extension, Wales) was united against what some saw as its internal coloniser, England. Mel Gibson's Tartan Western, *Braveheart*

(1995), simplistically prosecutes a case that Renton actively rejects. The question mark in the chapter's title points to the problematic question of nationhood that became critical to the decade, a question that would not go away after 1999, even with devolution that in part was invoked to hold the component parts of the United Kingdom together on the basis of mutual respect. In terms of Britain as a whole, Renton's position that the English colonised the smaller nations constituting the United Kingdom overlooks the complicated situation in Northern Ireland, English anxieties about English identity and the problematic question of Britain's own colonial past in terms of its former Empire. What complicates things even further is that Renton's rage is directed less at the English colonisers than at his own countrymen and women for being pathetic enough to be colonised. '"Ah don't hate the English"', he rages, '"They just git oan wi the shite thuv goat. I hate the Scots"' (78). Renton's caustic appraisal of his own people cautions against simple, self-deceiving nationalism. As if to underline the complicated timelines created by internal and external colonialism, Britain's long decline from imperial might was underscored humiliatingly by the handover of Hong Kong in 1997 to China.

Chapter 2, 'New Ethnicities', deals with the sometimes visibly changing face of Britain, a process that had been taking place for decades, but that in the 1990s gained a greater momentum. It is critical not to over-egg developments. As with the changing conception of nationhood in Britain, residual forces did not disappear, nor was long-standing racism consigned to history's dustbin. That said, in April 2001 British Foreign Secretary Robin Cook made the claim that chicken tikka masala was Britain's national dish. Whether factually true or not, the statement suggested an officially acknowledged and positively assessed culinary development. The New Labour government would help to celebrate the fiftieth anniversary of the arrival of the SS *Empire Windrush* from the Caribbean, which in 1948 had carried passengers from the Commonwealth eager to make their mark on and in the colonial 'motherland'. While largely unheralded at the time it arrived, the *Empire Windrush* now is generally understood as a key moment in the modern development of Britain. Not all aspects of the rethinking of ethnicity were positive, as the Rushdie Affair proved, but through the decade an increasingly heterogeneous Britain not so much emerged as simply presented itself openly and confidently. There was an undeniable cultural impact on British literature in the decade for writers who until the 1990s were still more likely to be grouped under what seemed a monolithic and perhaps derogatory term, 'black'. This chapter traces how during the decade that term became, in Paul Gilroy's words, 'multi-accentual' (cited in Proctor 2002: 318), only one – admittedly important – identifying signifier among many. Stuart Hall detected an important movement to 'new ethnicities' (Hall 1990), where earlier forms of alienation and marginalisation gave way to the possibility of a transformed, hybridic Britain. Only the possibility, though; real and lasting improvement and changes required ongoing negotiations about selfhood and belonging in relation to the national consciousness as a whole. Writers played their part in these cultural interactions by producing myriad narratives that collectively spoke to the lived experiences of migrants and their descendants, and which dramatised both the aspiration to be accepted primarily as British, and the real and concealed barriers to that aspiration.

Personal, political and historical ties with other nations were not, however, severed. If some of the reconsiderations of national identity examined in Chapter 1 were inward-looking, those by the writers examined in this chapter, such as Rushdie, Caryl Phillips, David Dabydeen and Moniza Alvi, were consciously and inquisitively connective, diasporic. The chapter understands developments in the 1990s as part of what Bruce King called the 'internationalization' (King 2004) of British literature, a process that had been taking place, though at a much slower pace, for decades. Which is not to pretend that problems of race and ethnicity had been resolved, real instances such as the murder of the young Londoner Stephen Lawrence in 1993 making plain the combative forces at work. The chapter examines these tensions in the work of the writers mentioned above, as well as in the poetry of Jackie Kay and the writing of Hanif Kureishi. What emerges are complex, tentative and sometimes contradictory dynamics both within and between real and what Benedict Anderson famously described as 'imagined communities' (Anderson 1983), influenced by generational, gender, class, religious, national and ethnic differences. The writers of the 1990s reflect upon renegotiated power arrangements in which 'black' characters are not simply integrated into the British community following an earlier period of alienation post-arrival in Britain, but increasingly are seen contributing to, and commenting critically about, the ongoing development of that community. The chapter strives not to paint an idealised picture at odds with the reality of social conditions, nor suggest that such literature existed on an equal footing with traditional writing in terms of its audience or its critical reception. Examples such as the television hit *Goodness Gracious Me!* or Kureishi's *The Buddha of Suburbia* record the often-unwitting humour generated by an interactive community in transition.

Chapter 3, 'Love in the Nineties', borrows its title and its epigraph from the song 'Girls and Boys', by one of the quintessential Britpop bands of the 1990s, Blur. The band's upbeat homage to the pleasures and perils of love in the nineties also addresses in semi-comic tones the complicated sexual politics of the period. When John Major called for a national move 'back to basics', one that celebrated traditional values of self-discipline and responsibility, he exposed the contradiction between the economic liberalism that was the mark of his government's policies and an entrenched and regressive social conservatism in line with its buttoned-down facade. Major's admission that he tucked his shirt into his underpants was taken as an unwitting but nevertheless devastating admission of sexual repression (making his later admission that he had had an affair with his Conservative colleague, Edwina Currie, all the more startling). The complexities of British gender politics and its treatment of sexuality in the 1990s can be seen in multifarious cultural responses: the problematic 'post-feminism' of the Spice Girls and Bridget Jones; the corresponding rise of 'laddism', exemplified in the prolonged adolescence glorified in the television series *Men Behaving Badly* and Nick Hornby's emotionally retarded Rob Fleming in *High Fidelity*; the homoerotic posturing of Dan and Larry in Patrick Marber's play *Closer*; Alan Hollinghurst's evocation of contemporary gay sexuality in *The Folding Star*; the exuberant exploration of sensuality by Jeanette Winterson in *Written on the Body*; the sustained and purposely shocking sexual aggression in plays by Sarah Kane and Mark Ravenhill, and Carol Ann Duffy's sharp representations of the complexities of married life from the perspective of the too-often-silent wife. Blur's wry observations about the breakdown or blurring of sexual and gender markers illustrated forces that, if not novel in the 1990s, was certainly more prevalent than ever before.

The 1990s saw the emergence of a New Brutalism in the theatre's depiction of sexuality and gender politics. Works such as *Blasted*, *Closer* and *Shopping and Fucking* depicted anal rape, masturbation, virtual sex, fellatio and beatings along a continuum that included suicide, cannibalism and attempts at self-strangulation. Many of these acts were performed or assessed with a disturbing lack of affect, or treated as part of overt and intense struggles for physical and psychological dominance. Paradoxically, the decade also was one in which romantic novels commanded a third of the paperback market. One of its iconic characters was Bridget Jones, whose hopeless, self-hating efforts to secure a man seemed indicative to some of the failure of feminist ideals such as independence and self-fashioning. Her male equivalent, Rob Fleming, from *High Fidelity*, proved equally inept in his quest for love, part of what was seen as an international crisis of heterosexual masculinity among Western men. Gay men endured the ongoing stigma of AIDS in a Britain where Section 28 of the Local Government Act of 1988 prohibited the promotion of homosexuality by schools and other government-run institutions. The absurdity of this law (a hangover from the Thatcher years, but not repealed until 2003) was confirmed with the dropping of the age of consent for homosexuals from twenty-one to eighteen in 1994, still higher than that for heterosexuals. The call for a more generous attitude to love by some of the key writers and musicians of the 1990s was reflected in some of the decade's most successful films, including the Mike Newell comedy *Four Weddings and a Funeral* (1994), in which a homosexual pair is accepted as the model loving couple, and Neil Jordan's far more confronting drama *The Crying Game* (1992), in which the complexities of sexuality are read through the seemingly intractable politics of Northern Ireland.

Chapter 4, 'Class Resilience', investigates the depiction of the working class and its relationship to one of the great myths of the decade: the aspiration for, or the reality of, a classless society. Propounded by both Major and Blair, but enacted by neither, the mistaken belief that a classless society was either achievable or desired was dismantled in the 1990s, where inequality increased rather than decreased. The Conservative Party could portray John Major as the embodiment of a successful rise from the working class to the highest office in the land, but Major's success was unique, rather than representative, the reality of social mobility being nothing like the rhetoric. This was recognised in the lived experience of British people, so that in one survey, over 80 per cent of respondents felt that class warfare was still operative (Adonis and Pollard 1997: 3). Inherent in the top-down argument was the need to dissolve the working class, or to absorb it 'up', a view captured in Deputy Leader of the Labour Party John Prescott's declaration, 'We're all middle class now', something that, Owen Jones later wrote, 'would be more fitting if he had been talking about his fellow politicians' (Jones 2011: 29). The fact that Prescott was a former union official measured the degree of bad faith required to accept the statement. Literary commentators such as Dominic Head record the decline of literature interested in class in the latter part of the twentieth century, and while this no doubt is the case, especially compared with the high-water marks of the 1950s and 1960s, class was neither discarded nor transcended, politically or culturally. Indeed, it morphed beyond the usual accounts of industrial hardship (though this was still addressed) to consider the lives of temporarily employed young Scottish girls like Alan Warner's Morvern Callar, or Kim, the sex worker in Carol Ann Duffy's poem 'Making Money'. The working class did not disappear, no matter the hopes and expectations of some. What seemed consistent was the workers' clear-eyed understanding that social and economic structures and processes were not configured in their favour.

More than simply survive, some of them even prosper, even if only temporarily. So, Chuckie Lurgan, in Robert McLiam Wilson's *Eureka Street: A Novel of Ireland Like No Other* makes a quick fortune in Belfast by selling low-grade giant dildos, while Jean, in John Godber's play about a northern England couple, the ironically titled *Lucky Sods*, wins the National Lottery multiple times. Mark Renton in *Trainspotting*, who signs on the dole under assumed names in Scotland and England to maintain his heroin habit, flees Britain after ripping off his friends after a drug deal, while the eponymous Morvern Callar strips her dead boyfriend's bank account to finance an extended spree in Europe. At the other end of the social scale, Sammy Samuels, in *How Late It Was, How Late*, like his Glaswegian counterpart, the unemployed alcoholic Joe Kavanagh, in Ken Loach's film *My Name is Joe* (1993), or Bob and Anne in Loach's *Raining Stones* (1993), are almost permanently struggling to survive and to stay ahead of the repossession men and within the legal norms of society. Jake Jackson acts as a Belfast repo man in *Eureka Street*, a role he abhors, but one that allows him a clear view of the economic determinants of society and the penalties built into late twentieth-century consumerism that he is tasked to inflict. As he notes, sardonically, 'they bought on, unsurprisingly. They were still allowed to purchase, to consume. They shored themselves up with comfort goods. They'd committed the crime of wanting what they could not have and they all came quietly' (Wilson 2015: 64). Across a range of financial circumstances and geographical locations, writers and filmmakers in the 1990s turned sharp and critical eyes upon lives of the working class, whose resilience in the face of a system loaded against them was mapped with precision and empathy.

Chapter 5, 'Celebrity Culture', broadens considerations of purely literary celebrity to consider cultural celebrity generally, for the decade of Princess Diana, Posh and Becks, and the Rushdie Affair witnessed the full flowering of celebrity culture in Britain. Some of the general dynamics at work seriously influenced what was published, and how it was sold and consumed. Despite jeremiads about the death of the book, such as Sven Birkerts' *The Gutenberg Elegies: The Fate of Reading in an Electronic Age* (1994), the 1990s in fact would see the revival of literature in Britain, especially popular literature. The most obvious, though unlikely, success proved to be the unprecedented and unexpected triumph of J. K. Rowling's stories about a young wizard, which catapulted her from single mum to reluctant international icon. The Potter books also helped to uncover a figure pronounced lost – the child reader. But even Rowling's literary celebrity paled next to that of Princess Diana, whose confected fairy tale life exemplified a glamour to which the decade seemed enthralled. One artistic group fully and at times unashamedly engaged with such superficiality, the Young British Artists, especially its undeclared leader, the *enfant terrible*, Damien Hirst. Hirst's brash, iconoclastic vitality was fused with a canny mercantilism that plundered art for gold, and gold for art. Yet, as Diana found, celebrity had its drawbacks, one of the literary victims of the 1990s being Martin Amis, whose outrageous and never-to-be-recovered advance for his 1995 novel *The Information* that he supposedly used to repair his teeth, made him, temporarily, a hate figure and a poster boy for the 'greed is good' mantra still echoing from Oliver Stone's 1987 film, *Wall Street*. Amis was also connected, via his father, Kingsley, with the scandal surrounding the publication of the racist and misogynist letters of Kingsley's friend, Philip Larkin. The magic wand of celebrity could transform instantly into a double-edged sword.

One of the more serious literary aspects of celebrity that preceded the 1990s but was substantially boosted during it was the commodification of prestige materialised in lucrative book prizes. The chapter examines the most famous and often the most controversial of these, the Booker Prize, exploring its considerable power to confer publicity and literary status on writers and texts. While clearly a vital part of literary celebrity in modern Britain, prizes can also be damaged by controversy, as can the writers and texts drawn into the cultural vortex such controversy can generate. Scandals such as the view by one Booker judge that *How Late It Was, How Late* was 'unreadably bad',[2] or that Graham Swift's *Last Orders* might carry the taint of plagiarism, or that Ian McEwan's Booker-winning *Amsterdam* was not particularly good, not only provided tabloid and 'posh' press fodder, but also called into question the point of prizes generally. These sometimes were seen merely to be part of the rituals required for the bestowal of cultural capital on the winner, and, in a virtuous circle, on the prize itself. That the Booker was run by a food company, rather than, as many a punter might think, somehow connected to the book trade, only underscored the whiff of venality behind the pomp and circumstance. The Booker was not the only prize available, the chapter acknowledging the importance of the Orange Prize, established in the 1990s to celebrate women's writing, itself a somewhat controversial move. The publicity activated by a prize can bring unwanted, as well as wished-for, attention: Ted Hughes's award of the Forward Poetry Prize for his collection *Birthday Letters*, which surveyed his tortured relationship with Sylvia Plath, placed it firmly in the public arena. It seems reasonable to think, though, that the publication of poems anatomising at length one of the great celebrity literary couples of the twentieth century would always have drawn partisan crowds.

Birthday Letters did much to resurrect a problematic past, while it simultaneously presented one contentious interpretation of events. Chapter 6, 'Rewriting the Past', assesses the rude health of historical literature in an age characterised by Fukuyama as inaugurating the end of history. Just to complicate matters, the 1990s was a decade in which postmodern history was claiming the attention, and sometimes the contempt, of British historians. Postmodern scholars argued that the field of history itself was more akin to creative literature than to a methodologically rigorous social science; traditional historians defended traditional methodology. Creative writers themselves approached their respective time frames from any number of angles to any number of purposes. Some aimed to recreate the past with due reverence and reference to actual events, while others invented historical events that they conveyed with a vivid and detailed realism. Writers linked the past to a later awareness (or lack of awareness) of the past, or playfully explored the limitations of the historical writing itself, employing and parodying the conventions of traditional history, or literary history. Hindsight proves that history (even in a Hegelian sense invoked by Francis Fukuyama) did not end with the collapse of the Eastern Bloc from 1989 onwards and the victory of Western liberal democracy. But one of the enduring elements of 1990s literature was its concern with history as the decade, century and millennium came to their synchronous close. Historical fiction necessarily explored the past, but in a decade more than usually interested in history, such work was also searched for what the past might reveal about the present.

A brief selection of texts considered at greater length in Chapter 6 provides an overview of the variety and creativity employed. Some were experimental in a metafictional sense, as with Martin Amis's *Time's Arrow*, where time advances backwards with disturbing implications, tracking the life of an ageing American doctor back to his problematic past performing Nazi experiments on innocent patients during the Second World War. Pat Barker's First World War *Regeneration* trilogy, one of the decade's most acclaimed historical narratives, utilises a relatively conventional structure, along with documents real and otherwise, and fictional as well as actual characters, to construct a complex group portrait of the war's psychological effects. It considers not only the combatants but also those charged to 'cure' their mental illnesses, if only so the latter can send the former back to war. Sebastian Faulks's *Birdsong* also deals with the First World War, but creates a larger historical frame, allowing readers to move back before the war and forward to a time close to, but not identical with, the present in which the novel was published. This structure provides for varying degrees of comprehension and proximity, creating a more tentative position for the reader that requires consideration of the process of interpreting history. Adam Thorpe's *Ulverton* is more ludic, focusing not just on time but also on a town, Ulverton, over four centuries. Each chapter has its own narrative mode, foregrounding the variety of documents by which history is transmitted, but also hinting at the inadequacies and partiality of those documents. As with so many 1990s historical texts, readers are encouraged and indeed required to reflect on their interpretive assumptions and processes. A. S. Byatt's *Possession* takes this idea even further, though in another direction, by making her major characters literary scholars piecing together a historical narrative whose plot lines and endpoint they do not know. Byatt employs literary scholarship (she was herself a literary academic) to build a plausible set of 'real' Victorian characters and documents that form the primary material for her contemporary literary critics, intertwining elements of detective, Gothic and romance genres to fashion an intricate and powerfully persuasive portrait of the past. Yet *Possession* is also a subtle and complex puzzle about the difficulties, if not the impossibility, of knowing that past.

This book argues that the 1990s as a whole was marked by an energised variety, an active dispersal of imaginative power that reflected a revitalised, confident and exploratory Britain. Chapter 7, 'Fantasiecle', explores critical aspects of this speculative power. As the World Wide Web opened up the possibility of virtual worlds and identities, advances in science such as chaos theory, that appear fantastic and assaulted our common sense, prompted imaginative writers to explore their almost unimaginable implications. At the same time, the success of Harry Potter and its ilk brought back older models of fantasy that deployed wands rather than lasers, flying brooms rather than flying saucers. The Harry Potter series helped to revive children's fantasy, elevating it to a worldwide phenomenon that fed traditional elements and tropes of British social and cultural life into the global mind. The same was true of a different order of culture in the hugely successful film *Shakespeare in Love*, which tapped audiences' knowledge of the Bard while playfully dismantling the aura associated with him, and indulging in an examination of the mysterious power of literature (specifically, theatre) to represent and help audiences understand the human condition through immersion in the fantastic. Salman Rushdie would attempt something similar in *The Moor's Last Sigh*, his intricate, multilayered assemblage of narratives centred on and told by a character destined to live his life at twice the normal rate. This personalised and perilous form of time travel gestures to the realm of science fiction, a realm inhabited by Iain M. Banks's *Excession*, part of his ongoing Culture series. The tendency for science fiction to run in series links *Excession* to Gwyneth Jones's *White Queen*, the first of her White Queen trilogy. But where the main action of *Excession* occupies the skies and involves malevolent aliens who threaten the Culture, *White Queen* primarily is set on Earth. Its essentially benign aliens, the Aleutians, who have arrived by accident, take over not by massive superiority in technology, but through superior social structures and more flexible identities. Even so, their arrival constitutes a futuristic form of colonisation, one that generates both acceptance and resistance.

Where *Excession* and *White Queen* fit unproblematically into the genre of science fiction, one criticism of some pieces of nineties fiction was that they were obsessed by science, incorporating lengthy scientific explanations that unsettled or occluded their narratives. Chapter 7 provides evidence to support that criticism in relation to two highly inventive texts, Jeanette Winterson's novel *Gut Symmetries*, and Tom Stoppard's play *Arcadia*. Both deploy elements of chaos theory into their narratives, two of the three main characters in *Gut Symmetries* being physicists, while there is one in *Arcadia*. The chapter argues, though, that in both cases the use of particle physics is not arbitrary, but is central to the major concerns of each work. Of the two, *Arcadia* integrates its bedazzling science in a far more sophisticated and entertaining way, partly because the nature of theatre (certainly of the type that Stoppard writes) allows for extended explanations performed as dialogue that is amenable to question, repetition and further explication. Essentially, as well, *Arcadia* benefits from Stoppard's humorous and intellectually impressive awareness of some of the implication of chaos theory. The play is a comedy of ideas in which both comedy and ideas are complex and self-aware. *Gut Symmetries* is rather more earnest and insistent in driving its main points home. Both works make the otherwise fantastic and bewildering theories digestible and illuminating, tribute to the spiritedly erudite quality of British creative writing in the last decade of the twentieth century.

The book's conclusion, 'Endings and Beginnings', looks back briefly over the decade, noting the salient points of difference between Thatcher's Britain and that of Blair's, while registering the continuities. It celebrates an outstanding period of literary experimentation and innovation, one that built substantially on the advances of the 1980s, so that writers who had emerged and quickly dominated that decade such as James Kelman, Salman Rushdie, Jeanette Winterson and Martin Amis played their parts in a more diverse and dynamic cultural scene. The decade had its failures and its false dawns (Cool Britannia; New Labour) but it also heralded genuine new talents and perspectives (Sarah Kane and A. L. Kennedy, Gwyneth Jones and Irvine Welsh, among many others). In Ian McEwan's 2005 novel, *Saturday*, written soon after the horrors of 11 September 2001, McEwan has his protagonist, neurosurgeon Henry Perowne, muse that 'the nineties are looking like an innocent decade' (32). Retrospection often allows this rather dismissive type of assessment, so that the first decade of the twenty-first century itself might now seem equally as innocent, and perhaps far more dangerously so. Likewise, we now know that the fears generated in the late 1990s that the prospect of the Millennium Bug might bring the cybernetic world to a close, as well as the hopes manufactured by the Millennium Dome, would prove illusory. What the book concludes, however, is that the 1990s was a decade of substantive literary, social and political invention and transformation, and that while certain established forces remained, emerging energies powered a long cultural devolution whose effects influenced the decade to come.

Notes

1. Available at <http://www.britpolitics.co.uk/speeches-sir-geoffrey-howe-resignation> (last accessed 16 August 2016).
2. Available at <http://www.nytimes.com/1994/11/29/books/in-furor-over-prize-novelist-speaks-up-for-his-language.html> (last accessed 18 August 2016).

Chapter One

United Kingdom?

Fuckin failures in a country ay failures. It's nae good blamin it oan the English fir colonising us. Ah don't hate the English. They're just wankers. We're colonised by wankers. We can't even pick a decent, vibrant, healthy culture to be colonised by. (Welsh 1993: 78)

Post-war Britain has long been seen as a nation in decline: the loss of imperial territory and international clout from 1945 onwards undeniable and inexorable facts that exposed the fantasy that Britain remained a Great Power. That fantasy was still viable during conferences at Yalta and Potsdam in 1945 that set the boundaries for a new, Cold War, geography. The Suez Crisis of 1956 is an oft-recited marker of decline, exposing the myth of British imperial reach, and prompting US Secretary of State's Dean Acheson's crushing evaluation that Great Britain had lost an Empire but had not yet found a role. The 1980s might be read as slowing the pace of decline, the Thatcher government under its forthright, pro-American leader attempting to re-establish Britain's credentials on the world stage. Partly this was plausible because of the close personal relationship between Thatcher and US President Ronald Reagan, whose 1984 'It's Morning Again In America' election campaign, with its highly romanticised, faux-folksy celebration of traditional values and optimism, signalled a drive to re-establish American pre-eminence after the bruising years of the Carter administration. There was no equivalent upbeat electoral message from the Conservatives, although their 1979 slogan, 'Don't just hope for a better life. Vote for one', was a muted attempt at imitation. Thatcher openly supported Reagan's belligerent take on the Soviet Union and would claim a part in the winning of the Cold War. But the always-tenuous belief in a mutually beneficial 'special relationship' between the United States and Britain – originally fabricated by Winston Churchill – quickly faded once Reagan and Thatcher left the scene, John Major never enjoying such a close relationship with

George H. W. Bush, or with Bill Clinton. Tony Blair, once he became prime minister in 1997, was able to buddy up to the equally young, telegenic centrist Clinton, but Blair was always, and obviously, the very junior partner. The 'Great' in Great Britain advertised past glories.

New Labour's own policy of internal devolution, foreshadowed in 1992 and implemented when the party won government, pointed to a recalibration of national identity. By 1999 there were independent assemblies in Belfast, Cardiff and Edinburgh, all inconceivable under Thatcher or even Major. Yet Mark Renton's caustic rant in *Trainspotting*, responding to his friend Tommy's patriotic promotion of the Scottish Highlands, reveals both entrenched tensions between the nations that made up Great Britain, and a diversity of views within the individual nations about their own identities. James Mitchell makes the illuminating general point that when 'the term "nationalism" is used in the UK it is more often assumed to refer to one of the sub-state nationalisms – Scottish, Welsh or Irish nationalisms' (Mitchell 2009: 3). English anxieties about English identity traditionally have been less prevalent or less openly paraded, possibly because the historical asymmetry of power in Britain, with so much political, economic and culture leverage centred on London, so clearly favoured the English. In similar vein the literary scholar James English highlights 'the repressed system of differences that had always underwritten the "United" Kingdom' (English 2006: 9). More specifically, Chris Rojek records that a 1997 survey showed only 52 per cent of all Britons described themselves as British, calling this part of longer-term 'desertion of British nationalism by the British themselves' (Rojek 2007: 7). In the 1990s the term 'Britain' in Great Britain came under telling scrutiny, prompting the question: in what sense was the 'United Kingdom' united?

A central aspect of Thatcher's 1980s diplomacy was suspicion and antagonism to Europe and the newly founded European Union. Although in many ways pro-Europe at the beginning of her leadership, Thatcher increasingly was seen as Europhobic, and saw the local political value in this belligerence, as did many of her parliamentary colleagues and party members. Yet that belligerence prompted Geoffrey Howe to resign. Where she attempted to create a self-image of Britain as geographically and culturally separate from Europe, and as interested primarily in economic alliances that favoured Britain, Major was more tempered and conciliatory, seeing a place for Britain within Europe. Quoting George Orwell, as noted in the Introduction, reflected Major's nostalgia for a bygone Britain. *The Independent* reviewed that speech in a lead article dismissively titled 'What a lot of tosh'.[1] In any case, Major slightly misquoted and misinterpreted Orwell, ignoring the fact that the quotation about the England of long shadows on cricket lawns came from Orwell's 'The Lion and the Unicorn: Socialism and the English Genius', a 1941 polemic that argues for socialist revolution, the nationalisation of industry, the dismantling of the House of Lords, and the closing of public schools. Orwell also regularly uses England as a placeholder for Britain. He acknowledges the problem, admitting early on that 'Welsh and Scottish readers are likely to have been offended because I have used the word "England" oftener than "Britain"', adding that 'A Scotsman, for instance does not thank you if you call him an Englishman' (Orwell 1998: 398). Five decades after Orwell, questions about British identity as a whole, as well as the relationships between the nations that comprised what was still officially the United Kingdom of Great Britain and Northern Ireland, were more complex and contentious. One suggestion was, that in the age of globalisation, with the end of the Cold War breaking down outmoded alliances, discrete nations themselves were less important than had been the case through the century. Perhaps in a world of financial integration and cultural homogeneity (code words for Americanisation) a post-national era was in the offing.

The election of Labour in 1997, with its slogan 'New Labour New Britain', promised a reassertion and a reconfiguration of British identity, and of its relationships to its allies. Where Thatcher had berated the French, in 1998 Blair became the first British prime minister to address the French National Assembly. Just as remarkably, he did so in fluent French, a gesture that enchanted the local audience. Internally, the political devolution mooted in Labour's 1992 manifesto was enacted with almost startling rapidity, so that 1997 referendums initiated a Welsh Assembly and a Scottish Parliament, while the Good Friday Agreement of 1998 set in train the Northern Ireland Assembly. Which is not to say that devolution was universally accepted, the devolution strategy having been tried unsuccessfully under James Callaghan in the late 1970s. The Welsh devolution vote in September 1997 was a surprisingly tight affair, the 'Yes' vote winning by only 6,721, a tiny percentage even in a population of just 3 million. Blair cannily exploited the fact that through much of Major's premiership the Conservative Party's electoral presence in Scotland and Wales was minimal. Again, this was partly a hangover from antagonisms stirred up by Thatcher's leadership. One infamous example was the so-called 'Sermon on The Mound' to the General Assembly of the Church of Scotland in 1988, when Thatcher interpreted the Bible through the lens of market economics to the most powerful figures in the Church. Another was the imposition of the poll tax on Scotland in 1989, a year ahead of its introduction in Wales and England, a point of antagonism until Major abandoned it in 1992. Although, to be fair, the poll tax was hugely unpopular through much of Britain, as a huge riot in London in March 1990 proved. Even out of office, though, Thatcher remained a much-loathed and demonised figure north of the Tweed River.

The situation was more problematic in Northern Ireland, where 'the Troubles' continued throughout Major's time in office, attempts at negotiations and outward signs of progress always prone to undermining atrocities from all sides. Once again Thatcher's turbulent relationship with one of the constituent parts of the United Kingdom defined that relationship in the 1980s, heightening contrasts with the following decade. Northern Ireland in the 1980s was marked by intransigence on both sides. A signal moment in 1981 was the death of Irish Republican Army (IRA) leader, prisoner Bobby Sands, who had won election to a Westminster seat from prison shortly before dying as the result of an extended hunger strike. As Richard English recounts:

> Even the IRA's flinty hunger-strike adversary, Margaret Thatcher, has observed that 'It was possible to admire the courage of Sands and the other hunger-strikers who died, but not to sympathise with their murderous cause. We had done everything in our power to persuade them to give up their fast.' (English 2003: 200)

English goes on to record that '100,100 [sic] people walked silently behind the coffin', with Sands' election agent Owen Carron giving 'the graveside oration: "It is hard to describe the sadness and sorrow in our hearts today as we stand at the grave of the Volunteer Bobby Sands, cruelly murdered by the British government"' (200). Three years later the IRA would attempt to blow up the Conservative conference in Brighton. The 1990s, however, ultimately proved the transformative decade of the post-war period in Northern Ireland. Tensions remained, but they were contained within a more resilient and tolerant set of expectations.

Robert McLiam Wilson's 1996 darkly comic novel, *Eureka Street*, captures the tenor of the times before these welcome advances. Its first-person narrator, Jake Jackson, notes dryly that in that earlier period

> Belfast shared the status of the battlefield. The place-names of the city and country had taken on the resonance and hard beauty of all history's slaughter venues. The Bogside, Crossmaglen, The Falls, The Shankhill and Andersontown. In the mental maps of those who had never been in Ireland, these places had tiny crossed swords after their names. (14)

He adds sardonically that 'When you considered that it was the under populated capital of a minor province, the world seemed to know it excessively well. Nobody needed to be told the reason for this needless fame' (14). But the violence that gained the city its needless fame spread out beyond Belfast and beyond Ireland, with the murder of Conservative Member of Parliament (MP) Ian Gow outside his home in England by the Provisional IRA in 1990 being one of the most 'successful' operations against the British government since the failed attempt to blow up the Conservative conference. Gow's death was only one among eighty-eight conflict-related deaths that year, figures that expose the literally deadly stakes involved. After years of surreptitious (and, for some, duplicitous) negotiations between the key parties involved, John Major signed the Downing Street Declaration with Irish Taoiseach Albert Reynolds in 1993 for a joint Northern Ireland solution. An IRA ceasefire came into effect. Hopes were frustrated, though, and by the beginning of 1996, Frank Millar observes, one reading of the Republican Movement's tactics acknowledged its 'impatience with an exhausted Major government', while another 'saw a republican leadership effectively marking time pending the commencement of fresh negotiations with an incoming Labour administration' (Millar 2007: 510). After many murderous false dawns, in 1998, via the Good Friday Agreement, Northern Ireland gained self-government, with the Northern Ireland Assembly meeting the following year, one of Tony Blair's early political triumphs. Oddly, for all the talk of New Britain, and while Blair reaped the political benefits from the devolution process generally, Iain McLean makes the telling point that 'the huge constitutional changes that occurred in Scotland and Wales during Tony Blair's time came almost casually. Blair showed some interest in process, but very little in policy. Devolution was a process he inherited' (McLean 2007: 487). To his credit, Blair did not squander that inheritance.

Renton's self- and nation-loathing cry in *Trainspotting*, that the Scots were colonised by wankers, also forcefully accuses the United Kingdom of being the ongoing site of internal colonial power, a claim that is problematic and illuminating on several levels. Katie Gramich quotes the Welsh poet R. S. Thomas's forthright view that 'Britishness is a mask. Beneath it there is only one nation, England' (Gramich 2003: 101). Thomas's retort might suggest, were one to accept the idea that England functioned and possibly still functions as colonial ruler over Wales, Scotland and Northern Ireland, that that rule was in some ways homogenous across the nations. Even a superficial comparison between Wales and Northern Ireland reveals important and undeniable differences between the extent and degree of 'colonial' rule in each; however, the standing military presence in the latter nation, its historical sectarian violence, and the accompanying deaths in the dozens each year exposed obvious and powerful distinctions. This is not to deny the sense felt by some Welsh (including Thomas) of being oppressed culturally and politically, but Gramich provides a sensibly qualified explanation for a colonialist reading of Wales and other 'British' nations:

> It is, of course, not a new idea that the Celtic countries, Wales, Scotland and Ireland, were in fact the first British colonies; historical and cultural similarities in their situations of those of more overtly colonised places (such as the Caribbean), tend to support this contention. It is, however, a highly sensitive area of discourse, for, as Ned Thomas has pointed out in his study of Derek Walcott, Wales was also part of Britain, and therefore a participant in the oppression of other peoples. This means that it is potentially insulting to allege that Wales, too, is a colony; compared to the enormity of slavery, the oppression of Wales has been a paltry thing. But it is still going on. (102–3)

The same complicity of the other 'Celtic' nations with England in the prosecution of British imperial rule over several centuries, with unprecedented and continuing economic benefits, is undoubtedly a reason for Caribbean countries in the twenty-first century to seek economic redress for the decades of exploitation whose effects still cripple them. One expression of the side effects of Britain's problematic history in the Caribbean, dealt with more fully in the following chapter, can be heard in the cultural theorist Stuart Hall's revelation that, before his move to Britain in 1951 to take up a Rhodes Scholarship at Oxford,

> I never once heard a single person refer to themselves, or to others ... as having being at one point in the past 'African.' It was only in the 1970s that the Afro-Caribbean identity became historically available to the great majority of Jamaican people, at home and abroad. In this historic moment, Jamaicans discovered themselves to be 'black' ... as the sons and daughters of slavery. (Hall 1990: 231)

Renton profanely proclaims his sense of being colonised; Hall describes a weird form of cultural blindness, itself the outcome of colonisation. A very rough internal equivalent, displaying a form of cultural deafness, was exposed in 1993 at the Welsh Conservative Party Conference. Conservative heavyweight John Redwood, recently appointed Secretary of State for Wales, was caught on television attempting to mime to the Welsh national anthem whose words he clearly did not know. Redwood was publicly ridiculed, although the humiliation was not enough to stop him challenging John Major for the leadership in 1995.

Redwood's inability to speak or sing Welsh fluently, if at all, was a deficiency he shared with the vast majority of Welsh people. The linguistic division among the Welsh unsettles facile notions of Welsh unity, sociologist Denis Balsom devising an influential 'Three Wales Model' to account for differences in Welsh speaking and self-perception. The three components, 'British Wales', 'Welsh Wales', and 'Y Fro Gymraeg' (Welsh-speaking Wales), measure the different importance given to language in terms of personal and national conceptions of identity. Balsom notes that most people in Wales preferred to define themselves as 'Welsh' rather than as 'British', even while most could not speak 'their' language. Wales was more fully absorbed within England than was Scotland, although, according to Keith Robbins, neither was 'absorbed in any simple fashion' (Robbins 1988: 12). James Mitchell places Welsh national sentiment in a long historical narrative, calling the sixteenth-century Acts of Union between England and Wales

> assimilationist, quite different from the treaty of Union of 1707 between England (and Wales) and Scotland. From Tudor times, Welsh counties had been run on English lines, subject to English law, with English as the official language and Wales given representation in parliament in return. (Mitchell 2009: 8)

One critical change came with the Welsh Language Act of 1993, which established that Welsh and English should be treated equally in the realm of public business in Wales. A Welsh Language Board was set up to promote the Welsh language and Welsh speakers were given the right in court to conduct themselves in Welsh, gaining symbolic and actual equality with English speakers.

In 1990, commercial sponsorship for the National Eisteddfod, the historic expression of Welsh language culture, topped £1 million. This sign of a healthy and developing national arts culture was complemented in 1992 with the establishment of the Wales Book of the Year, for the best Welsh or 'Welsh interest' books in Welsh and in English. The prizes formally promoted contemporary Welsh writers, in a decade when, as Chapter 5 explores more fully, prizes were critical to the celebrity culture, and where certain new prizes (most obviously, the Orange Prize for Women's Writing) offered fresh forms of endorsement and publicity for previously marginalised groups. The Welsh awards played a tangible role in rewarding creative excellence and in shoring up local publishing, increasingly under threat from large-scale producers swallowing up medium and small presses. The awards promoted an assortment of small independent presses such as Seren, and Gomer, presses that sustained local writing in Welsh and in English. They also foregrounded the critically important work of Gwasg Prifysgol Cymru, or the University of Wales Press, in encouraging and publishing local content and local writers. Welsh writers in English were able to publish with larger English language presses, of course, something that those capable of writing fluently in Welsh and choosing to do so were denied. For many young writers, especially, the local presses offered the best option. The choice to write in English or Welsh, or both, was a complicated affair, as it had long been the reality that, while the number of people competent in Welsh was growing in the 1990s, the figures remained relatively small. This was especially so in large cultural centres such as Cardiff, something that retarded the support and transmission of Welsh language writing.

Of the younger generation of writers emerging in the 1990s, Gwyneth Lewis addressed this problem directly, partly the result of her bilingual facility with Welsh and English. Growing up in a Welsh-speaking home in Cardiff (her parents originally coming from Welsh-speaking parts of the country) and learning English only from the age of two, Lewis won awards in successive years at the Urdd National Eisteddfod, the youth version of the national festival. Her first collections were in Welsh, including *Sonedua Redsa* – translatable as *The Sonnets of Redsa* – published by Gomer press in 1990, and *Cyfrif Un ac Un yn Dri* – translatable as *Counting One and One as Three* – by another local press, Barddas, in 1996. While she barely spoke English regularly before going to university, Lewis studied at Cambridge and would eventually gain a DPhil from Oxford, publishing separate collections of poetry in English during the 1990s: *Parables & Faxes* (1995) and *Zero Gravity* (1998). Both volumes were published by Bloodaxe, the radical Newcastle poetry press at the forefront of adventurous, internationalist volumes in the 1980s and 1990s. Bloodaxe's greater public presence and the English language in which these poems were written created a larger audience for Lewis, and an appreciative one: *Parables & Faxes* won the Aldeburgh Festival Prize and was shortlisted for the Forward Prize for Poetry, as was *Zero Gravity*. Both collections cover a great deal of territory (*Zero Gravity* metaphorically takes off into space, with poems about Lewis's American cousin, who worked repairing the Hubble telescope). Both also deal with the intricacies of languages at ground level. Lewis has written that 'the poetic line in English is always dragging you towards a pentameter or tetrameter, whereas this isn't a familiar sound in Welsh', adding that while 'lyricism and the music of words are nothing new in Welsh language poetry (in fact, an excess of music has been a problem with it) they *are* new in English verse' (Poole 1995: 28). In a 1995 article, 'Whose coat is that jacket? Whose hat is that cap?', a title that hints at cultural history, ambiguity and tensions embedded in language, Lewis writes that

> The smuggling of familiar material from one language to another seemed to me on reflection too easy a way of exploiting a Welsh subject matter in English. I wanted to be a full English language poet when I wrote in English,

and not just a translator of material which might not work in Welsh. (quoted in Williams 2003: 3)

Her poems deal not merely with material from one language or the other but with the lives and deaths of languages themselves, as in the sequence 'Welsh Espionage', which in part records the process by which her father began to teach her English, against the expected criticism by her mother:

> Welsh was the mother tongue, English was his.
> He taught her the body by fetishist quiz,
> father and daughter on the bottom stair;
> 'Dy benelin yw *elbow*, dy wallt di yw *hair*,
>
> *chin* ye dy ên di, head yw dy ben'
> She promptly forgot, made him do it again.
>
> (Lewis 1995: 42)

The fundamental relationship between language and the body, language and being, is complicated by the process of translating from the native and 'natural' Welsh to the learned and therefore more artificial English, the primacy of the former realised in the italicisation of the latter. Yet the rhymed first lines of the second stanza, the first ending in Welsh, the second in English, display mutually beneficial connections. Lewis realised, though, the insinuation of something problematic in the linking of language and fetishism, especially in terms of the father–daughter relationship, indicating that 'this was a way for me to explore the discomfort I felt about being torn between two cultures. Early on I had an acute sense of the cultural clash between the social values tied up in the two languages' (Williams 2003: 7). Engagement with the wider world, in which Welsh is neither spoken nor understood, produces traumatic possibilities, as another section of 'Welsh Espionage' exposes:

> This is how languages die – the tongue
> forgetting what it knew by heart, the young
>
> not understanding what, by rights, they should.
> And vital intelligence is gone for good.
>
> (Lewis 1995: 46)

Lewis's unusual facility in the two languages, when coupled with a vital intelligence alert to the possibilities and perils of two languages, asks questions of personal and, by extension, cultural identity inherent in the promotion or suppression of a native language.

Similar questions arise in a different medium with the major Welsh language film of the decade, *Hedd Wyn* (1992), which itself contained a vital literary component. Tracing the life of the Welsh poet Ellis Evans, who won the National Eisteddfod Chair for poetry after being killed at the Battle of Passchendaele in 1917 – the first writer to be awarded the prize posthumously – the film fuses a message on the senselessness of war with the lyricism of Welsh country life, specifically the farm near Trawsfynydd in west Wales, where Evans grew up. The fact that the film was spoken entirely in Welsh (with English subtitles), except by specifically English characters, was itself a major achievement. Given the hard-nosed economics of the film industry, especially for non-heritage films, British cinema has always struggled merely to get made. Two Welsh companies helped produce *Hedd Wyn*, one of them the Welsh television channel. The film paints a romantic picture of the untutored but talented poet from rural Wales, who feels inspired by Arianrhod, a mythological Welsh goddess. She appears to him and recites poetry at key moments. English soldiers practising artillery fire in preparation for the Great War ruin this bucolic idyll, while Evans' reluctant conscription puts him and other native Welsh speakers at odds with the English military hierarchy. One of the latter refers to them as 'ignorant Welsh peasants'. Welsh–English tensions pepper the film – Evans' mother, for example, pretends to speak only Welsh when the English conscription agent calls. Yet the film is not relentlessly anti-English; for all the severity of the English who run the conscription panel and who train their Welsh recruits with patronising military brutality, English soldiers retrieve the wounded Evans from the battlefield, and the upper middle class English officer who at first refuses to post Evans's poem to the Eisteddfod, partly because he cannot understand Welsh, later relents. The poem wins Evans the posthumous Bardic Chair. His deathbed exchange is with a Cockney soldier, who observes that Evans looks happy, a sentiment with which the dying soldier–poet concurs, possibly a gesture to Evans's pseudonym, 'Hedd Wyn', which means 'blessed peace'. The film is more a celebration of Evans's life and the Welsh culture that motivates him than a sustained attack upon the English (all nations are seen to suffer in the pointless battle) and this uplifting tone in part contributed to the film becoming the most successful Welsh language film in history. It won several awards, including six BAFTA Cymru Awards. Even more significantly beyond Wales, *Hedd Wyn* was nominated as Best Foreign Language film at the 1994 Academy Awards, the first British film to be so honoured. The category of Foreign Language film carries an undoubted irony, but there was a sting in the tale, the film failing to win a distribution deal in the United Kingdom. Foreign language films generally do poorly in Britain, but the critical acclaim the film received still sat oddly with its box office failure. The reality that Welsh would be understood as a foreign language within Britain underscores the peculiarities of British identity generally, and the many gradations of commitment to an overarching identity.

While Wales's situation was complex, it bore little comparison with the situation in Northern Ireland for much of the 1990s, with that nation's violent and historically embedded religious divisions generating distinctive and damaging allegiances with and antipathies to the Irish Republic and to the United Kingdom. The dividing or determining lines in relation to Northern Ireland were not only highly (and lethally) contested, but were more obviously geographical. Language was far less the issue in Northern Ireland than place, about who controlled what areas, for how long and by whose authority. Allegiance to a particular zone within the borders of Northern Ireland entailed allegiance to a place beyond those borders, whether to the rest of the United Kingdom of Great Britain and Northern Ireland (the title of which had the virtue of registering the existence of a distinct area with a distinct history and culture) or to the island of Ireland, which had a more geographical logic, but which threatened to erase critical elements of the peculiar history of the North. As Elmer Kennedy-Andrews observes: 'In Northern Ireland place is the site of division and dispute arising from conflicting claims to ownership and control. Meanings of place are tied up with questions of territoriality, belonging and social power.' While not merely a binary opposition for all the nation's inhabitants, for many that division was central to their self-perception, as Kennedy-Andrews explains:

> For nationalists, place is the essential ground of identity and a continuous, unified Irish culture. For unionists, Northern Ireland is their constitutionally established homeland founded to preserve their Protestant, British identity perceived to be constantly under siege from Catholic, Gaelic, 'Irish Ireland'. (Kennedy-Andrews: 2008: 2)

The meaning of place is never ahistorical, for the markers of allegiance are deeply embedded with historical meaning born out of the long and deadly saga labelled the Troubles. What was significant and in many ways wholly surprising in the 1990s was that, to an unprecedented and unlikely degree, the decade would mark the end of major conflict.

The distance that needed to be travelled can be captured in works from the early part of the decade, showing the links between place and history that function as forms of cultural scarring. Wilson's *Eureka Street* records the ongoing friendship between Catholic Jake Jackson and Protestant Chuckie Lurgan in Belfast. The novel is considered again in terms of questions of class in Chapter 4, but for now Chuckie's grimly insouciant comment, 'I liked the Troubles. They were like television' (48), marks with dark humour the psychological damage done by the state of constant, if only occasionally experienced, siege. Jake's assessment is more measured, more elegiac: 'Belfast is a city that has *lost its heart*. A ship-building, rope-making, linen weaving town. It builds no ships, makes no rope and weaves no linen. Those trades died. A city can't live without something to do with itself' (215). Birte Heidemann understands the novel as registering 'the shared sense of euphoria following the declaration of the first ceasefire of the Irish Republican Army (IRA) in 1994, but also points to the dangers and drawbacks of joining the bandwagon of global capitalism' (Heidemann 2016: 3). The strong implication is that the Troubles have in some ways masked how Northern Ireland has been excluded from mainstream political, economic and cultural changes that have transformed the global landscape. Relief at the apparent end of hostilities comes with recognition of the many different types of loss that the city, the people who inhabit it and the wider Northern Ireland population have suffered. The trades that have died are not linked to any religious group per se; global capitalism or many other forms of economic organisation have no need for the intense and antagonistic religious division the society has existed in and been modified by for decades.

Another of the younger generation of Northern Irish writers, Glenn Patterson, records something slightly different in *Fat Lad* (1992), the main character Drew Linden returning to his native Belfast after ten years, and quickly remembering some of the reasons behind his departure: 'The Belfast he left, the Belfast the Expats forswore, was a city dying on its feet: cratered sites and hunger strikes; atrophied, self-abased.' Belfast is a place far more put-upon than the mean housing schemes of Irvine Welsh's Edinburgh; it is a battle scene, even if the half rhyme of 'cratered sites and hunger strikes' suggests a familiarity affording a hard-edged poetry. Drew notices changes, though:

> But the Belfast he had heard reports of this past while, the Belfast he had seen with his own eyes last month, was a city in the process of recasting itself entirely. The army had long since departed from the Grand Central Hotel, on whose level remains an even grander shopping complex was now nearing completion. Restaurants, bars and takeaways proliferated along the lately coined Golden Mile, running south from the refurbished Opera House, and new names had appeared in the shopping streets: Next, Body Shop, Tie Rack, Principles. And his own firm, of course, Bookstore. (Patterson 1992: 5)

Against the grim and damaging stasis of the past, the Belfast of the novel's present demonstrates process, activity and, potentially, renewal. The levelling of the Grand Central Hotel, one-time barracks for the British Army, and the target of many an IRA bombing attack, clearly marks a move away from a certain form of British involvement (considered either as occupation or as protection). Yet the even grander shopping complex to come (Castle Court, that replaced it in 1990), would itself become a magnet for bombings during and after its construction. The process of complete recasting would still be long and vexatious, and Drew's positive take is tinged with anxiety, as though the hope that underpins the 'lately coined Golden Mile' might not be sufficiently resilient to withstand the dangerous historical and political undercurrents. Can 1980s chain stores offering consumerist glamour for the individual survive in this harsh cultural climate? The question has an oblique importance for *Fat Lad*, which was shortlisted for the Guinness Peat Aviation Book Award. Guinness Peat Aviation would almost collapse as the result of a disastrous share flotation in 1992, a cautionary note about capitalist facades. And the strained optimism of the early 1990s that *Fat Lad* records would be shattered several times before the oft-promised peace.

Two powerful and controversial early 1990s films presented the traumatic intra-British war in very different ways. As ever, given the mean rations on which the British film industry survived, the fact that such films were produced at all was miraculous, let alone that they dealt with material that did not in itself guarantee large audiences. Both their Irish-born writer-directors, though, were respected and had proven commercial success, and both films boasted casts with the all-important American box-office connection. Neil Jordan (*The Crying Game*, 1992) had been nominated for a Cannes Palme D'Or for *Mona Lisa* (1986), and *The Crying Game* starred American Forrest Whittaker, who played the title role in Clint Eastwood's lauded biopic of Charlie Parker. Jim Sheridan (*In the Name of the Father*, 1993) had directed the Academy Award-winning *My Left Foot* (1989), and the recipient of that award, Daniel Day-Lewis, was also a star of *In the Name of the Father*. That film ploughed a more conventional, if still stony, political field, recounting the true-life false arrest and imprisonment of the so-called Guildford Four for the bombing of a Guildford pub in 1974. The four were later freed, but not until having served sentences of up to fifteen years, based on confessions coerced by police. Powerfully acted by a stellar British cast including Emma Thompson and Pete Postlethwaite, *In the Name of the Father* was nominated for seven Oscars (although it failed to win any), and proved a critical and commercial success. Tellingly, though, American producers, Universal Pictures and Hell's Kitchen films, financed that film. *The Crying Game* had a budget one quarter the size, and was financed by British money. It reworked a reasonably standard plot about the IRA kidnap of a British soldier through the far more dangerous territory of sexuality. Jude, a female IRA operative, lures an unwitting British soldier, Jody, into a 'honey-trap'. While captured, Jody befriends one of his IRA captors, Fergus, and when Jody is killed by a British armoured carrier while trying to flee, Fergus repays a promise by finding Jody's London girlfriend, Dil, and telling her about Jody's love for her. Fergus then falls for Dil himself, before, in a dramatic surprise in a film made for a mainstream audience, she reveals herself as male. The intricate, highly charged combination of politics and sexuality, deception and revelation, intimacy and power, required Jordan's high risk brilliance and another top quality cast, that apart from Whittaker included Stephen Rea, Miranda Richardson and Jaye Davidson, nominated for an Academy Award for the role of Dil. While consciously controversial in its treatment of personal and political power, the film proved an international hit, winning an Oscar for Best Writing and a BAFTA for Best British film of 1993.

The relationship between Northern Ireland and the rest of the United Kingdom, England especially – keeping in mind that the majority of Northern Irish are, like the fictitious Chuckie Logan, Protestant – ensured that even after the formal end of the Troubles, suspicions remained. Wales was tranquil by comparison, while Scotland was positioned somewhere in-between, a large percentage of the population deeply ambivalent about the neighbours to the immediate south. Or, rather, about the Conservative faction of the English; for much of the 1990s, the Scottish National Party remained a fairly marginalised group itself. While it doubled the number of seats it won in the 1997 election over the previous effort in 1992, it only won six seats in total, fewer than the Liberal Democrats, and a minuscule return next to Labour's fifty-six seats. (Admittedly, the first-past-the-post system skewed things very much in Labour's favour.) The Conservatives, it needs be said, lost all their eleven seats. While Scottish Nationalists were insignificant politically, Scottish writing, especially its fiction, was enjoying the ongoing expansion that had begun in the 1980s with Gray's *Lanark*, and that harked back to an earlier renaissance in the 1920s and 1930s centred on figures such as Hugh MacDiarmid and Neil Gunn. Cairns Craig considers the new vitality within the 'repressed system of differences' noted by James English in his reading of the '"United" Kingdom'. Craig deals with established Scottish writers such as Gray and Kelman, along with the younger generation of writers who came of age in the nineties, among them A. L. Kennedy, Janice Galloway and Alan Warner. He places them within a far longer historical narrative going back to the generative work of Walter Scott. Despite the undoubted and long-standing vitality and variety of Scottish novelists, Craig argues, they traditionally have been demoted to 'regional versions of the development of the novel'. In open dispute with this marginalisation, Scottish writers had asserted the linguistic and larger cultural distinctiveness of Scottish life and Scottish perspectives, underlying the 'claim that Scotland had not, through the years of Union [from 1707] been successfully integrated into a unified British culture' (Craig 2006: 124). For Craig, 'the imagination is the medium through which the nation's past is valued' (Craig 1999: 10), so that culture itself played a vital role in the fashioning of new national possibilities. Richard Todd addresses a related aspect in a section exploring 'New Fiction from Scotland' from his 1996 study, *Consuming Fictions: The Booker Prize and British Literature Today* (1996: 131–63). Todd understands that the

> dilemma facing Scottish writers (and this applies equally to Irish, Welsh or distinctly regional writers on the British mainland) is the decision whether to support small local presses or surrender to the London publishers marketing muscle in order to reach a truly global audience. Many Scottish writers feel torn between loyalty to their own national roots and the desire for wider recognition. (132)

Gwyneth Lewis had to consider the same torn loyalties in terms of Welsh language publishers. But importantly, in the wake of the successes of work by Gray, Kelman, Welsh and others, publishers in Scotland and England were keen to promote Scottish writers.

The Picador Book of Contemporary Scottish Fiction neatly combines these elements, simultaneously advertising the continuing quality of contemporary Scottish writing and its attractiveness to a mainstream publisher. In his introduction to the collection, Peter Kravitz explains that

> Anyone looking for the country's authors in a Scottish bookshop [in the early 1980s] would have been pointed towards reprints of Neil Gunn and Eric Linklater. Publishers were more interested in resurrecting dead writers as opposed to looking for new ones. (Kravitz 1997: xii)

Kravitz ends by celebrating how,

> For the first time in centuries of insecurity and strife, Scotland has begun to stop defining itself by what it is not – England – and is with good humour facing up to what it is, both bad and good. Future generations will applaud the contributions which the writers in this anthology played in this process. (xxxvi)

The cultural confidence is palpable, and fed into an expansion of teaching and research on Scottish Literature. The four-volume *History of Scottish Literature* (1987–9), under the general editorship of Cairns Craig, provides one example of a growing body of critical work. Yet

Kravitz includes an important caveat in declaring that Scotland was facing up to what was good and bad. The Scottish literary renaissance was never a group exercise in national aggrandisement, and Mark Renton's disparaging review of his country and his co-citizens was not unique. At the other end of the scale, and itself a sign of complex times, the internationally successful film *Braveheart* presented one of the most positive reviews of Scottish culture produced in the 1990s, or perhaps in any decade. Part hagiography, part tourist brochure for the Highlands, part embellishment of the essential and unalloyed pride and rough-hewn goodness of the Scottish people, as well as exposé of the irredeemable ghastliness of the English nobility and their Scottish stooges, *Braveheart*'s call to Scottish nationalism was as simplistic and historically suspect as it was popular. The Scottish National Party employed Gibson's big screen myth-making quite openly and somewhat cynically in its advertising, asking prospective supporters: 'Are You A Braveheart?' Some clearly felt that they were, or that they would like to be, modern William Wallaces.

Carol Ann Duffy's poem 'Originally' provides a helpful bridge from such effusions to some of the harsher assessments made of Scottish contemporary life and history in the 1990s. The poet-critic Sean O'Brien writes of Duffy, born in Glasgow's Gorbals but brought up from early childhood in northern England, that 'Neither uprooted nor rootless, but not having taken root, Duffy can stand as an emigrant in the country of which she is technically a citizen' (O'Brien 1998: 160). He adds that

> The edge of estrangement is usually somewhere to hand in Duffy's work: it is part of what enables her to dramatise the experience of a wide variety of other strangers, many of them born here, who find themselves abroad in contemporary England. (160)

The speaker of 'Originally' carries the memory of a traumatic childhood move south from Scotland that exposes the undeniable, if troublingly indefinable, loss:

> We came from our own country in a red room
> which fell through the fields, our mother singing
> our father's name to the turn of the wheels.
> My brothers cried, one of them bawling, *Home,*
> *Home,* as the miles rushed back to the city,
> the street, the house, the vacant rooms
> where we didn't live anymore.
>
> (Duffy 1994: 65)

This could be any childhood move from one country to another, and the speaker generalises, noting how 'All childhood is an emigration', before distinguishing between moves that are 'slow' and those that are 'sudden. / Your accent wrong'. Amidst brothers bawling childishly, the speaker's analysis and response are more sophisticated and forcefully articulated, if still couched in childlike similes: 'My parents' anxiety stirred like a loose tooth in my head / *I want our own country*, I said'. The same speaker incorporates a longer historical perspective, explaining, how, over time, you

> forget, or don't recall, or change,
> and, seeing your brother swallow a slug
> feel only a skelf of shame. I remember my tongue
> shedding its skin like a snake, my voice
> in the classroom sounding just like the rest.
>
> (Duffy 1994: 65)

In lines that echo some of the sentiments in Gwyneth Lewis's 'Welsh Espionage', Duffy explores language's pivotal function in delineating identity, and, therefore, in recording sometimes radical changes over time. But while the notion of the tongue shedding its skin like a snake provides an arresting simile for linguistic change, the Scots word *skelf* (meaning 'a sharp sliver of wood') functions as the key marker of national distinctiveness, one that momentarily bamboozles those who can only guess at its meaning, while secretly locating the speaker's origins. *Skelf* is the marker of Scottishness that is also a way of excluding or perplexing those not 'in the know'. Where Lewis in part worries about the loss of linguistic knowledge and therefore of connections to origins, Duffy illustrates how one word on its own can act as an indelible signifier of origins that also functions precisely to define shame. The estrangement is also productive, subverting the cultural hierarchies encoded into language by introducing enriching novelty, and with it a realisation of previously hidden social and cultural differences.

A revealing quality of some Scottish literary characters in the 1990s is that, while they may venture beyond Scotland, they almost immediately seem riven by anxiety and self-doubt, especially if they end up in England. It is as though the confidence and adventure that precipitates their travel beyond Scotland quickly evaporates in the dank climate south of the border. This is true even among the hard nuts of Irvine Welsh's *Trainspotting*. So, for all his hatred of his native Scotland, Mark Renton quickly finds himself the dismissed and patronised outsider in London: 'The pub sign is a new one, but its message is old. The Britannia. Rule Britannia. Ah've never felt British, because ah'm not. It's ugly and artificial.' And yet the shrewd and subversive thought does not contain any recuperative sense of origin, of an identity wrapped in tartan: 'Ah've never really felt Scottish either' (1993: 228). He eventually returns, but only as part of his final escape from Scotland to Amsterdam, something examined in this study's discussion of class. Welsh's world is prototypically urban, mostly set in the mean, decaying and decadent housing schemes that supply a dangerously shadowy world at odds with the chocolate box Edinburgh beloved of Edinburgh Festival goers, whom Renton and his friends mock and abhor. *Braveheart* suggests that the almost primordially beautiful Highlands are the natural habitat of the indomitable, freedom loving Scots. When Tommy takes Renton, Sick Boy and Spud with him to the Highlands to proudly show off true Scottish beauty to them, however, their depositing on a lonely railway platform inspires not so much rapture as Renton's bitter and compromising assault on the identity, history and integrity of the Scottish. Tommy's naïve but entirely sincere love of nature and, more particularly, of Scotland, and the uplift that they give him, contrasts miserably with the heroin-damaged realities of his friends who happily choose to inhabit Edinburgh's forlorn corners. Renton is not alone in his instant and total dismissal of Highland pride, merely the one most capable of articulating his contempt. His response unwittingly attacks the empty myth-making so central to *Braveheart*. As Chapter 4 analyses more fully, Renton's position on the Highlands fits within a far wider, tough-minded rejection of the enticements of contemporary Scottish life and of consumerist life more generally. Amsterdam offers him not simply escape from his Scottish past, and the Scottish friends he betrays, but also the opportunity to become someone he cannot become in his homeland.

One of the immediate and obvious markers of Scottish identity in *Trainspotting*, especially for readers from outside Scotland, was Welsh's sustained and unapologetic use of various forms of Scots, for narration as well as for dialogue. James Kelman had employed vernaculars in his short stories and novels, as a way of giving voice and agency to those traditionally excluded from polite literary society. As Chapter 5 explains, this overtly political as well as aesthetic gesture proved controversial, possibly as Kelman intended. His use of Scots was far less varied than Irvine Welsh attempted in *Trainspotting*, Kelman's novels and stories usually being narrated by one character only. But many of *Trainspotting*'s sections are narrated in the first person by different characters, including, but not restricted to, the main figure, Renton, his hapless friend Spud, the cynical and exploitative Sick Boy, the psychopathic Begbie, and Renton's school age girlfriend, Dianne. Each has a unique linguistic vocabulary and rhythm, a private perspective and back story, and these elements contribute to the kaleidoscopic, polyphonic ensemble piece. The novel's global success internationalised the language of a tiny subgroup from a relatively small capital city, presenting a very different Scotland to the world than that proffered in *Braveheart*. Still other sections are told in the third person, at times in Standard English, including the final chapter, which ends: 'This thought terrified and excited him [Renton] as he contemplated life in Amsterdam' (344). Surprisingly, for a novel in which the linguistic connection to place is stressed and stretched to breaking point, *Trainspotting* ends as might any middle class *Bildungsroman*, its hero on the verge of lighting out for the territory.

For all that, *Trainspotting* was a bravura performance by Welsh, fizzing with hallucinogenic energy, unabashedly bawdy, irreverent and aggressive. Unique though it seemed in many ways, the novel fitted within a longer narrative of Scottish fictional adventure and achievement going back two decades and echoing the glory days of the Scottish Renaissance literature in the 1920s and 1930s. Gavin Wallace notes sardonically in the introduction to *The Scottish Novel since the Seventies: New Visions, Old Dreams* (Wallace and Stevenson 1993) that 'There is a sense in which Scottish fiction prospers in inverse proportion to the difficulties of the cultural and political situation which it confronts.' Wallace extends this wry cultural analysis, adding that 'the recent rude health of Scottish fiction might be taken to indicate that the life of the country itself must have been not just "inimical" but also fruitfully unendurable' (2). The world of Renton and others neatly exemplifies the fruitfully unendurable, a world given cinematic life in Danny Boyle's 1996 adaptation, a film that would itself quickly achieve cult status. The crazed energy ignites from the opening shot showing Renton and Spud careering down Edinburgh's Princes Street, dropping the books they have stolen from Waterstones bookshop. Security guards in pursuit, and with Iggy Pop's 'Lust for Life' as pounding mood music, this vibrant introduction ends in a montage of scenes from Renton's world as he rejects the 'Choose Life' mentality of the 1990s in favour of heroin. The film productively uses the novel's fragmented structure (or lack of structure), with its natural affinity to film scenes, to craft a realistically and comically unrelenting picture of low-life Edinburgh and its less illustrious denizens. Stand out scenes exploit the visual power possibilities of film, so that early on, Renton, having excreted suppositories into 'the worst toilet in Scotland', gags at the effluvia before sliding into it and slowly diving to the bottom of a fantastic lake to retrieve them. Later, Tommy takes him, Sick Boy and Spud to the Highlands and eulogises about the 'great outdoors', asking 'Doesn't it make you proud to be Scottish?' This sets off first Sick Boy and then Renton, who launches into his tirade against Scotland and the Scots. In the novel, these critical thoughts are directed against people like Begbie (Welsh 1993: 78), but in the film Renton shouts them dismissively at Tommy, adding that 'It's a shite state of affairs to be in, Tommy, and all the fresh air in the world won't make any fuckin' difference.' Those words, in this setting, spoken in a film released only a year after *Braveheart*, appear a conscious effort on the part of screenplay writer John Hodge and director Danny Boyle to obliterate the romantic outpourings of the earlier film. For the characters in *Trainspotting*, the real Scotland of the 1990s resides not in mist-smothered glens but in heroin-ravaged schemes.

Margaret Hamilton, in A. L. Kennedy's first novel, *Looking for the Possible Dance* (1993), lives in rather different circumstances in urban Glasgow. Like Renton, she plots her escape, although in her case the initial prompt is her loving but overbearing and dangerously clingy father. Margaret's first real flight from home involves studying at an English university. This breakout fails because, in a new habitat potentially full of possibilities, she automatically is paired with another Scot, Colin, who will prove even more dangerously self-absorbed and self-destructive than her father. The novel's title alludes to Margaret's search of the elusive 'possible dance', the dance move 'to beat them all', one that might offer some form of transcendence out of her drab existence. But her efforts inevitably are shackled by her native culture, harshly anatomised in her understanding that she,

> like many others, will take the rest of her life to recover from a process we may summarise thus:
> THE SCOTTISH METHOD
> (FOR THE PROTECTION OF CHILDREN)
> 1. Guilt is good.
> 2. The history, language and culture of Scotland do not exist. If they did, they would be of no importance and might as well not.
> …
> 6. Pain and fear will teach us to hurt and petrify ourselves, thus circumventing further public expense.
> 7. Joy is fleeting, sinful and the forerunner of despair.
> …
> 10. Nothing in the country which is nothing, we are only defined by what we are not. Our elders and betters are also nothing: we must remember this makes them bitter and dangerous. (Kennedy 1998:16)

This acidly comic view of the authentic and historical Scottish culture places the blame for Scottish miserable-ism not with the perfidious English over the border, but internally, initiated by and maintained through the historically established workings of the church and the deeply embedded and damaged psyche that results from its prolonged and malignant influence. Margaret is firmly encased in what Peter

Kravitz would accept as the 'bad'. For all her first efforts to break free to the supposedly safe and perhaps post-national space of university, Margaret eventually returns to Scotland with Colin, enduring again the crushing and perverting effects of her 'native' culture, with his own brand of violent misogyny to add to her depressing wide experience of such behaviour. Scotland is not an accommodating place for women. Once Colin has ritually committed suicide, Margaret can escape by train in order to save herself, and begin to become something other than the self imposed upon her. But it takes Colin's brutal act to shock her into action and, after repeated suffering at the hands of a representative posse of men also repressed by <u>THE SCOTTISH METHOD (FOR THE PROTECTION OF CHILDREN)</u>, to propel her towards some freedom. The drug-fuelled exuberance of Welsh's Edinburgh's underclass is nowhere in evidence in the despairing Glasgow Kennedy evokes, so that, for Margaret, England represents the possibility of renewal, rather than oppression. It might be the case that joy will be fleeting and the forerunner of despair, but the possible dance could exist beyond the book's pages, and beyond the nation's border.

Brutal suicide, in this case an unnamed boyfriend, also launches the title character of Alan Warner's 1995 novel *Morvern Callar* beyond her origins in the small seaside town of Oban in the west of Scotland. The novel is dealt with briefly in terms of issues of class in Chapter 4, but here what matters is that Warner's first person narrative relates with a chilling matter-of-factness Morvern's muted response to her boyfriend's unforeseen act of self-annihilation in the kitchen of their flat. Her failure to think or speak her boyfriend's name announces a worrying detachment, but that boyfriend merely functions as a catalyst for her own adventures and aimless journeying. Rather than recoiling from or running away from the ghastly discovery, Morvern calmly and systematically disposes of the body, appropriating her boyfriend's recently completed novel and replacing his name with her own. This piece of literary larceny allows her to use the proceeds of an agent's advance to engage permissively in the Mediterranean rave scene. She taps into the same milieu of youth, music, sex, alcohol and drugs that activate Irvine Welsh's characters, her actions similarly random and driven by primal urges, amorality and the chasing after instant and sometimes dangerous gratification. In this way Morvern connects not with anything particularly Scottish, but with a global, or at least Western, youth culture high on risk and illicit substances. Unlike characters in *Trainspotting*, with whom she shares certain obvious similarities, Morvern's narratorial voice is rendered in something close to Standard English, as in the grim first sentences: 'He'd cut His throat with a knife. He's chopped His hand with the meat cleaver. He couldn't object so I lit a Silk Cut' (1). Only occasional idiomatic phrases give away any sense of place, and even the dialogue, so much the marker of national identity in *Trainspotting*, is recorded without the phonetic transcription that characterises Welsh's novel. In contrast to the dialects and patois consciously employed by Welsh and (from a different location and with characters of different socio-economic standing) by Kelman, Warner erases most linguistic signals of national identity, allowing Morvern her own individualised and internationalised place in the world.

Writers in Northern Ireland, Wales and Scotland, exploring the cultural psyches of their respective nations, painted vivid if unromantic portraits that added meaningfully to the overall sense of the United Kingdom in the nineties as a nation where the so-called 'margins' mattered. For the largest, most populous, and historically the most powerful of the four nations, England, the decade was to prove more problematic, a time for reappraisal that necessarily marked Britain's (and therefore England's) long decline from imperial might to middle-range power. That self-examination could suggest England itself as regionally divided, with the powerhouse of London more psychologically than geographically distant from, say, 'the North'. Jeremy Paxman suggested the southern bias of dominant senses of England in his 1998 account, *The English: A Portrait of a People*, writing that

> If you had to guess the lane, small cottage and field of grain, where there'll always be an England, you'd decide pretty quickly where it was not. You could instantly rule out places like Northumberland and Yorkshire, where fields have dry-stone walls and are more likely full of sheep anyway. (Paxman 1998: 156)

More morbidly, the philosopher and social commentator Roger Scruton's *England: An Elegy* (2000) looks back in fond memory to a nation that, in the opening chapter 'What on Earth was England?' he conceives of in the past tense, asking rhetorically; 'What was England: a nation? A territory? A language? A culture? An empire? An idea?' (Scruton 2000: 2). Perhaps unsurprisingly for a conservative, Scruton follows John Major in quoting from Orwell's *The Lion and the Unicorn*, indeed from the same passage, noting that for Orwell, as for himself, 'England was not a nation or a creed or a language or a state but a home. Things at home don't need an explanation. They are there because they are there' (16). The mix of tautology and nostalgia is revealingly enervated, but Scruton notes a more modern literary account of England's demise on the bookshelf of historical studies: 'Unique among the many obituaries is that of Julian Barnes, whose witty account of represented and re-presented England (in *England, England*, London, 1998) contains a strangely moving evocation of the old tranquillity' (ix). Although Scruton correctly discerns the novel's witty take on Englishness, his view that it offers a strangely moving account of the old tranquillity seriously misreads *England, England*'s dark account of nostalgia and the state of the nation at the end of the century.

Barnes creates a fantasy world that reduces Englishness to a set of historical and cultural clichés and contrivances. Built on the Isle of Wight by the entrepreneurial Sir Jack Pittman (his name resonant of a lost industrial past), 'England, England' is the name given to a commercial enterprise that aims to provide a distillation of Englishness for the discerning tourist. As befits such a venture, the process begins with market research that invites potential investors from twenty-five countries to list 'six characteristics, virtues or quintessences which the word England suggested to them' (83). The resulting list of 'Fifty Quintessences of Englishness' is revealing:

1. ROYAL FAMILY
2. BIG BEN/ HOUSES OF PARLIAMENT
3. MANCHESTER UNITED FOOTBALL CLUB
4. CLASS SYSTEM
5. PUBS
6. A ROBIN IN THE SNOW
7. ROBIN HOOD AND HIS MERRIE MEN
8. CRICKET
9. WHITE CLIFFS OF DOVER
10. IMPERIALISM
...
46. EMOTIONAL FRIGIDITY
47. WEMBLEY STADIUM
48. FLAGELLATION/ PUBLIC SCHOOLS
49. NOT WASHING/BAD UNDERWEAR
50. MAGNA CARTA. (83–5)

The novel's premise provides Barnes the opportunity to turn a coldly satirical eye on England, the English, as the perception of England and Englishness held by outsiders. The overwhelming view, encoded in this list, is of a nation locked in a circumscribed past. And yet the idea of marketing some form of cod England to a paying public sits comfortably within a postmodern sensibility, as a 'French intellectual', brought in to address the Project's Co-ordinating Committee, explains:

> We are talking about something profoundly modern. It is well-established ... that nowadays we prefer the replica to the original. We prefer the reproduction of the work of art to the work of art itself, the perfect sound and solitude of the compact disc to the symphony orchestra in the company of

the thousand victims of throat complaints, the book on tape to the book on the lap. (53)

Ironically, then, the construction of a replica England, or, rather, the replica of those aspects of England a customer survey deems quintessential, is simultaneously regressively nostalgic and neatly *sympatico* with the end-of-the-century zeitgeist. Critically, and again in tune with the nineties comfort with commodities, customers would be willing to pay for a taste of history. As the Project's Concept Developer tells its Official Historian, the media historian Dr Max, the point is not so much that paying customers learn about England's history as that they are made to '*feel* less ignorant. Whether they *are* or not is quite another matter, even outside our jurisdiction' (70). Dr Max later realises a 'paradox: that patriotism's most eager bedfellow was ignorance, not knowledge' (82). And, it might be added, comfort over contestation.

Barnes's take on the marketing of England for a paying (if primarily foreign) public, wryly assesses the sort of branding exercises more broadly visible in the Young British Artists and Britpop labels or the New Labour reboot. He sees comic implications rather than cutting-edge thinking, a notable example being the Gastronomic Sub-Committee's approval of such dishes as 'Yorkshire Pudding, Lancashire hotpot, Sussex pond pudding, Coventry godcakes, Aylesbury duckling' (90) and the like, while it bans

> porridge for its Scottish associations, faggots and fairy cakes in case they offended the pink dollar, spotted dick even when renamed spotted dog. Devils- and angels-on-horseback were in; toad-in-the-hole and cock-a-leakie out; Welsh rarebit, Scotch eggs and Irish stew were not even discussed. (91)

Ultimately, the success of England, England the concept comes at the expense of what comes to be called Old England, whose 'tourist-based economy collapsed' as a result of competition for its more concentrated, customer-driven replica. As a consequence, 'A resurgent Scotland purchased large tracts of land down to the old northern industrial cities; even Wales paid to expand into Shropshire and Herefordshire' (251). 'Mass depopulation' takes place, and people of 'Caribbean and Subcontinental origin began returning to the more prosperous lands from which their great-great-grandparents had once arrived' (252). Depopulation increases to a point where the European Union withdraws the right of the Old English 'to free movement in the Union', while 'Greek destroyers [patrol] the Sleeve to intercept boat people' (252). Attempts at 'Renewal' come to naught, Old England eventually withdrawing from the European Union, and declaring its separateness from the rest of the globe and from the Third Millennium by changing its name to Anglia.

The world began to forget that 'England' had ever meant anything except England, England, a false memory which the Island worked to reinforce; while those who remained in Anglia began to forget the world beyond. (253)

This, presumably, is the decline Roger Scruton lamented, without taking account of the satirical tone and texture of Barnes' ludic rendition of a Little Englander dream that finally becomes a 'reality' – if only (at least at time of writing) a fictional one.

The eclipse of British global power was underscored in July 1997 by the handover, after a century of British rule, of Hong Kong to China. The transfer of a small island in Asia to a genuine regional superpower was overseen by the establishment figure Chris Patten, the quintessentially English former Chairman of the Conservative Party. Patten was architect of John Major's surprise victory in 1992, though he lost his own seat in the English heartland of Bath. As compensation, Patten was named the last Governor of Hong Kong, a suitably symbolic individual to mark emblematic losses of power. While Britain gave up or gave back an external colony in the late 1990s as part of its shrinking reach beyond its shores, the relationships between the nations that made up the United Kingdom were beginning to transform during the decade. Devolution was still a novelty by the end of 1999, but its activation quickly generated forces that slowly began to reconfigure the identities of Northern Ireland, Scotland, Wales and England, and their interrelationships. It is important not to overstate the impact of these political changes in the 1990s, especially given the asymmetric nature of power in Britain deriving from the financial and cultural dominance of London, in tandem with the political dominance of Westminster. Power was not easily ceded. Yet even before these substantial (and, from the perspective of 1990, miraculous) changes, the decade witnessed diverse and dispersed energies that displayed new cultural alignments. Peter Kravitz's 1997 assessment that 'Scotland has begun to stop defining itself by what it is not – England' was also increasingly true for Wales and Northern Ireland. Kravitz accepts that the process has only begun, but the reality of that beginning was undeniable.

Note

1. Available at <http://www.independent.co.uk/voices/leading-article-what-a-lot-of-tosh-1457335.html> (last accessed 23 August 2016).

Chapter Two

New Ethnicities

> [C]ultural identity is not a fixed essence at all, lying unchanged outside history and culture. It is not some universal and transcendental spirit inside us on which history has made no fundamental mark. It is not once-and-for-all. It is not a fixed origin to which we can make some final and absolute Return. Of course, it is not a mere phantasm either. It is *something* – not a trick of the imagination ... If identity does not proceed in a straight, unbroken line, from some fixed origin, how are we to understand its formation? (Hall 1990: 226)

The previous chapter suggested that the United Kingdom was less united, and perhaps less of a kingdom, in 1999 than 1990, partly the result of the redistribution of political power via the different acts of devolution that opened up new forms of self-determination to the constituent nations of Britain. That chapter also argued that these political and bureaucratic changes reflected complex and often subtle changes in the ways that Britons understood themselves as Welsh, Scottish, Northern Irish and English. These developments were not solely the product of the decade, but were accelerated by some of the cultural energies and arguments that came to the fore in the 1990s. Within the national subgroups were other divisions and distinctions that complicated individual and group senses of identity and relationship, particularly in terms of perceived colonial power imbalances. While the notion of English colonial control was a critical element in the ways in which people understood themselves and worked towards new forms of organisation, the idea of internal colonialism was problematic given that Scotland, Wales and Ireland had in various ways prospered mightily from being part of the British imperial project. This complicated history was made more intricate still by the ways in which, as Britain's colonial power waned after the Second World War, former members of the Empire were encouraged to participate in the reconstruction of what they saw, and were actively encouraged to see, as the 'Mother Country', as 'Home'.

The British Nationality Act of 1948 had reconfigured citizenship within the single category of 'British subject: citizen of the United Kingdom and Colonies', allowing people from those colonies to migrate to the Imperial centre. The initial uptake was small, but, in hindsight, one of the most symbolic moments was the arrival at Tilbury Docks on 22 June 1948 of the ship the *Empire Windrush*, carrying mostly young men from the Caribbean eager to start new lives in Britain. Naturally, these were not the first West Indians to arrive in Britain, for while some of the new arrivals stayed in hostels, others stayed with friends who had made the journey before them. Black Britishness, a term that gained increasing currency in the 1990s, clearly did not begin with the *Empire Windrush*. Bruce King explains the change in terms of literary impact, noting that

> England over the centuries had people of colour and at times they had contributed to its literature, but the size of this new movement would have a lasting effect on British culture, remaking England into a multiracial society and giving its literature a new internationalism when, with the collapse of its empire, it risked narrowing its perspective to Little Englandism. (King 2004: 14)

The slippage between 'England' and 'British' is instructive, as is King's use of the pejorative term Little Englandism to denote the restricted and antagonistic perspective reminiscent of Enoch Powell's 1968 address to the West Midlands Conservative Political Service Centre. Better known as the 'Rivers of Blood' speech, in which the famously erudite Powell used a reference from Virgil's *Aeneid* (foretelling 'the River Tiber foaming with much blood'), the speech also quoted one of his constituents prophesying that 'in 15 or 20 years times the black man will have the whip hand over the white man' (Powell 2001: 13). The reality proved very different, so that thirty years on from Powell's speech, Prince Charles spoke at the official 'SS Empire Windrush Reception' at St James's Palace. Barbara Korte and Eva Ulrike Pirker suggest that

> The Empire Windrush has evolved into a foundation myth. David Myles refers to it as the 'mythical ark of West Indian emigration – their Mayflower' ... but the ship is now hailed as an 'icon' of British history along with the Notting Hill Carnival. The iconicity is all the more striking if one considers that, before the late 1990s, the Windrush had practically slipped from British consciousness. (Korte and Pirker 2011: 26–7)

The word 'slipped' insinuates that British people had forgotten about the *Empire Windrush* over the intervening half-century. In fact, as Korte and Pirker reveal, the overwhelming majority of Britons had not heard of the ship, let alone saw it as pivotal to the identity of the contemporary Britain they inhabited. Prince Charles admitted himself in his official speech that 'I had little idea of what the name Windrush signified', adding 'so preparing for this afternoon has been an education. Many other Britons, black and white, would have been through the same process over recent weeks' (Korte and Pirker 2011: 7). Charles probably spoke the truth – for the majority of non-Caribbean Britons in 1998 the *Empire Windrush* was less a myth than a revelation. But his speech and the reception reflected a broader recognition of important changes to notions of British identity.

These changes were not simply about the makeup of the British population, but also heralded transformations of British culture. Speaking to the Social Market Foundation in April 2001, British Foreign Secretary Robin Cook declared that 'Chicken tikka masala is now Britain's true national dish'. Developing a thesis that to some in the audience might have come as a surprise, Cook explained that this was so 'not only because it is the most popular, but because it is the perfect illustration of the way Britain absorbs and adapts external influences'. He expanded on these broader cultural implications: 'Chicken tikka is an Indian dish. The masala sauce was added to satisfy the desire of British people to have their meat served in gravy'.[1] Cook's theory about the origin of the dish is disputable – other claimants include a Bangladeshi cook in Glasgow – but the general thrust of his argument in what became known as the 'Chicken Masala Speech' was clear: Britain at the start of the twenty-first century was a multicultural country that celebrated its diversity. Another public example of the improved and approved status of blacks in Britain was a national conference organised in 1999 by the Arts Council under the title 'Whose Heritage? The Impact of Cultural Diversity on Britain's Living Heritage'. The Secretary of State for Culture, Media and Sport, Chris Smith, in his opening address, declared that 'diversity is a fundamental feature of Britain, and it is what makes it, in many ways, rather special' (cited in Korte and Pirker 2011: 21–2). Nor were Cook and Smith alone in foregrounding cultural diversity. A four-part BBC documentary in 1998 celebrated the fiftieth anniversary of the arrival of the *Empire Windrush* in 1948, and the revision of British identity that it began, starting with images of the British Olympic team captain Linford Christie holding aloft the British flag, footballer Ian Wright scoring a goal for England, the female group Eternal singing their international soul hit, 'Angel of Mine', and Trevor McDonald reading the BBC news, a voiceover declaring that 'A Britain without these faces would, today, be hard to imagine' (Upshal 1998). This had not always been the case: John Major's 1993 preference for the more mono-cultural world of the 1950s was only one of the decade's more benign instances of a less inclusive stance.

On a less positive note, the shadow of the Rushdie Affair fell over the 1990s, a measure of more contested social space. Salman Rushdie's startling rise from his breakthrough novel, *Midnight's Children*, in 1981, to the literary elite in Britain by the end of that decade, seemed to signify an increasingly ethnically heterogeneous Britain. It was also emblematic of the undeniable cultural impact on British literature by writers who until the 1990s were still more likely to be grouped under the monolithic and reductive term, 'black'. This chapter traces how during the decade 'black' became, in Paul Gilroy's terms, 'multi-accentual' (Procter 2000: 318), merely one – admittedly important – identifying signifier among many. Stuart Hall detected an important movement in the period towards 'new ethnicities' (Hall 1990) in Britain. Alienation could give way to the possibility of a hybridic Britain, one that incorporated, rather than rejected, difference. The creation of hyphenated identities during the period – including 'Black-British' and 'Asian-British' – suggested ongoing negotiations about selfhood and national character, not merely within immigrant communities, but within Britain itself. This is not to suggest a happy ethnic melting pot. As well as the turmoil that swirled about *The Satanic Verses*, the 1990s was also the decade when Brixton residents protested about deaths in police custody, where casual racism did not evaporate magically and in which Stephen Lawrence was brutally killed by racist thugs. Benjamin Zephaniah provided a necessary caution in his 1999 poem, 'What Stephen Lawrence Has Taught Us', performed on Channel 4 news:

> We know who the killers are
> We have watched them strutting before us
> As proud as sick Mussolinis,
> We have watched them strut before us
> Compassionless and arrogant,
> They paraded before us
> Like angels of death
> Protected by the law.
>
> (quoted in Procter 2000: 259)

The poem does not only call out injustice and indifference, institutionalised racism and police complicity, for it ends with a plea to Paul Condon, the Commissioner of the Metropolitan Police from 1993 to 2000, to

> Pop out of Teletubby land
> And visit reality,
> Come to an honest place
> And get some advice from your neighbours,
> Be enlightened by our community,

> Neglect your well-paid ignorance
> Because
> We know who the killers are.
>
> (quoted in Procter 2000: 261)

This is the voice of anger and protest, surely, but is also the voice of someone who feels part of a larger community, someone asserting the desire and the right to equal treatment. Those desires clearly have not been satisfied, but neither are they abandoned as wildly utopian. For all the shortcomings, and the slow pace of change, instances such as the government-backed 'Whose Heritage?' conference suggest discernible progress. It would have been unlikely before the 1990s, and demonstrates how the recognition of cultural diversity had become part of the mainstream of social thinking and process. Tony Blair, speaking about his sense of Britishness in March 2000, made plain that modern Britain resulted from 'a rich mix of different ethnic and religious identities and religious origins over the centuries'.[2] That mix became even richer over the 1990s.

If some of the reconsiderations of national identity examined in the previous chapter were inward looking, those by the writers examined in this chapter, such as Rushdie, Caryl Phillips, David Dabydeen and Moniza Alvi, were consciously and inquisitively connective, diasporic. In cultural terms the notion of diaspora, deriving from the term 'dispersal', recognises that movements of individuals and of peoples over time necessarily create important new implications for the places left behind and the places journeyed towards. As with 'internal' movements within Britain, some of which were considered in the previous chapter, these changes can be traumatic and unsettling, relocation entailing varying degrees of dislocation. They can also be interactive and productive, creating new forms, new ways of being and understanding. They can be understood as part of what King calls the 'internationalization of English literature' (King 2004) that had been taking place, though at a much slower pace, for decades. What emerges are complex, tentative and sometimes contradictory dynamics both within and between real communities, and what Benedict Anderson famously called 'imagined' communities, influenced by generational, gender, class, religious, national and ethnic differences. British writing in the 1990s displayed renegotiated power arrangements, in which 'black' characters were not simply integrated into the British community following an earlier period of alienation post-arrival in Britain, but increasingly were seen contributing to, and commenting critically on, the development of that community, and its changing identity.

While the decade offered vivid and often daring explorations by writers of new identities and territories, it was also a decade reflecting, whether consciously or not, the theoretical advances made under the general auspices of post-colonialism. The academic institutionalism of these ideas was advertised through university courses on the topic that sprouted in the late 1980s and especially in the 1990s. The seeds of these courses were planted earlier, key texts including Edward Said's *Orientalism* (1978) and Gayatri Chakravorty Spivak's 1988 essay, 'Can the Subaltern Speak?' One of the more referenced 1990s works was Homi Bhabha's *The Location of Culture* (1994), in which Bhabha argued, along similar lines to Stuart Hall in this chapter's epigraph, that

> what is theoretically innovative and politically crucial [in contemporary theory], is the need to think beyond narratives or originary and initial subjectivities and to focus on those moments and those processes that are produced in the articulation of cultural differences. The 'in-between' spaces provide the terrain for elaborating strategies of selfhood – singular or communal – that initiate new signs of identity, and innovative sites of collaboration, and contestation, in the act of defining the idea of society itself. (2)

The notion of the 'in-between' would drive many subsequent accounts of post-colonial literature well beyond British shores, as one might expect, many of the actual writers themselves being definable in those terms, sometimes as a result of their lived experience and because of the focus of some, or most, of their work. While a spatially oriented metaphor, the idea of 'in-between' spaces also suggested energy and movement, the tell-tale hyphen in this instance reflecting the to-and-fro of thought and deed encapsulated in the term 'strategies of selfhood', with consequent forms of personal and communal development.

A telling sign of the arrival of Post-Colonial Studies as an active and activist academic field was the production of texts that were meant primarily as university textbooks to underpin the new courses being created and expanded. As with other theories employing the 'post' prefix, arguments arose about whether or not to include a hyphen, whether the term following the hyphen was capitalised or not, let alone the specific question of when the colonial experience began and ended (if indeed it had ended). Perhaps the most referenced of the new theoretical texts for teaching to students was *The Empire Writes Back: Theory and Practice in Post-colonial Literatures* (1989), by Bill Ashcroft, Gareth Griffiths and Helen Tiffen. This provocative work presented a comprehensive account of the current state of post-colonial play on the cusp of the 1990s. *The Empire Writes Back*, as the authors declare in explaining some of the motivation for post-colonial literary studies, drew its title from Salman Rushdie:

> A characteristic of dominated literatures is an inevitable tendency towards subversions, and a study of the subversive strategies employed by post-colonial

writers would reveal both the configurations of domination and the imaginative and critical responses to this condition. Directly and indirectly, in Salman Rushdie's phrase 'the Empire writes back' to the imperial 'centre', not only through nationalist assertion, proclaiming itself central and self-determining, but even more radically by questioning the bases of European and British metaphysics, challenging the world-view that can polarize centre and periphery in the first place. (Ashcroft, Griffiths and Tiffen 1989: 32)

Centre and periphery (along with marginalisation) were key terms in much post-colonial thinking (the spatial aspect carrying geographical implications). The three authors would later edit *The Post-Colonial Studies Reader* (1995), its reprinting several times before the end of the decade proof of the reader's initiating quality and the rapid development of the field. Patrick Williams and Laura Chrisman in *Colonial Discourse and Post-Colonial Theory: A Reader* (1994) acknowledge the change, admitting that 'even a few years ago, a book of this nature might well have seemed a strange proposition', before countering that 'this is not now the case, thanks on the one hand to a greater awareness and on the other hand of the remarkable output of people working in the post-colonial field in recent years' (Williams and Chrisman 1994: ix). The similarly titled *Colonial Discourse/Postcolonial Theory* (1994) edited by Francis Barker et al., Ania Loomba's *Colonialism/Postcolonialism* (1998) and Derek Walder's *Post-colonial Literatures in English: History, Language, Theory* (1998) advertised the success of post-colonial studies not only in opening up new intellectual territory but also in prompting a re-evaluation of more mainstream or canonical literature. Walder's text also carried in its title the pluralising of the term literature, undercutting conventional ideas in the field of English Literature (single) by adding to the stock of possibilities, and (in this instance) by replacing what might be construed as the imperious dominance of the English in the term 'English Literature' with the less hierarchical, more inclusive, 'Literatures in English'.

Although post-colonial theory was in many ways constitutive of new ways of understanding literature, the primary, creative texts themselves and the writers who produced them also supplied innovative ways of addressing identity and ethnicity that were themselves in flux, and were contributing to fresh knowledge and more informed and nuanced responses. Cultural texts, including literature, film, television and music, created and maintained dialogue between groups that at times were still wary of each other. This wariness was not fully overcome in the nineties, as the Rushdie Affair would prove, but participants on all sides were able to contribute to more enlightened attitudes that promised greater awareness than before. Hanif Kureishi, born in Bromley, London, in 1954, of parents who had migrated from Pakistan, recorded his ambivalent relationship to Britain in the 1985 screenplay that made his name commercially: *My Beautiful Laundrette*. Set in South London, the film traced the rise of young English-born Omar Ali, son of a Pakistani journalist, once-famous but now a broken alcoholic. Omar's entrepreneurialism clashes with his father's left-wing past, but meshes with his uncle's Thatcherite success in Britain. Omar's path to success, he thinks, can be achieved through refashioning a rundown launderette into something beautiful and commercially viable, but this impetus is stalled and confused by a sexual relationship with his white working class friend, Johnny, who is trying himself to escape his neo-fascist past. Despite some highly charged political and social drama, *My Beautiful Laundrette* is also a comedy that satirises notions of racial or ethnic purity. Kureishi enjoys exposing social absurdities, and his first novel, *The Buddha of Suburbia* (1990), adopts a wry comic mode from the outset:

> My name is Karim Amir, and I am an Englishman born and bred, almost. I am considered a funny kind of Englishman, a new breed as it were, having emerged from two old histories. But I don't care – Englishman I am (though not proud of it), from the South London suburbs and going somewhere. Perhaps it is the odd mixture of continents and blood, of here and there, of belonging and not, that makes me reckless and bored. Or perhaps it was being brought up in the suburbs that did it. (Kureishi 1990: 3)

The qualifications in the opening paragraph arrest any simple ethnic profiling on the reader's part, Kureishi playing with the tension between Karim's name and his assertion that he is 'an Englishman born and bred'. The word 'almost' provides the rhetorical and social punchline. Ambivalent though it pretends to be, Karim's first person narrative allows him to control that ambivalence, to choose which parts of the 'two old histories' that he claims to belong to best suit him. His name might suggest that the second history is that of Pakistan, but he quickly establishs that his father is Indian, having arrived in 1950 largely ignorant of the country to which he was migrating, and becoming a lowly civil service clerk. The novel's title suggests other possibilities, the ironies embedded in *The Buddha of Suburbia* combining the allure of 'Eastern' religion to the 'progressive' white middle class with the drabness of London suburbia in 1970s Britain where the narrative begins. Karim's father is the eponymous Buddha, who fuses together a mishmash of oriental philosophy and religion for an 'enlightened' English crowd searching for release or enlightenment. Key among these is Eva Kay, the organiser of the groups to which the Buddha preaches, whose motives are more sexual than spiritual, providing Kureishi with the opportunity to lampoon the West's attraction to Eastern spiritual enlightenment:

> I didn't recognise Eva Kay when she greeted us at the door, and for a moment I thought we had turned up at the wrong place. The only thing she wore was a full-length, multi-coloured kaftan, and her hair was down, and out, and up. She had darkened her eyes with kohl so that she looked like a panda. (8–9)

Eva's multi-faceted if dubious desire for things Eastern provides Karim's father with the escape he needs from his dull but dutiful English wife, entirely satisfied with suburbia and a diet of British television.

Karim is the archetypal young man on the make, the novel's two parts, 'In the Suburbs' and 'In the City', charting his move from what he perceives as stifling periphery to active and enticing centre. As a teenager, he casually explores his bisexuality, the latest music trends from Soft Machine to Pink Floyd, Led Zeppelin to jazz, avant-garde French and Black Panther philosophies, especially with his intellectually free-spirited cousin Jamila, whose adventurous spirit is stifled by her being required to fit traditional roles for females. Karim negotiates a changing world still inherently warped by racism, in which his uncle Ted, taking him to watch a Spurs match, dismisses Herne Hill and Brixton as 'where the niggers live. Them blacks' (43). Unsurprisingly, Karim himself is the focus of abuse, called Curryface at school, and told to 'Eat shit, Pakis'. And he understands the hypocritical local attitudes to people like him and Jamila: 'The thing was, we were supposed to be English, but to the English we were always wogs and nigs and Pakis and the rest of it' (53). Escape from the suburbs to the inner city proves liberating, but his never entirely convincing aspirations to be an actor are compromised when the major role he wins is that of Mowgli, the Indian boy in a stage version of Rudyard Kipling's *The Jungle Book*. Kureishi depicts the theatre world comically as one of fragile or monstrous egos, pretention and insincerity, but Jamila's response to *The Jungle Book*, calling it 'neo-fascist', 'disgusting' and 'just pandering to prejudices' (157), exposes the problematic shadow of racism in the text. For all that, the naïve Karim enjoys the role for the recognition it affords, and acting will take him to the real global cultural centre, the ultimate 1970s city, New York. Kureishi has the satirist's eye for the hypocrisies and absurdities of all his characters, especially those looking ostentatiously for 'meaning', or indulging in empty posing. An example of the former provokes Karim's surprise finding towards the end of the narrative: 'I'd always thought that Dad's guru business would eventually fall off in London, but it was clear now that he would never lack employment while the city was full of lonely, unhappy, unconfident people who required guidance, support and pity' (279).

The observation blends cynicism with humanist empathy. Posing is mocked when Karim returns to London and visits a new club in Covent

Garden. Fashions have changed, so that hippies and punks are passé, the club instead filled with people aping John Major's favourite author: 'It was like being in a room full of George Orwell lookalikes, except that Orwell would have eschewed the earrings' (270). Lonely people and lookalikes populate a book where authenticity is sometimes sought but rarely found.

The world of the theatre, which provides Karim with considerable pleasure, proves emblematic of this often shallow, manipulative and showy world, offering him the potential simultaneously to reveal and hide his true self. That would be easier were he to know fully what that self was, but, like other characters in *The Buddha of Suburbia*, Karim's moments of insight are usually dulled by idiocy or superficial hedonism. In the finale, his father and Eva marry, as befits what essentially is a comedy that considers interethnic relations. This prompts Karim to 'think about the past and what I'd been through as I'd struggled to locate myself and learn what the heart is. Perhaps in the future I would live more deeply' (283–4). The urge for a more profound life comes freighted with intrinsic qualifications. To this can be added the reality that the novel's title, much of its action and Karim's own passage from innocence to experience are marked by him being a 'funny kind of Englishman'. While he might be a 'new breed' and the product of 'two old histories' in his own eyes, in the world of 1970s and 1980s Britain the novel recaptures, he understands that he remains 'an odd mixture', a state of affairs determined not by him but by those around him. As in the theatre, the 'audience' has a complex and often determining effect in accepting or rejecting those on stage, in making the final discrimination, so to speak. That does not mean that progress and valuable change are impossible or doomed. Early on, for example, Karim describes his father's Buddha outfit: 'He was certainly exotic, probably the only man in southern England at the time (apart, possibly, from George Harrison) wearing a red and gold waistcoat and Indian pyjamas' (31). In the final scene, in an expensive Soho restaurant where the marriage between Eva and his father is announced, Karim comments that 'Eva persuaded Dad into his Nehru jacket, collarless and buttoned up to the throat like a Beatle jacket, only longer. The waiters would think he was an ambassador or a prince, or something' (282). The 'exotic' might be misinterpreted, but (in this case, drawing from an early decade on the celebrity of The Beatles) misinterpretation can also convey cultural power.

The Buddha of Suburbia dissects assorted and mutable connections and contradictions between identity and context, satirically assessing the desire for meaning within a nation still riven with ethnic tension and misinterpretation. This fluid sense of identity resonates with the idea of 'new ethnicities' that Stuart Hall detected:

> If the black subject and black experience are not stabilised by Nature, or by some essential guarantee, then it must be the case that they are constructed historically, culturally, politically – and the concept that refers to this is 'ethnicity'. The term ethnicity acknowledged the place of history, language and culture in the construction of identity, as well as the fact that all subjectivity and discourse is placed, positioned, situated, and all knowledge is contextual. (Hall 1996: 447)

This angle on ethnicity necessarily incorporates the identity of 'white' subjects, recognising them also as constructed historically. In one sense, the types of questions and problems addressed in the previous chapter indicate how those supposedly stable national identities were themselves increasingly under scrutiny. As before, it is important not to exaggerate the importance of the 1990s in bringing such questions and concerns to the fore; as the example of the Scottish Renaissance in literature in the 1920s and 1930s makes plain, such questions have long, often highly complicated, narratives. At the same time, it is worth noting how the nineties aided a new and often more sophisticated conception of ethnicity, one incorporating real world experience and imaginative literary interventions. By way of counterargument, power imbalances had typically and historically done much to entrench white advantage. Erasing one's ethnicity, assimilating to the prevailing cultural norms, proved one way of overcoming this imbalance. Yet Jung Min Choy points out that 'Assimilation involves abandoning one identity and accepting another. What this suggests is the gradual eradication of ethnicity. The implication is that by ridding themselves of their former traits and accepting an Anglo identity, minorities will be significantly improved' (Choy 1997: 116). The difficulties of such abandonment and acceptance are manifest, but the subtle and sometimes playful literary rejections of limited and policed notions of authenticity and origin in Britain were more likely in the 1990s than ever before.

One contemporary sign of this disregard for limitations was a BBC radio sketch show (1996–8) later adapted as a television show: *Goodness Gracious Me!* Its title was taken from the song sung by Sophia Loren and Peter Sellers in the 1960 film *The Millionairess*, in which Sellers plays an Indian doctor, Ahmed Al Kabir. Sellers (made up to look 'Indian') sings his part of the song in what, for 1960, was accepted by audiences as a 'funny' Indian accent. By re-appropriating what by the 1990s was an out-dated stereotype, the show's four creators – all of Indian descent, but born respectively in Kenya, Mumbai, London and Wolverhampton – indelibly mark the cultural distance between the decades. The television show, first shown in 1998, reached an audience far greater than that achieved by the original radio version. Its success allowed the presenters to launch individual careers that began to normalise Indian faces on television and in film. The show mocked traditional attitudes to, or ignorance of, Indian culture generally, sometimes by exposing prejudice through reverse perspective. So, in what would become a series of sketches, a group of drunken Bombay Indians 'go for an English' at a restaurant, their inappropriate and culturally ignorant behaviour parodying that shown by drunken English going to an Indian restaurant. Another regular skit featured 'Mr Everything Comes From India', a character lampooning those British Indians who tried to claim Indian primacy in all things. One of the most subversive regular skits dealt with the hypocrisies of assimilation: two British Indian couples, the Kapoors and the Rabindranaths, represent themselves as the Coopers and the Robinsons, openly if feebly denying their Indian heritage. This pretence requires not only that they adulterate their true identities to fit into what they take to be English norms, but that they also perform to each other as their fake 'English' selves. These excruciatingly funny acts of bad faith inevitably create vortexes of self-loathing and ludic pretence. In one instance, they meet by chance in a pub. 'St John Cooper' (real name, Sanjay Kapoor) confidently orders 'three pints of Cobblers and a yard of ale'. When hostile white locals tell them to leave, and then threaten to murder them, the Kapoors and the Rabindranaths pray for their lives using cod Christian phrases. A West Indian man who enters the pub saves them, not by any act he performs, but by being an even greater figure of hatred than the Indians. The open relief of the Kapoors and the Rabindranaths, that a West Indian might be even more unpalatable to the English than Indians desperately pretending to be English, deftly illustrates the edgy and complicated ethnic and racial politics of the time. That they, as Indians, feel no solidarity with another 'black' figure (indeed, they openly look down on him) adds an extra nuance to what is a charged comic situation. This type of tough-minded and unsentimental humour reflected a cultural politics that noted changes and subtleties, but also acknowledged ingrained prejudice on all sides. The satire worked in several directions and for several audiences simultaneously, while activating an awareness of distinct perspectives and justifications. The show also gave a voice to generational difference, the younger age group distancing itself from the entrenched view of its migrant predecessors. *Goodness Gracious Me!* critically evaluated Indian Britons of all generations, proving how intolerance could work both ways, as well as between generations and different ethnic groups. The show's success in scoring satirical points with well-crafted humour was rewarded in a host of prizes and the addition of phrases such as 'kiss my chuddies' and 'going for an English' to the British lexicon.

The outward confidence and exuberance exhibited by Kureishi and the writers and performers of *Goodness Gracious Me!* were not the only positions adopted by writers. Jackie Kay provides a telling example of a different experience of being black in Britain in the poem 'In My Country', from her 1993 Bloodaxe collection, *Other Lovers*. Kay was born in Edinburgh in 1961 to a Scottish mother and a Nigerian father, eventually being adopted by two white Glaswegians. She read English Literature at Stirling University. This unconventional upbringing creates sometimes unintentionally comic situations, as Kay explains:

> People often ask me where I'm from, even in my own country – I seem to have a whole collection of strange anecdotes of people doing that. I'm going to sit down in a pub on a chair in London and this woman went 'You cannae sit in that chair. It's my chair.' And me saying to her, 'Oh right, you're from Glasgow, aren't you?' And she says, 'Aye, how did you know that?' And I said, 'I'm from Glasgow myself,' and she went, 'You're not are you? You foreign looking bugger!'[3]

While the ethnic diversity in parts of England and especially of London was customary in the 1960s, that in Scotland was far less established. Kay's first collection of poetry, *The Adoption Papers* (1991), dealt with some of the autobiographical issues surrounding her circumstances, addressing adoption from the perspectives of the child, the birth mother and the adopted mother. It won one of Scotland premier literary prizes, the Saltire Society Scottish First Book Award, an award given to 'living authors of Scottish descent or residing in Scotland' or where the book's subject is 'the life or work of a Scot or with a Scottish question, event or situation'.[4] Previous winners included A. L. Kennedy. *The Adoption Papers* also won a Scottish Arts Council Book Award. *Other Lovers* ventures more broadly, dealing with the slave-based identities of Afro-Caribbeans, and with the American blues singer, Bessie Smith. It also contains a poem that addresses the lived reality of a black woman in Scotland:

In My Country

> walking by the waters
> down where an honest river
> shakes hands with the sea
> a woman passed round me
> in a slow, watchful circle
> as if I were a superstition;
>
> or the worst dregs of her imagination,
> so when she finally spoke

her words spliced into bars
of an old wheel. A segment of air.
Where do you come from?
'Here,' I said, 'Here. These parts.'

(Kay 1993: 24)

The poem neatly exposes the tinged ambiguity of the speaker's situation, the first lines setting up an almost lyrical account of place characterised by connection ('My country'), ethics ('an honest river') and mutual respect ('shakes hands with the sea'). The speaker's connection to the landscape, subtly underlined by the alliterative link between 'walking' and 'waters', gets abruptly troubled by the second half of the stanza in which an anonymous – and, therefore, worryingly representative – woman passes in an almost magical 'slow, watchful circle', Kay emphasising her crone-like qualities in the term 'superstition'. But by this point of the poem the speaker is the one under scrutiny, agency undermined. Various meanings of superstition have hardened in the speaker's realisation, contained in the phrase 'the worst dregs of her imagination', of the woman's horrified menace. To this point, no words have been spoken by either party, but the dramatic tension slowly activated in the phrase 'so when she finally spoke' sets up the expectation of release encountered in the final two lines. Kay enhances the rhetorical force of the demand-question, 'Where do you come from', by italicising it, giving the words typographical energy and intimidation. The speaker literally has the last word and the last words, the repetition of 'Here' (along with its capitalisation) functioning successfully as a counterclaim of personal value and belonging. As a consequence, the now-dynamic speaker forces home the advantage by claiming, in the insistent connection to 'These parts', a fundamental and identity-confirming allegiance to the place that both inhabit at that moment. The possession of territory and the absence of any subsequent recorded comeback marks a substantive victory for the speaker. The poem never explains the cause of the woman's animosity, universalising beyond a reading that would restrict 'In My Country' to Kay's own situation. By being less specific, less openly auto-biographical, the poem speaks for all those challenged to justify themselves in a space where they are deemed by the self-confident 'local' to have no place.

Moniza Alvi's poem 'I Would Like to Be A Dot in A Painting by Miró' from her first collection, *The Country on My Shoulder* (1993), later incorporated into the collection *Carrying My Wife* (2000), offers a different slant on the importance and perils of place and identity in relationship to it. Born in Pakistan to a Pakistani father and English mother, Alvi's family moved to England when she was a baby. *The Country on My Shoulder* in part deals with questions of belonging. It gained Alvi sufficient acclaim so that she was included in the *Poetry Review*'s 1994 'New Generation' promotion. The poem begins:

> I would like to be a dot in a painting by Miró.
> Barely distinguishable from the other dots,
> it's true, but quite uniquely placed.
> And from my dark centre
> I'd survey the beauty of the linescape
> and wonder – would it be worthwhile
> to roll myself towards the lemon stripe,
> Centrally poised, and push my curves
> against its edge, to get myself a little attention?
> But it's fine where I am.
>
> (Alvi 2000: 118)

The muted tone and ambition of the speaker – 'would it be worthwhile' – has almost Prufrockian echoes, without J. Alfred's paranoia and self-loathing. There is a restrained confidence in the wish to be barely distinguishable while knowing one is quite uniquely placed, as though the speaker is willing to accept the limitations for the simultaneous advantages of being a dot or a line in a work by Miró. Alvi draws on the importance of the placement of dots, lines and assorted and fantastic shapes in Miró's art to underscore the virtues of stillness and balance. Identity resides in the appreciation of connections and distinctions, of difference ('my dark centre', 'the lemon stripe') and a commonality that makes that difference barely distinguishable.

'The Double City', from her 1996 collection, *A Bowl of Warm Air*, also in *Carrying My Wife*, presents a far more dynamic and disturbing consideration of politicised social space:

> I live in one city,
> But then it becomes another.
> The point where they mesh –
> I call it mine.
>
> Dacoits creep from caves
> In the banks of the Indus.
>
> One of them is displaced.
> From Trafalgar Square
> he dominates London, his face
> masked by scarves and sunglasses.
> He draws towards him all the conflict
> Of the metropolis – his speech
> A barrage of grenades, rocket-launchers.
>
> (Alvi 2000: 69)

This first section of the poem situates the speaker geographically, politically and emotionally at the intersection of newly terrorised space. The displacement of the gang member from caves on the banks of the Indus River reconfigures London as a double city that simultaneously continues blithely on and unwittingly is under threat, where 'there are fluid streets / and solid streets. On some it is safe to walk'. The uncertainty over which streets are safe and which not intensifies the oppressive mood. Alvi sharpens the focus by dealing with a specific court case, that of an Indian woman in London who burned her abusive husband to death. Against the rather generic (though still worrying) image of the terrorist, the actual legal controversy that involved contrasting cultural codes of subservience and independence heightens even further the tension and menace of the double city:

The women of Southall
champion the release
of the battered Kiranjit
who killed her husband.
Lord Taylor, free her now!
Their saris billow in a storm of chants

(Alvi 2000: 69)

The naming of Southall gives this part of the poem cultural and social specificity that acts as a communal refusal to be oppressed, the italicised plea (a typographical breach of legal norms) recalling Benjamin Zephaniah's call for Police Commissioner Paul Condon to visit the world of Stephen Lawrence. The italics here energise the final line, fusing political and cultural agency. Kiranjit Ahluwlia, the wronged woman in the poem, eventually had her life sentence overturned.

Less fortunate was Salman Rushdie, who had to endure a storm of antagonistic chants, rather than be bolstered by them. Rushdie's literary reputation as one of the best writers of his generation, a place gained initially with *Midnight's Children*, remained largely undiminished in the 1990s. Indeed, *Midnight's Children* won the Booker of Bookers in 1993, an award to celebrate the twenty-fifth anniversary of Britain's most prestigious literary prize. The ongoing international cultural and religious furore over *The Satanic Verses* would haunt him through the nineties, chiefly, of course, because he was under constant threat of assassination. The Rushdie Affair points to fault lines in any overarching myth of easy or comfortable acceptance in Britain of difference, and indeed the sometimes consciously disruptive discourses opened up new divisions that had little to do with the actual contents of the novel itself. Many who condemned *The Satanic Verses* had not read it; that might be true for some who supported it. The overtly religious concerns the novel addressed, made plain in its title, created much of the antagonism, both within Britain and abroad. Only a decade earlier than the fatwah against

Rushdie, Monty Python's *Life of Britain* (1979) had been accused of a blasphemous misrepresentation of the life of Christ, and had been banned in parts of Britain – including Aberystwyth, where the ban was only lifted in 2009. Religious controversy in the cultural arena was not unknown.

Rushdie had come to England as a boy to attend Rugby School and then Cambridge University, where his lawyer father had also studied, giving him a substantially different background from many poor migrants from the Commonwealth. Kenan Malik suggests that 'Rushdie always saw himself as a man inhabiting a world "in-between" three cultures: India, Pakistan and England' (Malik 2013: vii). In the light of the previous chapter, the use of 'England' rather than 'Britain' explains the specificity of Rushdie's affiliations. Malik continues that what Rushdie

> wanted to discover through his fiction was how to 'connect the different worlds from which he had come', by exploring *'how the world joined up*, not only how the East flowed into the West and the West into the East, but how the past shaped the present while the present changed the understanding of the past, and how the imagined world, the location of dreams, art, invention and, yes, belief, leaked across the frontier that separated it from the everyday, "real" place in which humans mistakenly believe they lived'. (Malik 2013: vii–viii)

This relative privilege fed into a more general charge made against Rushdie during *The Satanic Verses* controversy, based on the tensions between his origins (he was born in Bombay into a Muslim family) and his later British citizenship. David Lawton, in his 1993 study, *Blasphemy*, suggests that one reaction was that 'Rushdie, coming from a Muslim background, knows Muslim culture and its ethos. But having become acculturated in British Society, and protected by its institutions, he is holding up his abandoned culture to scorn' (Lawton 1993: 184). Lawton traces the genealogy of the term 'blasphemy' over several centuries, arguing vigorously that 'There is manifestly nothing in the book to support a view that Rushdie has "become acculturated in British Society".' Instead, Lawton contends, 'One of the themes of the book is the impossibility of such acculturation without freer movement between communities and the social commitment for transculturing.' For Lawton, 'it is for such acculturation that Saladin Chamcha is satirised in the early part of the book' (85). The failure or foolishness of acculturation needs to be contextualised by remembering that the controversy was ignited in India before the book was originally published in Britain late in 1988. As Daniel Pipes notes, Muslims in India

> learned about the book from two magazines, *India Today* and *Sunday*, which in their mid-September [1988] editions provided reviews of the book,

excerpts, and interviews with the author. With prescience and understatement, Madhu Jain predicted in *India Today* that *The Satanic Verses* 'is bound to trigger an avalanche of protests from the ramparts'.

It did not take long. Syed Shahbuddin and Khurshid Alam Kahn, Muslim members of the Indian parliament, did not like what they had read of the book, so they began a campaign to have the book banned in India. (Pipes 1999: 19)

Shahbuddin would not read the novel, arguing that 'I do not have to wade through a filthy drain to know what filth is' (quoted in Pipes 1999: 20). His reaction was echoed by many over the subsequent years. Lawton adds an interesting and informative piece of information that might further explain the extreme reaction, commenting that 'when the title is translated into Arabic it reads as "The Satanic Qu-ran", or "The Quran is Satan's Work"', adding that 'There is therefore a very strong possibility that the book would have escaped such serious trouble under another title' (Lawton 1993: 183). Rushdie would survive the 1990s, but another of the cruel absurdities of *The Satanic Verses* affair was that others were killed, including (in 1991) the Italian and Japanese translators of the novel. Rushdie's own responses to the unprecedented pressures were humanly contradictory, including in 1990 an apology to Muslims for any offence, and an essay in the same year, 'In Good Faith', in which he tried to explain what he had written and why he had written it. One problem Rushdie faced in making his case was that the global audiences for and against him were diffuse and mutually antagonistic, so that, for all the intelligent and tolerant arguments that he made, intolerance was not assuaged.

Other authors born in former British colonies, such as David Dabydeen and Caryl Philips, supply more positive examples of the fate of such writers in the 1990s. Dabydeen was born in Guyana in 1955, when the nation was still a plantation economy known as British Guiana. It became an independent republic in 1966 and is the only South American nation with English as an official language. Dabydeen emigrated to England with his father, eventually reading English Literature at Cambridge and obtaining a PhD at University College, London. As well as being a creative writer, Dabydeen became, and continues to function as, an academic. His output as a writer moves between the academic and the creative. Works such as *The Black Presence in English Literature* (1985) and *Black Writers in Britain 1760–1890* (1991), an anthology of primary texts he edited in collaboration with noted postcolonial authority Paul Edwards, attesting to his expertise in the area, as well as to the rising interest in the subject at the time. His critical overview as an academic on the situation for black writers in the English or British setting, and their particular difficulties associated with the process of writing and publishing, are worth extended quotation. By 1990 Dabydeen was a highly regarded poet, his first collection, *Slave Song* (1984), winning the Commonwealth Poetry Prize. In the provocatively titled essay 'On Not Being Milton: Nigger Talk in England Today', Dabydeen wrote that

> The pressure now is also towards mimicry. Either you drop the epithet 'black' and think of yourself as a 'writer' (a few of us foolishly embrace this position, desirous of the status of 'writing' and knowing that 'black' is blighted) – that is, you cease dwelling on the nigger/tribal/nationalistic theme, or you cease *folking* [sic] up the literature, and you become 'universal' – or else you perish in the backwater of small presses, you don't get published in the 'quality' presses, and you don't receive the corresponding patronage of media hype. (Dabydeen 1990: 12–13)

The scare quotes and italicisation illustrate the distinct and somewhat distant situation of the 'black' writer required to take into account and to some degree internalise the prevailing literary and cultural forces that structure and propel or retard the publication and the reception of literature. The rejection of those forces is possible, Dabydeen suggests, but the impact is likely to be severe and damaging to the writer's attempt to attract publishers and readers. Inherent in the tensions between authenticity and popularity, universality or marginality, are real life implications for the possibilities of surviving as a writer, a precarious enough existence in itself. The essay attempts to educate readers in what otherwise might not be obvious to a 'non-black' audience, the implication being that black writers are required to deal with issues that do not impinge upon most white writers, or not to the same degree. As was noted in the previous chapter, a writer such a Gwyneth Lewis must make conscious and consequential choices about the language or languages in which she writes, but those choices are less loaded than the ones Dabydeen foregrounds.

In addition to these overarching concerns, Dabydeen has written insightfully about the actual subject matter that black writers might deal with, especially in terms of an established English literary canon that includes writers such as John Milton and Joseph Conrad. The latter's novella, *Heart of Darkness*, provides the basis for the title of Dabydeen's 1991 novel, *The Intended*, that epithet being given to the woman Kurtz was meant to marry and whom Marlow visits at the finale. In an interview, Dabydeen explains that with *The Intended*

> I wanted to show how the [main] character misrepresents what England is by taking on official English definitions of themselves. The English define them-

selves in terms of a heritage of language, a very glorious heritage of achievement, of order, of civilisation. This black character, who wants to be English, gravitates towards the myth of England rather than trying to seek out the reality of England. (Dabydeen 1995: 85)

Dabydeen's focus on English, rather than British, definitions and heritage creates a targeted ambivalence, one that also surfaces in an explanation of his novel *Disappearance* (1993), in which a young Guyanese engineer struggles to arrest the erosion of a Kentish coastal village, by building up its defences against the disappearance of its cliff faces. Again, Dabydeen observes the problems faced by writers from outside an established tradition, in this case problems based not simply on those of representation, but on the relation of the writer to place:

> When ex-colonial writers deal with England, they are terrified of confronting the English landscape, the English rural landscape, so the bulk of writing is set in cities. No black writer, apart from V. S. Naipaul, has ever dealt intimately with the English rural landscape, with village life and this is because the English landscape is an archetype of the English identity and we are still made to feel that we are immigrants and therefore outsiders. (Dabydeen 1995: 80)

This dislocation from location – again, a specifically English location – adds another component of marginalisation, even if Dabydeen, as an 'ex-colonial writer', is not willing to concede defeat entirely, adding 'Although I can't yet live the rural experience, I can describe it' (81). The erosion of landscape is a key motif in *Disappearance*, symbolically the defining boundary between England and the outside world, highlighting the multi-faceted importance of a colonial subject from Guyana metaphorically, and to some degree literally, attempting to shore up that boundary.

While Dabydeen's combination of ex-colonial writer in Britain and academic was unusual in the 1990s, it was not unique. Caryl Philips was born in 1958 in St Kitts, a tiny island in the West Indies, with a population of less than 50,000. His family migrated to Britain when he was a baby. Philips recorded one effect of this diasporic move, commenting that

> I grew up in Leeds in the sixties and seventies, in a world in which everybody, from teachers to policemen, felt it appropriate to ask me – some more forcefully than others – for an explanation of where I was from. The answer 'Leeds' or 'Yorkshire,' was never going to satisfy them. Of course as a result, it was never going to satisfy me either. (quoted in Walters 2005: 130)

Yet Philips prospered, studying English at Oxford in the 1970s, producing plays and, after graduating, writing two plays that were staged in

London. In his twenties, he returned to St Kitts, and for the next decade lived at times there and in England, producing the novels *The Final Passage* (1985), *Higher Ground* (1988) and *Cambridge* (1991). The last of these novels captures the symbolic power of the journey back and forth between England and the West Indies, dealing with the double narrative of Emily, a young middle class English girl who visits her father's West Indian plantation, and the eponymous Cambridge, a slave transported to England. Cambridge converts to Christianity, becomes a missionary and then is captured on his return to the West Indies, made a slave again, gets charged for murder and is hanged. *Cambridge* juxtaposes Emily's textual record, her journal, with the internal thoughts of Cambridge (whose real name, he tells the reader, is Olumide, although other European names have been imposed upon him over time). The novel's title clearly suggests other possibilities than those the reader encounters, and this undermining of beliefs, and the requirement that modern readers critically engage with their own knowledge (or lack thereof) of the slave experience and of plantation life for the colonial masters, propels and complicates the plot. Imposing names on slaves was a long-established part of a consciously dehumanising process devised to eradicate an identity while claiming English control over the individual so renamed. But the name also foregrounds the importance of place and displacement, the ways in which voyages, chosen or brutally imposed, are themselves transformative, defining and redefining notions of personal and communal identity, and of conceptions of 'home' and its relation to selfhood.

Similar themes illuminate Philips' 1993 novel, *Crossing the River*, one of the more challenging examinations of ethnic relationships, dealing as it does with the impact of slavery on African, British and American characters over several centuries. Its title incorporates several possible interpretations: the journey of the dead across the river Styx; Heraclitus' view that it is impossible to step in the same river twice, the sense of endless change incorporating both infinite fleeting moments and something inherently eternal; the difficulties faced by African characters as they cross literal and metaphorical boundaries; the possibility or impossibility of return to a home that may not even still exist. The novel is filled with journeys made, and, just as importantly, not made, chosen and imposed through slavery, exploration, colonisation and war. It subtly assesses ways in which such journeys have an impact not only on those who make them and the people they encounter as a result, but also on those who do not make the journey, who are haunted by the loss that diaspora imposes on those left behind. *Crossing the River* begins with an unnamed, archetypal father in Africa, lamenting that he had to sell his three children, Nash, Martha and Travis, into slavery, because the crops failed:

> Children. I am your father. I love you. But understand. There are no paths in water. No signposts. There is no return. To a land trampled by the muddy boots of others. To a people encouraged to war among themselves. To a father consumed with guilt. You are beyond. Broken off, like limbs from a tree. (Philips 1993: 1–2)

This doleful invocation fits with Stuart Hall's belief in the impossibility of unproblematic return; the person or character who returns is changed, as is the place to which they return; stability of identity, whether of person or of place, is a denial of lived history. The father's lament registers the transformative nature of diaspora, especially, as is often the case, when that dispersal is enforced. Philips fashions a provocative example of the harsh reality that the dispersed characters in his novel must discover and deal with, a launching into other-worldliness requiring that readers deploy both empathy and critical adventurousness. Successive sections of the novel trace the narratives of characters with the names 'Nash', 'Martha' and 'Travis', the children the father addresses in his opening cry. Given the historical sweep of the novel over two and a half centuries, from the initial slave trade, through to the Second World War, it eventually becomes clear that the 'Nash', 'Martha' and 'Travis', central to the respective sections, are representative rather than real figures. Philips adds levels of complexity by integrating the stories of these characters with the voices of 'white' characters integral not only to the lives of these characters, but also to the way they see themselves and are seen in the societies they inhabit. Consequently, relationships between the characters both within specific time periods and across time activate networks of historical, political, psychological and ethnic connection.

Crossing the River is composed of four sections – 'The Pagan Coast', 'West', 'Crossing the River' and 'Somewhere in England' – located on two continents (North America and Africa) and one country (England). Each offers an actively off-centre take on transatlantic black experience. 'The Pagan Coast', for example, relates Nash's tale, that of a freed slave returning to Africa from the United States in the early nineteenth century as an emissary of the American Colonization Society, an attempt to establish a colony of freed American slaves in the newly formed African nation of Liberia. The ironies of this endeavour are complex, including the re-colonisation of Africa by *avant la lettre* African-Americans who are themselves freed slaves, the naïve homogenising of the prolific variety of African continent as though it were one country, and the related and mistaken hope that a return to a place as immense and disconnected as

Africa can be a return 'home'. Added to these complexities is the fraught relationship between Nash and his former master, Edward. Edward functions as Nash's lost father figure, revealed in a series of poignant letters sent back by Nash to the United States; but Edward secretly lusts after his erstwhile slave. 'West' is Martha's story, again a surprising one given the common belief that white settlers opened up the United States in the nineteenth century. Martha is another imposed name, its bearer an African whose husband and daughter are sold at a slave market, and who escapes from Kansas slave owners for a new life in California. That place provides the quintessential site of hope and renewal in the larger myth of America's Manifest Destiny, which proclaimed that God had gifted Americans a new Eden for them to cultivate. The reality is less idyllic, ingrained prejudice ensuring that Martha never reaches the promised land. 'Somewhere in England' recounts Travis's narrative as a black American soldier in England during the Second World War, seen through the eyes of Joyce. She is a young northern England white woman, shoddily treated by her first husband and family, and attracted by Travis's novelty, vitality and gentility. She retains the wariness of her generation to outsiders, commenting that 'I didn't like to ask too much because I didn't know much about Americans. Or Coloureds' (202). Still, the prospect of new life in the United States, far away from the anonymous boredom and insularity that the section's title, 'Somewhere in England', conveys, points to another adventurous transatlantic journey, another transformation of identity, this time for Joyce as a representative 'war bride'. Travis's vigour and civility function as alluring counterpoints to the cramped, Little England attitudes from which Joyce hungers to escape in the hope of reimagining herself. *Crossing the River* ends, appropriately enough, with the father whose foolish act in selling his children 'created' the narrative: 'A many-tongued chorus continues to swell. And I hope among its survivors' voices I might occasionally hear those of my own children. My Nash. My Martha. My Travis. My daughter. Joyce. All. Hurt but determined' (237).

This belated and figurative recognition by the father of the voices of those figurative children places them with an incalculable multitude of narratives spoken and sung over two-and-a-half centuries by an incalculable multitude of real people. Extrapolating from his own fictional characters to the world beyond, Philips achieves a fascinating reconciliation in *Crossing the River*, one that places literature firmly in the centre of the realisation and representation of new, multiracial ethnicities. Wendy Walters sees Philips as a writer enabling readers to 'perceive a sustaining passion, to consider the ways in which survival is possible, and to imagine new futures' (Walters 2005: 133). From a slightly different perspective, Bénédicte Ledent observes that *Crossing the River* charts

> an ever-evolving process in which fixity and an assertive homogeneous identity have no place ... exemplified again and again, not only in the novel's multi-focused narrative, but in its meaningfully polyphonic and open-ended structure. ... The multiple physical and cultural passages experienced by all the characters constantly challenge the roles traditionally imposed upon them by class, race, gender or nation. (Ledent 1995: 58)

Crossing the River won the 1993 James Tait Black Memorial Prize, one of the most respected literary prizes in Britain. Philips had already won *The Sunday Times* Young Writer of the Year Award in 1992, and was included in the *Granta* list of 'Best Young British Novelists' in 1993. Chapter 5 considers in more detail how *Granta*'s initial 1983 list heralded writers such as Martin Amis and Pat Barker who were to become central to the direction of contemporary British writing. In the celebrity-enamoured 1990s, making the 1993 list was an important signal of Philips's critical success. Ironically, by that stage Philips had himself 'crossed the river', taking up a teaching post at Amherst College, Massachusetts, while moving between St Kitts, England and the United States. By 1998 he was Henry R. Luce Professor of Migration and Social Order at Columbia University in New York. But to show that he had not severed his connections with Britain, or it with him, in 2000 he was elected a Fellow of the Royal Society of Literature (a body set up in 1820 to award writers of the highest merit). David Dabydeen was elected a Fellow in the same year, these accolades small but indelible signs of recognition and respect that the 1990s conferred on writers born beyond British shores.

The nineties was a complicated but transformative decade for writing by individuals who had 'crossed the river', or were the recent descendants of those who had made that adventurous journey. Transformative not only for those who had travelled, but also for the Britain that they increasingly and insistently called home. The degree of affiliation was different for different individuals, as were the responses of established Britons. But Enoch Powell's furied predictions of mass violence and his irresponsible quoting of the view that in fifteen to twenty years the black man would have the whip hand over the white man, had been proved false; the intellectually brilliant can be fools. Britain had moved on. In his classic 1987 study, *There Ain't No Black in the Union Jack*, Paul Gilroy focused a sharp critical lens on British racial politics, the title itself alluding to the strong element of racism in play. In the 1990s, black was far more visible, metaphorically, in the Union Jack, than it had been before. This had less to do solely with importation of other ways of seeing or being 'black', than with the undoubted ways in which blackness by the end of 1999 was far more part of what defined 'Britishness' than was the case in 1987. Gilroy's new 2002 introduction to *There Ain't No Black in the Union Jack* does not relent on criticising the state of the nation, noting that

> The outrages, deaths and dogged campaigns of resistance and recognition so evident during the intervening years [between 1987 and 2002] have created just enough hope to sustain the fragile belief that a restored and healthier Britain might one day teach the rest of the world something about what will have to be done in order to live peacefully with difference. (Gilroy 2002: xxxvii)

This highly qualified optimism from one of the sharpest critics of entrenched British attitudes marks admittedly the small but still discernible distance travelled in a relatively short time.

Notes

1. Available at <https://www.theguardian.com/world/2001/apr/19/race.british identity> (last accessed 18 January 2017).
2. Available at <http://news.bbc.co.uk/2/hi/uk_politics/693591.stm> (last accessed 19 January 2017).
3. Available at <http://www.poetryarchive.org/poem/my-country> (last accessed 26 September 2016).
4. Available at <http://www.saltiresociety.org.uk/awards/> (last accessed 26 September 2016).

Chapter Three

Love in the Nineties

Love in the nineties
Is paranoid
On sunny beaches
Take your chances
Looking for

Girls who are boys
Who like boys to be girls
Who do boys like they're girls
Who do girls like they're boys

(Blur 1995)

The lyrics from Blur's 'Girls and Boys' advertise a simultaneously troubling, ambiguous and celebratory reading of love and sexuality in the nineties. The clip that accompanied the song revels in the festive and (apart from two ambiguous shaven headed figures tongue kissing) the heterosexual, mostly featuring partying British teenagers and twenty-somethings. The words that precede those quoted above – 'Streets like a jungle / So call the police / Following the herd / Down to Greece / On holiday' – explain the paranoia somewhat, while presenting a garish snapshot of the slightly mindless hedonism of British youth. The words immediately following those quoted above – 'Always should be someone you really love' – sanction sexual freedom, while requiring some level of emotional responsibility. The playful and slightly risqué ambiguity of girls who are boys who like girls to be boys also reflects the increasing acceptance of diverse sexualities. This broadmindedness was not necessarily indicative of the nation as a whole, where Section 28 of the Local Government Act of 1988, prohibiting the promotion of homosexuality by schools and other government-run institutions, remained the law of the land. If Blur's popular laddishness addressed facets of nineties sexual politics, the far more commercially successful Spice Girls conjured up others, their debut hit single 'Wannabee' (1996) mixing 'Girl Power' solidarity – 'If you wanna be my lover / You gotta get with my friends' – with a confident sensuality – 'If you wanna be my lover / You gotta, you gotta, you gotta, you gotta, you gotta / Slam, slam, slam, slam (make it last forever).' Girl Power was one of the slogans of the nineties, but the question remained whether it offered young girls, especially, confident role models, or represented a robotic mantra that masked consumer-driven sexism. The more strident and subversive Grrrl Power of the same time provided something more radical, aggressively challenging gender norms and larger social realities, while exuding a self-assured knowingness about the need for conscious public action.

A substantially less confident take on female identity, personal relationships, and sex, materialised in one of the phenomena of the period, 'Chick Lit'. Inaugurated by Helen Fielding's *Bridget Jones's Diary* (1996), a romantic comedy exposing the anxieties of contemporary heterosexual courtship through the jaundiced eyes of the eponymous thirty-something singleton, Chick Lit for some registered the degree to which the period was postfeminist, a moving on from, or a turning away from, the demands and advances of second wave feminism of the 1960s and 1970s. The definitions of postfeminism (or sometimes 'post-feminism', to emphasise historical discontinuity) were varied, but the belief remained that a generational shift had occurred, that nineties girls, and young women especially, understood the world differently from their mothers and grandmothers. Men, particularly heterosexual men, could also be seen to exist in a postfeminist world, one in which feminist gains sometimes were treated as having created a more responsive New Man, one attuned to the needs of his female partner, and willing to openly express emotion. A less positive reading of the New Man indicated someone who felt emasculated or at least confused about his new role and about his relationship with postfeminist women. A marketable literary version of these anxieties, lazily if inevitably branded 'Lad Lit', was exemplified in Nick Hornby's *High Fidelity* (1995), in which thirty-something singleton Rob Fleming struggles to deal with the breakup with his long-standing girlfriend, Laura. *High Fidelity* and its ilk seemed to expose a general crisis in British heterosexual masculinity.

The relatively good-humoured and upbeat attitudes of these bands and writers sit at odds with the darker elements of 1990s theatre, the New Brutalism flaring from plays to which Aleks Sierz gave the memorable title of 'In-Yer-Face Theatre' (Sierz 2001). Consciously confrontational works such as Sarah Kane's *Blasted* (first performed in 1995) and Mark Ravenhill's *Shopping and Fucking* (1996) display explicit sexuality that compels audiences to experience unvarnished depictions of damaged and damaging figures, much of the aggression enacted through sexual acts predicated on violence designed to unsettle and perhaps repulse audiences. The desire to shock and provoke worked, the *Daily Mail*, only one example, calling *Blasted* 'This disgusting piece of filth.' Ken Urban notes wryly: 'The result of such "bad" press? The play's short three-work run immediately sold out, overnight Sarah Kane became a *cause célèbre*, and *Blasted* became the most talked about, least seen play of the decade in her home country' (Urban 2011: 65). The attimes literally naked aggression and sexuality of such works placed them in open conflict with John Major's earlier call, at the 1993 Conservative conference, for a return to 'the old values – neighbourliness, decency and courtesy', that he believed were 'still alive'. Major added with all sincerity that it was 'time to get back to basics, to self-discipline and respect for the law, to consideration for others, to accepting a responsibility for yourself and your family', and that the Conservative party stood for 'self-reliance, decency and respect for others'.[1] His call was at odds with the increasingly liberal mores of the time, as were hangovers from the previous decade such as Section 28. Because Section 28 did not create a criminal offence, no person was prosecuted, and in fact the age of consent for homosexuals was dropped from twenty-one to eighteen in 1994, but the regulation promoted a climate of fear and hypocrisy in terms of sexual behaviour. (It was not repealed until 2003.) Alwyn Turner quotes the Conservative director of communications saying in the wake of the 'back to basics' speech that Major 'was intent on rolling back the permissive society', and the journalist Matthew Parris as writing that 'Within seconds, journalists were asking sceptical questions about divorce, adultery and waywardness among Major's colleagues' (Turner 2013: 205). Those questions might have been directed elsewhere had reporters known of the prime minister's own affair with Edwina Curry.

Major's desperate and ineffectual cry for a return to conservative and Conservative social values, as with his evocation of the idyllic England of the past, argued for a connection with a more tranquil era. This nostalgia politics was being rejected in several ways, one being the ushering in of an era of post-feminism, the replacement, or rejection, or moving beyond the political and social engagement of the 1960s and 1970s that Major so abhorred. Elaine Aston argues that Sarah Kane's

> theatre figures the generational feminist shift from [Carol] Churchill's second wave understanding of '*what I feel is quite strongly a feminist position*' to what one might rephrase as 'what I feel is quite strongly the *loss* of a feminist position (sic)'. (Aston 2013)

While careful to wrap the question of gender in scare quotes, Aston adds that 'Kane is representative of the 1990s "woman" playwright who is genealogically connected to feminist theatre histories, but is generationally divorced from an "old" style of feminist attachment'. *Blasted*, she contends, 'figures the fault line between a "personal as political feminist past" and a "personal without a feminist political present/future"' (Aston 2013: 21). One might see another approach in Carol Ann Duffy's 1999 collection of poetry, *The World's Wife*, which reviews the lives of famous real, fictional and mythical men through the eyes of wives largely erased from historical or cultural accounts. Or rather, silenced, for Duffy gives voice to a range of characters from the mythical Mrs Aesop, bored witless by her fable-creating husband, or Mrs Midas, traumatised by the possibility that her husband might touch her, through to Mrs Darwin, whose caustic assessment of her husband and her own unacknowledged contribution to his thinking are recorded with witty brevity:

> 7 April 1852.
> Went to the Zoo.
> I said to Him –
> Something about that Chimpanzee over there reminds
> me of you.
>
> (Duffy 1999: 20)

The World's Wife functions both as a set of creative 'personal' statements from the wives who are keen not to praise famous men, and as a social critique of the silencing and sidelining of women that has a long and inglorious history. Where the Spice Girls' 'girl power' was patently in some ways a marketing slogan to entice girls and young women to part with cash and (in some cases) agency, Kane, Duffy and others proposed more challenging possibilities for girls, women, and, by extension, for men as well. Both denied that they were 'women writers'. Kane, for her part, declared: 'I have no responsibility as a women writer because I don't believe there's such a thing' (quoted in Stephenson and Langridge 1997: 134).

Duffy and Kane might be taken to characterise post-feminist writers in their questioning acceptance that fundamental change in emotional relationships requires a more thorough-going recalibration of personal relationships and power imbalances. The term 'post-feminist' itself was, as was the case with post-national and post-colonial, a problematic term, hinting at an advance beyond the achievements of second wave feminism; or a reactionary rejection of feminism and a return to more traditional arrangements; or, yet again, a conscious redirection of feminist energy. Angela McRobbie, for instance, who understands post-feminism as originating in the 1990s, argues that elements of feminism have been taken into account, and have been incorporated into political and institutional life. Drawing on a vocabulary that includes words like 'empowerment' and 'choice', these elements are then converted into a much more individualistic discourse, and they are deployed in this new guise, particularly in media and popular culture, but also by the agencies of the state, as a kind of substitute for feminism. These new and seemingly 'modern' ideas about women and especially about young women are then disseminated aggressively, so as to ensure that a new women's movement will not re-emerge. (McRobbie 2009: 1)

She interprets the film of *Bridget Jones's Diary* (2000) as exemplary of feminism being taken into account, but as a 'ghostly presence', one relegated to the wings in favour of the 'celebratory post-feminism' of consumer culture. This entails light-hearted fun at a 'hen's night' with male strippers, revelling in wedding culture, and including gay men and lesbians. These signals subtly, or not so subtly, whisper: 'thank goodness, girls can be girls again, that time of dourness and censoriousness [the 1970s and 1980s] is over' (McRobbie 2009: 8). In this reading of the film adaptation of Fielding's novel, post-feminism is the dissembling mask worn by those wanting to de-radicalise feminism in order to refit it for more commercially exploitable purposes, in line with the nineties promotion of individualism and consumerism. This interpretation suggests that the novel's success, as with the equally popular film, records the muting of criticism, and the stifling of important and necessary social change.

The original novel gets further treatment later in this chapter, but for the moment we can begin to map the diversity of approaches to gender and sexuality in the 1990s, dealing with two plays that exemplify the new energy and raw sexuality of the time: Sarah Kane's *Blasted* (1995) and Patrick Marber's *Closer* (1997). Ken Urban notes that in 1991 *The Guardian*'s Michael Billington had lamented that 'new drama no longer occupies the central position it has in British theatre over the past thirty-five years'. Billington criticises new writing for its 'small scale nature', which 'increasingly privatises experience' (quoted in Urban 2011: 65). Billington spoke too soon, for the 1990s is now appreciated as a decade when a startlingly aggressive and confrontational theatre appeared, written by a new generation of writers as bold and actively insurrectionist as the fabled Angry Young Men of the 1950s. One noticeable point of distinction was that there were also Angry Young Women, writers such as Kane willing to deal with confrontational issues such as rape, torture, madness, domestic violence and war, and to require that audiences experience approximations of the same. The tenor of this highly charged theatre is captured in labels like New Brutalists, New Jacobeans and, more regularly, In-Yer-Face Theatre, commemorating writers who threw aside the complacency and timidity of much contemporary theatre in ways that appalled some and thrilled others. Such work drew a new young audience to the theatre and reset the coordinates for British theatre. In-Yer-Face playwrights turned away from the 'state of the nation' approach epitomised by the plays of David Hare, plays such as *Racing Demon* (1990), which critically examines the Church of England; *Murmuring Judges* (1991), focusing on the British legal system; and *The Absence of War* (1993), which anatomises the inner workings of the Labour Party. Although they advertise a leftist 'message', Hare's acceptance of a knighthood in 1997 seemed to confirm him as a pillar of the establishment. Young writers also spurned the unapologetically intellectual and aesthetic sophistication and polish of Tom Stoppard, who in brilliant works such as *Arcadia* (1993; examined in Chapter 7) and *The Invention of Love* (1997) dealt with chaos theory, and the love life of Victorian poet A. E. Housman, respectively. Looking back nostalgically but with great critical acuity and intensity, Stoppard's plays exemplified an unapologetically middle class, high-brow experience that illuminated and entertained. In-Yer-Face theatre was a metaphorical gob in the face of these minutely crafted and highly successful plays, this well-made theatre.

Blasted was a cultural phenomenon from the outset, upsetting audiences, critics and those who had only heard about the play second-hand. As a debut play by a young, unknown writer, *Blasted* came with no pre-publicity, and was first performed in the small sixty-two seat) Theatre Upstairs at the Royal Court theatre. While Jack Tinkler's *Daily Review* is best remembered, other critics were no less scathing, *The Guardian*'s Michael Billington musing about 'how such naïve tosh managed to scrape past the Royal Court's normally judicious play-selection committee' (quoted in Urban 2011: 65). His reaction is not surprising, given that the play relentlessly forces audiences to experience discomfort, disgust, terror, uncertainty, much in the manner of European Theatre of the Absurd and the Theatre of Cruelty. Billington would later reject his initial response, recognising the play's virtues and its moral engagement. Urban detects a set of resemblances that include the importance of shock in language and imagery; the 'investment in cruelty'; the exploration of gender roles and sexual mores, especially pertaining to the 'so-called 1990s "Crisis of Masculinity"'; a general suspicion of partisan politics, political correctness and restrictive identity labels; and the acceptance of theatre's role as a commodity (69–70). As Chapter 5 explains, some of these attributes could also be discerned in the Young British Artists, and entailed a similar rejection of established and establishment models, though to very different effect.

Blasted opens in a suitably commercial world: the notes explain the setting as 'A very expensive hotel room in Leeds – the kind that is so expensive it could be anywhere in the world' (Kane 2011: 3). Ian and Cate (he, a forty-five-year-old journalist, she, a twenty-year-old woman) enter into what might seem, certainly to an innocent audience, a common setting for a relatively simple sexual fling. What seemingly begins in this way descends vertiginously into a brutal, twisted tussle. The gun-wielding Ian, his weapon a potent and simultaneously pathetic emblem of his sadistic masculinity, indulges in racist and nihilistic machismo that tears at Cate's troubled vulnerability. Desperately in need of validation and love, that is repeatedly undermined by his misogynistic callousness, Cate from the outset seems dangerously at Ian's worldly, power-fuelled mercy. Her refusal to eat meat and her fainting spells function, it appears, as signs of weakness next to his uber-male posturing. Yet, even though he tells her he is dying, when he strips naked and asks her to 'Put your mouth on me' (7), she stares at first and then 'bursts out laughing' (8), before collapsing. The stage directions instruct that 'Ian attempts to dress, but stumbles with embarrassment' (8), before retreating to the bathroom to dress. Cate repeatedly resists his sexual advances, although he forces her to masturbate him, and eventually to fellate him in the second scene. Even performing this act she resists, biting his penis 'as hard as she can' (31). The interplay between violence and intimacy or love runs through the play, Ian's proposal of marriage, or the presentation of flowers at the end of scene one, undermined by the opening of scene two where the flowers are 'ripped apart and scattered around the room' (24), suggesting that Ian has raped Cate overnight. Power shifts back and forth between them, Ian's sexist domination challenged by sexual neediness and his admission that his wife 'fucked off with a dyke' (19), Cate's subservience counterbalanced by her having a boyfriend, Shaun, and the fact that she agrees to spend the night in the hotel only because she is worried for Ian.

Kane uses the confined space of the stage to ratchet up the tension and oppression, but in the second scene the outside world intrudes viciously with the arrival of Soldier. The otherwise unnamed figure transforms the room into a war zone, 'marking' it by urinating on the pillow and claiming that this is 'our town now' (39). Cate has escaped through the bathroom window, but a bomb hits the room, a bridge to the third scene where the space now has a gaping hole and Soldier starts to exert his damaged power. Unlike the blustering, insecure Ian, Soldier has been permanently warped by war, performing and witnessing extreme acts that he begins to introduce into the relatively benign hotel space. His own girlfriend, Col, having been murdered by a soldier, Soldier enacts revenge on the much-reduced Ian, anally raping him before sucking out and eating his eyes. Horrific as these events are (and they are meant to be repellent) they are no more extreme, for example, than those in Shakespeare's *Titus Andronicus*, hence the general label New Jacobean for such 1990s plays. Soldier berates Ian for sensitivity about being raped. He plausibly claims to have performed the act many times, then kisses Ian sensitively on the lips, as though he were Col, complicating the dangerous nexus of power, extreme violence, intimacy and love. By scene four Soldier has shot himself, and Cate returns with a baby, recalibrating again the relations of power and love. Ian tries to reassert his dominance, telling Cate that Shaun will see her as 'soiled goods' (52), but when this fails tries to shoot himself. Cate has taken out the bullets, telling him that he has been saved by 'fate' (57). Initially a victim of what (over time) is revealed as Ian's hollow power, Cate slowly gains the ascendancy in the war-torn scenario. Her application of a classical notion of order in the idea of fate, one that plays against the sustained chaos around them, gets undermined when she realises that the baby, a possible emblem of redemption, hope and female fecundity, has died.

The final scene begins with Cate burying the baby under the floorboards of the room and going in search of food from the soldiers who control the world beyond the room and, as Soldier has graphically demonstrated, within it. Alone, abused and powerless, the bereft Ian performs a series of desperate and perverse acts: masturbating, defecating, laughing hysterically, attempting to strangle himself, hugging Soldier, and, in a hugely controversial act (one with rough parallels to *Titus Andronicus*), eating the baby before occupying its grave, dying, as the stage directions instruct, 'with relief' (60). Rain, which has appeared in various forms at the end of each scene (sequentially as spring, summer, autumn and winter rain) falls through the roof on him as Cate returns with food and drink, the blood running between her legs suggesting the sexualised struggle needed to gain such things in wartime. After feeding herself, she feeds Ian, who is resurrected, saying 'thank you' (61) in a first and final gesture of gratitude. This ends the perverse series of power struggles, in which sexual acts and sexuality expose dark, essential truths. Ian's crisis is less that of someone insecure with the new sexual coordinates of society than of someone desperate to re-impose primordial notions of masculinity on women. His own insecurities and inadequacies, over the course of the play, are rigorously exposed. This happens first tentatively, through his initial interactions with Cate, and then more explicitly with forceful entry of the psychotic Soldier. Both a terrifyingly generic character and one individualised by his horrifying experiences, Soldier ultimately cannot bear the psychological weight that knowledge has imparted. Cate, vulnerable and damaged in the early scenes, taps inner strengths that enable her to survive. Perhaps this is the best that can be hoped for in a relentlessly aggressive, almost primal world, seemingly dominated by men who are themselves vulnerable and damaged. *Blasted*'s raw examination of power, love, sexuality and damage proved hugely confrontational. But while some critics initially reacted with horror or contempt, the play was quickly recognised as conveying something vital and uncompromisingly true.

Shopping and Fucking, Mark Ravenhill's 1996 play, addressed sex and sexuality in ways that shocked some of its first audiences (while thrilling others). Sex in *Blasted* is in some ways militarised, partly through the employment of guns as means of enforcing sexual and other forms of domination, partly through the slowly engulfing wartime setting. In Ravenhill's play sex is more monetised, a form of transaction linked with elements of economic power and class, something dealt with in the next chapter. Dan Rebellato suggests that in Ravenhill's plays the sexual explicitness 'is part of his scandalised portrait of an apolitical generation with no values but economic ones, media-fixated and self-obsessed, fucking while Rome burns' (Rebellato 2001: xiii). Certainly, there is a degree of self-obsession in *Shopping and Fucking*, but there is also an ongoing concern with intimacy and different forms of attachment that investigate the significance and intricacies of relationships. Some of these are based on power imbalances, or are otherwise troubling, as in an early scene where a corrupt businessman, Brian, tries to use a job interview to make a young woman, Lulu, strip; when Mark, in an institution to deal with his addictions, pays to lick the arse of a fellow inmate; or when Gary, a rent boy, tells of how his stepfather regularly raped him. For all the sex, actual, remembered or intimated in the play, very little involves pure pleasure. For Mark, monetising sex for much of the time saves him from engaging in real intimacy, and when he admits to Gary that he loves him, Gary contemptuously rejects that genuine expression of emotion. Gary's own problematic sexual history with his stepfather eventually prompts him to beg Mark to fuck him with a knife or a screwdriver to annihilate the pain, Gary declaring: 'I've got this unhappiness. This big sadness swelling like it's gonna burst. I'm sick and I'll never be well.' Pleading further that he wants 'it over. And there's only one ending', he adds that if Mark accepts, 'I'll say "I love you"' (Ravenhill 2001: 85). Gary stress tests to breaking point Mark's troubled longing for love, replacing physical intimacy with a crudely mechanical form of self-destructive punishment.

The first meeting between Mark and Gary gestures to a future only slowly emerging in the 1990s, one that suggested a novel form of intimacy. Gary's first words in the play reflect the new possibilities for rent boy hook-ups, and by implication for all first dates: 'course any day now it will be virtual'. He then shows himself to have the requisite 1990s entrepreneurial spirit by commenting that he is 'Looking to invest. The Net and the web and that', following this up with a canny prediction: 'Couple of year's times and we'll not even meet. We'll be holograph things. We could look like whatever we wanted. And then we wouldn't have to meet 'cos we might not look like our holographs' (22). The beginnings of the World Wide Web in the early nineties connected people in an unprecedented manner, including offering the ability to contact strangers. A decade before Facebook added a new dimension to notions of personal identity and community, the Web introduced people to each other in innovative ways with unforeseen promises and threats. Given human ingenuity and desire, it was not long before some internet chat rooms morphed into sites for virtual meetings, contacts that could then be upgraded to face-to-face encounters. Pornography very quickly colonised a substantial and lucrative area of the internet. In *Shopping and Fucking*, the young Gary quickly sees the implications of this novel form of intimacy, while the older Mark remains largely ignorant, having picked Gary for the already slightly dated pre-digital reason that 'I liked your voice' (22). Other characters engage with the lurid side of the internet, although not by choice. In order to pay Brian off for money lost in a botched sale of drugs, Lulu and her boyfriend Robbie are required to work phone sex lines. Scene 10 is a relatively short but hilarious set of interactive calls as Mark and Lulu move between mobile phones and clients, telling one: 'And you want me and I want you and it's man on man and I'm Adam and you're Adam'; in another: 'Bite. Yes. Your tongue. The apple. Good. The forbidden fruit'; and in one that charts technological changes, 'You can call as often as you like. Oh good, yes, that's a good idea, a cord that reaches the bed' (51). The sexual world Ravenhill conjures up is multidimensional and permissive, dangerous and funny, tender and sinister, drawing new maps of tenderness and oppression rather than going 'back to basics'.

Another of Sierz's In-Yer-Face playwrights, Patrick Marber, focused on four characters in rather more conventional and realistic circumstances in *Closer*, a dark romantic comedy that explores ancient questions of fidelity, chance, deception and the nature of love, through the contemporary prism. Over the years between 1993 and 1997, Dan (thirties; an obituary writer); Larry (early forties; a dermatologist); Alice (twenties; a self-professed 'waif', later revealed as a stripper); and Anna (thirties; photographer), fall in and out of love and lust. The play's title points ironically to a desire for intimacy that the characters manipulate in others for their own benefits, a situation enhanced by the chance ways in which they meet. Dan and Alice, for example, literally and metaphorically meet by accident, when he sees her knocked down by a London cab, and takes her to hospital, where the play begins. Her youth and beauty captivate him, and in line with his natural inclinations he begins to flirt, even while admitting that he has a girlfriend, Ruth. He and Alice engage in the quick-fire hard-edged banter that gives *Closer* its vitality and tangy flavour:

> Alice: Men want a girl who looks like a boy. They want to protect her but she must be a survivor. And she must come . . . like a *train* . . . but with *elegance*. (Marber 1997: 10)

The challenge to heterosexual male sexuality in the ambiguity of men liking girls to look like boys unconsciously echoes Blur's 'Girls and Boys', but the interchange also canvasses more traditional notions of emotional connection:

> Dan: What do *you* want?
> Alice: To be loved.
> Dan: That simple?
> Alice: It's a big want.
> *She looks at him.*
> Do you have a girlfriend?
> Dan: Yeah, Ruth . . . She's called Ruth. She's a linguist.
> *He looks at Alice.*
> Will you meet me after work? (10)

The interchange underscores Alice's greater emotional insight and Dan's naïve possessiveness. If love in the nineties is not paranoid, it can be a sharp, chancy game in which traditional roles (waif/protector) are actively evoked and forensically scrutinised. In *Closer*, sex is a narcissistic performance, particularly for the men, even if Alice's job as a stripper seems to present her as the literal embodiment of performance. Her work, though, requires a knowing inauthenticity.

Scene 2 kicks to 1994, with Dan at a photo shoot for his upcoming book on Alice's life. Here he falls for the photographer, the more experienced Anna, who rebuffs him, before telling him that she found Alice's story '*accurate* . . . About sex. About love' (14). The conflation of sex and love works as one of *Closer*'s thematic pivot points, with the women having a clearer sense both of the complications and dangers in play. Dan and Larry, by contrast, treat relationships in terms of possession, with the women as sexual and emotional trophies to be won and displayed. The women understand this problematic rivalry, attempting to negotiate for something approaching genuine love. Dan next appears memorably in Scene 3, which captures the early use of virtual reality hinted at in *Shopping and Fucking*. By the time the play was first performed, there were still only 1,500 internet cafes worldwide.[2] Larry and Dan connect, by chance, on the suitably explicit LONDON FUCK website. The two are shown simultaneously on different parts of the stage, Dan in his flat, Larry in his office, while their typed 'dialogue' 'appears on a large screen simultaneous to their typing it' (21). The large screen visually realises their virtual interaction, isolating and connecting them, exposing their private fantasies voyeuristically for the audience's pleasure. The younger Dan, understanding the fantasy possibilities, renames himself after the woman who earlier has spurned his charms, Anna. 'Anna' quickly employs pornographic clichés to arouse Larry, whose admission that this is his '1st time' causes 'Anna' to reply 'A Virgin. Welcome' (21). Alone in his flat, with his secret female identity, Dan enjoys the game of teasing Larry sexually. But the adoption of a dominating female persona, while vital to his fun, reveals something of Dan's own polymorphous sexual identity and desires. What they both take to be private activities also expose their pornographic and misogynist attitudes, although not before Marber has fun with the possibilities the newish technology creates. So, when Larry types an early question 'Nice arse?' and Dan replies 'Y', Larry's insistent follow up 'Becos i want 2 know' causes the more experienced Dan to smile, before he types: 'No, "Y" means "Yes".' Larry's apologetic 'O' shows him to be embarrassingly inexperienced with the new cyber lexicon. His desperate attempt to appear tech-savvy is undermined again shortly after:

Dan: Well hung?
Larry: 9£
(*Speaking*) Shit.
(Typing) 9"
Dan: GET IT OUT. (22)

Closer is largely made up of this type of stichomythic dialogue, a form of verbal attack and parry usually reserved for moments when characters are in conflict. Here, though, it functions to display a cynical, narcissistic superficiality that reflects the self-absorption of the men, and the way in which language is deployed to win or dominate interpersonal transactions, rather than to reveal emotional depths. These and other interchanges are funny, no doubt, but blended with the humour are darker forces, as when Larry's typed fantasy involves being tied up and teased as six women 'fight over me', while Dan, as 'Anna', imagines pleasuring a queue of strangers who ultimately humiliate her. The sexual arousal Dan gets from this fantasy of his own domination as a 'woman' causes him to type 'wait, have to type with 1 hand ... I'm cumming right now ...' (24) before a prolonged sequence of random letters and symbols typographically represent Dan's orgasm to Larry and the audience. There is then a stage direction, 'Pause. Larry, motionless, stares at this screen after which Larry asks/types, 'was it good?' (24) Again, a revealing if brutal humour operates here, as well as a worrying revelation about the essentially masturbatory and aggressive nature of cybersex generally and perhaps heterosexual male sex more specifically. For all their dangerous competitiveness, though, Dan and Larry are inadequate, and these inadequacies, shallow motives and self-destructiveness are revealed and explored with acerbic precision, their respective jobs as obituary writer and dermatologist indicative of a level of morbid superficiality they continue to display throughout the play.

Alice and Anna, stripper and photographer, also function in some way on surface levels. But where Larry and Dan operate (however superficially) in the realms of life and death, the women are alert to the dangerous and deceptive allure of facades (especially female beauty), as they dance for men, in Alice's case, or see through their duplicitous self-confidence, as in Anna's first encounter with Dan. Both want to be loved, in Alice's words, while both understand that this might involve confronting and manipulating confrontational and manipulative men. They do enjoy the comparative independence available to post-feminist women, while still having to perform in a world of considerable repressive male power. Both couples swap partners several times during the play, mostly at the instigation of the competing men, and the multiple betrayals, based on jealousy, lust and revenge, mortally complicate the ideal that love or truth provide a necessary or workable basis for relationships. While who wins and who loses in these ugly struggles is often undetermined, both women are compromised, and compromise themselves. By the beginning of the penultimate scene Dan is with Alice, Anna with Larry. In that scene, set in January 1997 at an airport hotel, as they prepare to fly to the United States, Dan demands to see Alice's passport (which she refuses to show him), asks her when she will stop stripping, and then confronts her about how, as a stripper, she once had danced for Larry. He asks whether she had slept with Larry, a 'victory' over him that Dan clearly cannot abide. Dan demands the truth, telling her that 'without it we are just animals'. But her truthful reply, 'I don't love you any more', stuns him. She adds: 'I've left. I've *gone*. I don't love you any more. Goodbye', before admitting that 'I fucked Larry. Many times. I enjoyed it. I came. I prefer *you*. Now go' (100). He tells her that Larry had already told him this, his motive as the bested male being to test her commitment to the truth. But the truth is too damaging for both of them, and a tough verbal and physical tussle ends the scene:

> Dan: WHO ARE YOU?
> Alice: I'M NO ONE.
> *Alice spits in his face. He grabs her by the throat, one hand.*
> Go on, hit me. That's what you *want*. Hit me, you fucker.
> *Silence.*
> *Dan hits Alice.*
> *Silence.*
> Alice: Do you have an original thought in your head?
> *Blackout.* (102–3)

For all the contemporary edge of their relationship, it ends with the replaying of ancient enmities.

The final scene, occurring in 'July 1997', two months after the play was first presented at the Cottesloe auditorium at London's Royal National Theatre, looks back to a different past. It returns to Postman's Park, a tranquil space in central London that houses a Memorial to Heroic Sacrifice, and that Dan and Alice earlier had talked in at the beginning of their relationship. The park commemorates ordinary people who had sacrificed themselves for others, an ironic setting given the selfishness shown by all the characters at some point. Here we find that Anna and Larry have split again, and that he now is in a casual relationship with a nurse, Polly, replicating Anna's first husband's betrayal of her for a younger woman. Larry fails to comprehend the edge to her comment 'I always knew you'd end up with a pretty nurse' (104), and attempts to pick Anna up, an advance she rebuffs with a jokey 'Fuck off and die, you fucked up slag' (104). But Larry finds that Alice has taken her identity from one of the people commemorated in the park, a young woman who sacrificed herself to rescue children from a burning building. When Dan appears (Larry quickly leaves), he reveals that Alice's real name was Jane Jones and that she has been killed in a New York car accident. In the longest speech in the play Dan reveals in a halting manner Alice's true identity, her death, and how when his fellow obituary writer callously wondered '"Who's on the slab?", I went out to the fire escape and cried like a baby. I covered my face – why do we do that?' (105) Where the ever-dominant Larry never shows empathy, Dan can show his 'feminine side', carrying a bunch of flowers that he will place to commemorate Alice. Able to display authentic emotions for the first time, he is incapable of comprehending the suppressed depths from which they surface. Anna and Dan part at the end of the scene that ends the play. His simple 'Goodbye' contrasts with her 'Yes. Goodbye' (109), a more emphatic request for closure in a play whose title marked the contemporary world's desire for love and measured the unbridgeable gap between people. The final stage directions

> *They exit separately.*
> *Empty stage.*
> *Blackout.* (109)

underscore the mutual recognition of emotional estrangement.

Closer, for all of its undoubted rawness, is far less confrontational than *Blasted* or *Shopping and Fucking*, and perhaps in part for that reason was more commercially successful, eventually being adapted into a 2004 film by American director Mike Nichols, starring a top flight transatlantic cast of Julia Roberts, Jude Law, Clive Owen and Natalie Portman. *Closer*'s success on stage and screen was dwarfed by Helen Fielding's *Bridget Jones's Diary* (1996), a 1990s' publishing phenomenon and primary 'Chick Lit' text. Never a novel with literary aspirations – though Fielding admitted the obvious, that it reworked key aspects of Jane Austen's *Pride and Prejudice*, the television series of which had recently been a massive hit – *Bridget Jones's Diary* reflected one form of post-feminism noted above by McRobbie. The novel, revealingly, was adapted from Fielding's column in *The Independent*, and charts a largely calamitous year in the life of its eponymous heroine, a self-lacerating thirty-something London single woman obsessed with body image and her floundering career. Surrounded by damaged relationships, Bridget desperately searches for a man to marry. The diary begins with an excessively hopeful list of New Year's Resolution admonishments and aspirations:

> I WILL NOT
> Drink more than fourteen alcohol units a week.
> Smoke.
> Waste money on: pasta-makers, ice-cream machines or other culinary devices which I'll never use; books by unreadable literary authors to put impressively on shelves; exotic underwear, since pointless as have no boyfriend . . . (Fielding 1996: 2)

> I WILL
> Stop smoking.
> Drink no more than fourteen alcohol units a week.
> Reduce circumference of thighs by 3 inches (i.e. 1½ inches each), using anti-cellulite diet . . . (3)

The dysfunctional catalogue introduces the faux-diary mode for the rest of the book. While suitably self-absorbed and unwittingly self-revelatory, this contains more detail than any actual diary might logically contain (long sequences of dutifully recorded dialogue are included, for example), blurring formal lines between novel and diary. Yet the diary form has its advantages, providing a rough and ready narrative structure, and accentuating the first-person voice that gives *Bridget Jones's Diary* its rapid pacing and earthy flavour, combining often embarrassingly intimate private thoughts with the accounts of equally embarrassing social actions that constitute ongoing comic humiliation. For instance, Bridget somewhat uncharacteristically asserts herself against the advances of her boss, the priapic Daniel Cleaver, whom she simultaneously loathes and lusts after. Embellishing her actions to her supportive friends Sharon, Tom and Jude, she accepts their approval and writes:

> 5pm ... feeling v. empowered. Tremendous. Think might read bit of Susan Faludi's *Backlash*.
> 5am. Oh God, am so unhappy about Daniel. I love him. (77)

The failure to read Faludi situates Bridget, and the novel as a whole, as essentially post-feminist.

Faludi's 1991 international bestseller, *Backlash: The Undeclared War against American Women*, opens with a proposition: 'To be a woman in America at the close of the 20th century – what good fortune' (Faludi 1991: 5). But Faludi, herself an award-winning journalist, argues instead that

> Behind the celebration of American women's victory, behind the news, cheerfully and endlessly repeated, that the struggle for women's rights was won, another message flashes. You may be free and equal now, it says to women, but you have never been more miserable.

And Faludi's sketch of the reality for contemporary American professional women draws evidence from the media:

> Professional women are suffering 'burnout' and succumbing to an 'infertility epidemic'. Single women are grieving from a 'man shortage'. The *New York Times* reports: childless women are 'depressed and confused' and their ranks are swelling. Newsweek says: Unwed women are 'hysterical' and crumbling under a 'profound crisis of confidence'. (5)

Faludi rejects as 'absurd' the case that feminism is to blame for these woes, noting that, despite the hype, true sexual equality in terms of pay, conditions and status is nowhere in sight. She charges that the feminist goals of economic independence and self-determination have been channelled in the neoliberal world into an egotistical striving for individual self-improvement, a consumerist-infused hijacking of feminist aspirations that amount to a powerful social backlash against true empowerment of women. *Mutatis mutandis*, the diagnosis for the American professional woman seems appropriate for Bridget Jones. Her failure to read *Backlash* and her speedy emotional retreat into the clutches of the sexist Cleaver illustrate how far she is from the independent woman she aspires to be. And yet she is at the cutting-edge of the developing intersection of emotion and technology, her dealings with Cleaver regularly carried out via the relatively new form of sending and receiving messages: emailing. The novel representation of emailing, in a novel, requires a different font from the italics used for the running diary of Bridget's weight, alcohol and cigarette intake, and calories accumulated. Her reaction to the first virtual contact made by Cleaver registers the undoubted power of this new form of contact: 'Yesssss! Yessss! Daniel Cleaver wants my phone no. Am marvellous. Am irresistible Sex Goddess. Hurrah!' (26). Despite the new technology, age-old disappointment looms.

Nick Hornby was Helen Fielding's male equivalent in the adjacent field of 'Lad Lit'. The women's version of the subgenre far outsold the men's, so, where *Bridget Jones's Diary* sold 15 million copies, and was a global hit, Hornby's *High Fidelity* 'merely' sold over a million copies, by most standards a remarkable achievement. Women read *High Fidelity*, of course, but it seems likely that Hornby uncovered or even helped to create a largely untapped reservoir of male adult readers willing to complete a novel that explored the intricacies and exposed the fundamental failing of a certain form of male social and emotional life. Hornby's novel in fact was published a year before *Bridget Jones*, and while they were both first time novelists, this was his third book. His second, *Fever Pitch* (1992), an autobiographical account of Hornby's devotion to Arsenal Football Club, was in many ways the nonfiction version of Lad Lit. It also sold over a million copies in the UK, winning the William Hill Sports Book of the Year award. *Fever Pitch*, *High Fidelity* and Hornby himself were signal examples of the 'New Lad' phenomenon, an important subset of male cultural behaviour, distinct from the 'Iron John' and 'New Man' figures who also populated the territory of 1990s heterosexual masculinity. The 'New Lad' was upbeat, youngish and happily juvenile, out for a good time with his mates, into football, lager, 'birds' and soft-core porn magazines such as *Loaded* and *Maxim* that enjoyed huge success in the decade. The 'New Man', by contrast, was responsive to the demands of feminism and worked actively to de-programme himself from traditional patriarchal norms. Yet, in 'getting in touch with their feminine side', to employ the reductive and somewhat disturbing refrain of the time, the so-called 'New Man' had deteriorated to an emasculated husk. The 'Iron John' archetype, imported from the United States in the form of poet Robert Bly's international bestseller, *Iron John: A Book about Men* (1991), tried to reclaim and powerfully assert what Bly presented as evolutionary, fundamental and necessary 'male' attributes. Martin Amis tries to explain the state of play in a 1991 review of *Iron John*, lampooning the New Man as

> becoming the old man, perhaps prematurely, what with all the washing up he's done; there he stands in the kitchen, a nappy in one hand, a pack of tarot cards in the other, with his sympathetic pregnancies, his hot flushes and 'contact' pre-menstrual tensions, and with a duped frown on his ageing face. The time is ripe. And now the door swings open and in he comes, preceded by a gust of testosterone and a few tumbleweeds of pubic hair: the Old Man, the Deep Male – Iron John. (Amis 1991b: 3)

Iron John is the mythical figure Bly employs to represent the Old Male virtues of strength, camaraderie and sexual potency. No stranger to accusations of misogyny himself, Amis mocks the American excesses of the Iron John archetype in his review. But if transatlantic differences are discernible, and the hyper-macho Iron John type seemed more suited to the more performative American culture, Amis does not write off the idea that British men might also feel undermined and anxious.

Robert Crawford's 1995 poem 'Male Infertility', part of his 1996 collection, *Masculinity*, catches some of the farce inherent in the chasm between socially sanctioned notions of masculinity and base reality, here focused on a representative 'he'. Crawford employs the iconography of the male (and possibly female) fantasy figure of James Bond as a tuxedoed yardstick to examine male inadequacy. 'Male Infertility' begins with Bond-like iconography, 'Slouched there in the Aston Martin / On its abattoir of upholstery / He escapes / To the storming of the undersea missile silo / The satellite rescue', but ends in self-aware confusion:

> Suddenly he had this vision
> Of a sperm in a boyhood sex-ed film
>
> As a speargun-carrying tadpole-flippered frogman
> Whose visor fills up with tears
>
> And of living forever in a dinner jacket
> Fussier and fussier about what to drink
>
> Always, 'Shaken, not stirred.'
> Chlorine-blue bikinis, roulette tables, water skiing
>
> Show me that scene in *Thunderball*
> Where James Bond changes a nappy.
>
> (Crawford 1996: 13)

Overt references to masculinity in the title of the poem and the collection as a whole hint that these considerable and anxiety-producing topics are not simply personal apprehensions, but also register contemporary fears and uncertainties. The flashback to the film *Thunderball* (1965), when Sean Connery's athletic and assured masculinity was never in doubt, transports the reader back to a time when second-wave feminism had yet to break fully on the cultural shores. That fantasy also locates the poem historically in the world of Crawford's own childhood (he was born in 1959), and perhaps even to his, and Connery's, Scottishness, which, as A. L. Kennedy shows, comes with its own endemic problems regarding gender relations. Note Crawford's use of the nappy to signify emasculation, the failure to achieve Bond-like independence and insouciance. Bond never has to perform the demeaning (because traditionally female) domestic chores associated with child rearing – his forte is sex, not procreation per se. Interestingly, in Amis's review of *Iron John*, he also uses the nappy as a signifier of emasculation. Both he and Crawford are tongue in cheek, neither of them defending the Iron Johns or James Bonds, but where Amis's acerbic take on the Deep Man does nothing openly to investigate his own masculinity, the very title 'Male Infertility' encodes the speaker's disabling failure to measure up on the most basic procreative function. Within the poem itself, the complexities and anxieties are manifest: the contrast between the vision and the visor filled with tears, the quasi-Freudian linking of sperm and speargun, the timorous undertones of inadequate masculinity embedded in the classic Bond Martini request that it be 'Shaken, not stirred'. For all the self-mocking criticism, there is possibly defiance or even rejection of an infantile fantasy of Bond-like control in the final challenge to be shown the scene in *Thunderball* when James Bond changes a nappy. The scene does not exist, as the speaker well knows, allowing us to read the challenge as a rebuttal of Ian Fleming's now out-dated secret agent, and praise for the new codes of fatherhood, or as rendering the slightly haunted awareness of the New Man's domestic bondage. Crawford probably did not know it would happen, but, after a hiatus of six years, a new Bond film, *Goldeneye*, with Pierce Brosnan playing a new but still confidently macho Bond, was released the same year that 'Male Infertility' was published.

Popular culture in the shape of the Spice Girls offered other gender models, or stereotypes, part of another 1990s phenomenon, Girl Power. Jessica Taft provides four meanings for the term Girl Power, something she argues that 'constructs barriers to both girls' activism in general and girls' engagement with feminist politics' (Taft 2004: 70). These are anti-feminism, post-feminism, individual power and consumer power. Taft makes the point that 'The depoliticizing meanings of Girl Power are more visible due to their location in dominant media institutions' (70).

In their own book, *Spice Girls* (1997), the group (or their producers) make the claim that

> Girl Power is when . . .
> You and your mates reply to wolf whistles by shouting, 'Get your arse out!'
> You wear high heels *and* think on your feet,
> You know you can do it and nothing's going to stop you
> You don't wait around for him to call. (1997: 6)

This playful (or worryingly ambiguous) assertion of Girl Power points to the Spice Girls' own problematic place in the sexual politics of the decade. Whatever their aspirations to independence and to forms of self-assertion, the group was intrinsically and perhaps terminally compromised by a message that came with a price tag, an association with traditional and regressive forms of female identity that belied the crafted 'power' the group strove to embody. Was the group simply, as some alleged, 'tools of patriarchy', unintentionally undermining a progressive feminist message? Or was the group, in brashly asserting their working class and lower middle class roots and multiracial composition, presenting a flawed and sometimes-contradictory affirmative message about self-realisation to a mass audience? Champions of both views had evidence to support their contending cases; what is undeniable is that for a short period the group held the attention of many girls and young women who bought their music and merchandise in quantities that challenged and at times surpassed figures racked up by The Beatles.

The nineties certainly offered variety. Where the Spice Girls played to stereotypes (while possibly undermining them), and Sarah Kane dispassionately explored the excesses of sexuality, Jeanette Winterson dealt more playfully with sensuality and passion. Winterson had burst confidently on to the literary scene in the 1980s with her quirky comic semi-autobiographical novel, *Oranges Are Not the Only Fruit* (1985), where Old Testament Christianity provided an ironic structure, as well as the ammunition for symbolic, cultural and linguistic playfulness. She engaged with more experimental concerns in follow-up works *The Passion* (1987), an exuberant mix of magic realism and historical metafiction set in the Napoleonic Wars, and *Sexing the Cherry* (1989), which explored desire and gender power relationships in another richly creative and playful text. *Written on the Body* (1991) is in many ways a more restrained work than *The Passion* and *Sexing the Cherry*, restricted to the contemporary world and to modern relationships. A quasi-philosophical exploration of love, haunted by the possibility of its loss, *Written on the Body* presents a consciously ungendered narrator who wryly examines affairs and relationships with a number of women.

The uncertainty about whether the narrator is female or male activates an intriguing androgynous undercurrent, as the narrator excavates not only the physicality of desire but also (as the title hints) the language through which love is represented and communicated, the ways in which different forms of love, attraction and attachment are expressed. This concern with language inevitably deals with a literary vocabulary drawn on to articulate emotions, from clichés to highly evocative and activating phrases. While the undeniable, if sometimes perplexing, physicality and sensuality of love are celebrated, Winterson also gives space to the complementary and at times competing realm of consciousness: critical, suspicious, exuberant, and all-too conscious of the ambiguity of emotional responses. And, of course, there are the consciousness, desires and bodies of sexual or emotional partners, let alone the already-written narratives of previous lost loves. Dominic Head astutely reads what he sees as a 'key passage', where

> a simplistic computer culture is equated with an alternative and dangerous kind of fantasy, exemplified in the possibilities of Virtual Reality. Rejecting the possibilities of Virtual sex, the narrator states the preference for 'a real English meadow' as a site for romance, thus renouncing the solipsistic fantasy world of the computer. (Head 2002: 103)

Ravenhill had touched on the evolving potential for virtual sex and virtual identity in *Shopping and Fucking*, while Marber had explored at greater length how (in this case) men might use the lewd and ludic possibilities opened up by the internet to indulge in power struggles carried out by other means than face to face conflict. Marber was also alert to the voyeuristic pull of such technology, its capacity to foreground the multi-faceted allure of seeing. Winterson's characters enjoy looking at each other, too, but they also celebrate the sensuous physicality of the body that can only be experienced corporeally. As her character 'Sappho' advertises in Winterson's *Art & Lies: A Piece for Three Voices and a Bawd* (1995): 'I AM A SEXUALIST. In flagrante delicto. The end-stop of the universe. Say my name and you say sex. Say my name and you see white sand under a white sky white trammel of my thighs' (51). The subtitle discloses Sappho as only one voice among three (the other two are 'Handel' and 'Picasso'), this shared workload maintaining the vivid power of each. As an extended one-person show, by contrast, *Written on the Body* loses its vitality, becoming a slightly narcissistic riff on the attractiveness of its narrator. While exploring the undoubted pleasures of sensuality for that character, the novel sometimes fails to convey that pleasure with sufficient precision, or to give strong enough voice or agency to the array of females the narrator encounters.

Edward Manners, the protagonist of Alan Hollinghurst's James Tait Black Award-winning novel, *The Folding Star* (1994), is also somewhat self-absorbed and manipulative, though also more self-critical. An English teacher taking up a job in Flanders, he is also an incessant voyeur, as the novel's opening reveals:

> A man was waiting already on the narrow island of the tram-stop, and I asked him falteringly about the routes. He explained, politely, in detail, as if it were an interest of his; but I didn't take it in. I was charmed by his grey eyes and unnecessary smile, and the flecks of white paint on his nose and dark-blond hair. I nodded and smiled back, and he fell into a nice pensiveness, hands in pockets, looking down the empty street. I decided I would follow him. (Hollinghurst 1994: 3)

Manners' stand-offish sensuality trips him up in this case – having got on a tram after the man, and felt the man's breath on the back of his neck from the seat behind, he finds that the man is meeting a woman. Hollinghurst adroitly renders his nuanced acceptance of this reality: 'My friend jumped off and trotted her away under his arm, whilst the doors folded with a sigh' (3), the final word neatly blending sound and sensibility. The man, of course, is no friend at all, the newly arrived Manners an observing and engaged outsider, but a stranger in a strange land, nonetheless. A self-styled 'pudging, bespectacled English teacher' (22) in a world whose social and sexual codes he is trying with varying degrees of success to read, Manners becomes obsessed with one of his pupils, the sensuous, gifted and troubled Luc, whom he follows and whose clothing he steals, becoming, in his own terms, 'a reckless addict of the laundry basket' (192). Their eventual sexual relationship ends when Luc disappears.

Hollinghurst intertwines this contemporary story with an artistic tale of obsession, that of the Flemish symbolist painter Edgard Orst for a model, Jane Byron. She would eventually drown, but Orst would paint her again and again. The connections between love, loss and obsession in the stories of Orst's model and Luc are complemented by a third narrative that takes up the second section of the book. This concerns Manners' own past, primarily his relationship with his great juvenile love, 'Dawn'. Dawn is the name his friend Ralph had become associated with by chance at school, but which Ralph then 'blossomed into . . . like a drag name' (192). Dawn's death in a car accident brings Manners back to England, prompting him to contemplate his own youthful desire for rich and nuanced experience, encapsulated in seeing the evening star, a 'solitary ritual, wound up incoherently with bits of poetry said over and over like spells'. He recalls a poem in which he'd seen that first star referred to as the folding star, and the words haunted me with their suggestion of an embrace and at the same time a soundless implosion, of something ancient and evanescent; I looked up to it in a mood of desolate solitude burning into cold calm. I lingered, testing out the ache of it: I had to be back before it was truly dark, but in high summer that could be very late. I became a connoisseur of the last lonely gradings of blue into black. (216)

The blend of connoisseurship and loneliness, of sensuousness and seemingly inevitable loss, is made more concrete one evening when, immediately after these thoughts are conveyed, Edward recounts the night that Dawn comes to the same place and confidently seduces him under the trees. Edward's initial thought, '"But that's where the queers go", imagining some nice distinction between what they did there and whatever we were going to do' (219) captures the contrast between 'something ancient and evanescent' and earthy quotidian existence. The novel's stylish, dense and evocative account of love and loss was shortlisted for the Booker Prize.

Despite the contradictions of Clause 28 and hypocrisies deriving from it, despite the fears AIDs still produced, and despite John Major's 'back to basics' speech, homosexuality itself was less socially stigmatised than it had been in the 1980s. Prejudice was still rife and potentially humiliating and dangerous, of course, but a greater degree of acceptance was slowly emerging for gay and lesbian relationships, helped by novels such as *The Folding Star* and *Written on the Body*, the national and international successes of films like *The Crying Game* (looked at in Chapter 1) and one of the most successful comedies of the 1990s, *Four Weddings and a Funeral* (1994). The latter film showcases screenwriter Richard Curtis's capacity to portray the foibles and allure of the middle and upper middle classes (embodied in the tongue-tied bungling of Hugh Grant), and, as with the even more successful *Notting Hill* (1999), to cannily play to the lucrative American audience by having Grant fall in love with an American – Andie McDowell in *Four Weddings and a Funeral* and Julia Roberts in *Notting Hill*. *Four Weddings and a Funeral* exemplifies the conservative traditions of romantic comedy, with Grant as the likeable but ineffectual Charles, unwilling and unable to commit while those around him marry. But while the film revels in the standard romcom tropes, it is the relationship between Matthew and Gareth that produces the funeral of the title, after Gareth dies of a heart attack during the groom's toast at the third wedding. At Gareth's funeral, Matthew gives the oration, halting from his own thoughts and declaring: 'Perhaps you will forgive me if I turn from my own feelings to the words of another splendid bugger, W.H. Auden. This is actually what I want to say.' He then recites W. H. Auden's poem 'Funeral Blues', which includes the lines

> He was my North, my South, my East my West,
> My working week and my Sunday rest,
> My noon, my midnight, my talk, my song;
> I thought that love would last forever: I was wrong.
>
> (Auden 1950: 258)

In a film notable for its upbeat light-heartedness, the oration is easily the weightiest emotional moment. Unable themselves to marry under the prevailing laws of the 1990s, Matthew and Gareth have been accepted by their friends throughout the film as exemplars of a full, loving relationship. The recognition of genuine, long-standing emotional commitment stands out amidst all the frivolous courtships and Grantish buffoonery. Love in the nineties was as messy as it has always been, but in a decade where social conservatism was wheeled back in for a last hurrah, the case for honest, if sometimes In-Yer-Face, accounts of troublesome sexuality and sensuality was repeatedly and persuasively made.

Notes

1. Available at <https://www.theguardian.com/politics/1993/oct/09/conservatives.past> (last accessed 19 January 2017).
2. Available at <http://www.encyclopedia.com/topic/Cybercafe.aspx> (last accessed 21 August 2016).

Chapter Four

Class Resilience

> Megabucks. Wages. Interest. Wealth. I sniff and snuffle
> from a whiff of pelf; the stench of an abattoir blown
> by a stale wind over the fields. Roll up a fiver,
> snort. Meet Kim. Kim will give you the works,
> her own worst enema, suck you, lick you, squeal
> red weals to your whip, be nun, nurse, nanny,
> nymph on a credit card. Don't worry.
> Kim's only in it for the money. Lucre. Tin. Dibs.
>
> (Duffy 1994: 72)

Alwyn Turner's compendious study, *A Classless Society: Britain in the 1990s* (2013), ends after 574 richly observed pages seemingly contradicting its title. Turner writes of John Major and Tony Blair, that 'both had sought to create a classless society, both had failed, with wealth inequality increasing and social mobility decreasing, and both found themselves ill at ease with the kind of classless culture that emerged instead' (574). Turner adds that Major and Blair (and before them, Margaret Thatcher) had aimed to refashion Britain as a meritocracy, where ability was more pertinent and consequential than family background and traditional networks of social power. They hoped, he suggests, for a new elite based on talent, but that instead: 'The dominant strand of culture that emerged in the 1990s was very anti-elitist, as expressed through the National Lottery, reality television, the internet and the celebration of Princess Diana and David Beckham' (574). In bracketing Diana and Beckham, Turner blurs two conceptions of class: one, that of some vaguely understood but easy to concede aspect of 'quality', that both might exhibit due to supposed gifts of grace and beauty, or sporting prowess; the other, the division of a population in terms of socio-economic position and status. While both Diana and Beckham were certainly celebrities (the focus of the following chapter), and therefore drew upon the cachet that such status conferred in the 1990s, in British terms the son of an East End kitchen fitter and a hairdresser came from a very distinct and discernible social class than the daughter of British nobility, who seemed destined to become Queen of England. (The only writer to achieve anywhere near this sort of celebrity was Salman Rushdie, although not for his recognised skill with words.) Turner captures something about how in the 1990s what could be described as highbrow culture lost its dominant position and the extent to which culture in broad terms was democratised, so that both a princess and a premier league footballer could be celebrated by the public at large. Certainly, the steady movement from an economy founded on manufacturing to that dominated by services had gained pace in the previous decades and accelerated again under Margaret Thatcher, eroding long-established economic distinctions and community affiliations that had underpinned notions of class in Britain. But as Carol Ann Duffy's poem 'Making Money' (above) makes plain, the new service economy did not erase established hierarchies, nor fundamentally challenge inequities of power. Labour Deputy Leader, John Prescott, sometimes ridiculed as the token working class member of the Blair leadership team, and as a sop to the unions, claimed in 1997 that 'we are all middle class now'.[1] The implication seemed to be that the traditional working class had in some way been absorbed, had ceased to exist in any socially meaningful sense. In its way, Prescott's declaration was as remarkable as Margaret Thatcher's claim that 'there is no such thing as society'. The lived experience of many Britons in the 1990s refuted both statements; the working class endured.

As the Introduction noted, the Conservative Party advertised its somewhat surprise leader in 1990 as a testament to the party's capacity to choose that person on merit, rather than on social background. The implication was that John Major represented the successful striving of the individual that Thatcherism promoted. As historian David Cannadine observes in the conclusion to his significant contemporary study of the decade, *The Rise and Fall of Class in Britain* (1999),

> Thatcher's constantly and determinedly negative rhetoric was very successful in discrediting class and class conflict as the languages and concepts of political discussion, and it is not coincidence also in these years that they disappeared as the languages and concepts of historical enquiry. (Cannadine 1999: 180)

Cannadine argues that, although Thatcher tried to replace the language of class and productive labour with that of the consumer and the customer, and despite her 'deep-rooted dislike of the traditional aristocracy' and the 'traditional working class, especially organised labour', her confrontationist approach did not erase class from political discourse or social reality, or at least not to the degree hoped. John Major immediately defined himself as a prime minister wanting to create a 'classless society', but whereas 'Thatcher's "classless society" was the product of confrontation and struggle and victory; Major's "classless society" was one way everyone would try to be nice to each other' (185). Cannadine's early assessment of New Labour and Tony Blair was astute: 'Like the Conservatives, New Labour nowadays talks the language of individual "consumers" and "citizens" rather than that of collective "workers" or "producers" or "classes"' (187). The language of conciliation replaced the language of confrontation. The title of Andrew Adonis's and Stephen Pollard's *A Class Act: The Myth of Britain's Classless Society* (1997) speaks for itself, its authors quoting a Gallup poll from 1995 in which, when confronted with the proposition 'There used to be a lot of talk in politics about "the class struggle". Do you think there is a class struggle in this country or not?', 81 per cent of those sampled replied 'Yes' (3). Which is not to say that the combatants in this struggle had not changed, Adonis and Pollard emphasising the rise of what they labelled the new 'Super Class',

> a new élite of top professionals and managers, at once meritocratic and yet exclusive, very highly paid yet powerfully convinced of the justice of its rewards, and increasingly divorced from the rest of society by wealth, education, values, residence and lifestyle. (67)

This group was not purely a product of the nineties, but the benefits it was reaping in that decade were the stuff of public scandal: the salary of the chair of British Telecom, for example, went from £84,000 in 1984 to £663,000 by 1994, while that of British Gas's Cedric Brown in 1994 was increased by 75 per cent to £475,000 (70). Ironically, one of the authors of *A Class Act* came to exemplify aspects of the book's argument. Adonis, a columnist on the *Observer* when the book was published, would later become a minister in the Blair government. As if to underline his transformative rise, Blair in time would confer upon Adonis a life peerage, making him the grandiloquent Right Honourable the Lord Adonis.

Blair would declare in December 1998 that 'slowly, but surely, the old establishment is being replaced by a new, larger, more meritocratic middle class' (Marwick 2000: 370). But while traditional class markers such as trade union membership fell, housing prices rose, and the supposedly meritocratic 'Super Class' prospered, Arthur Marwick noted that 'At the bottom of society a recognizable "underclass" of the unfortunate, those dependent on state benefits, casual worker and the badly paid ... was also clearly established' (84–5). For those at the base of a rapidly growing pyramid, the reality was stark. The poverty rate, for example, barely improved (from 22 per cent in 1990 to 20 per cent in 1997–8); it had been 13 per cent in the last year of the Callaghan government (Jackson and Saunders 2012: 274). Unemployment at 1.8 million in 1990 was 1.9 million in 1997, having peaked at over 3 million in 1993 (271). For all the rhetoric of meritocratic change, none of the substantive actions that Major or Blair might conceivably have taken to bring about a classless society – Cannadine suggests such basics as the abolition of titles, the dismantling of the House of Lords, the eradication of the division between state and private education systems – were taken on with any great conviction in the 1990s. As Chapter 1 noted, George Orwell had advocated many of these steps five decades before in *The Lion and the Unicorn*. Class would remain a remarkably resilient component of self-perception, mutual perception, social perception and literary representation.

As commentators appreciate, 'class' is simultaneously difficult to define and undeniably important to understanding aspects of British history, politics and culture, the impossibility of providing a clear explanation of the term not invalidating it as a helpful explanatory concept. This chapter sketches in some of the outlines of the changes in the depiction and reception of class. Those responses, naturally, were varied, although an obvious bias derived for the fact that writers, publishers and the reviewers who acted as cultural gatekeepers were predominantly middle class creatures with predominantly middle class concerns. Virginia Woolf put this point bluntly in a 1940 essay, 'The Leaning Tower', declaring: 'Take away all that the working class has given to English literature and literature would scarcely suffer; take away all that the educated class has given, and English literature would scarcely exist' (Woolf 1967: 168).

Woolf tempers this provocatively blunt assessment with the qualifier that workers in 1940 were unlikely to receive the expensive type of education freely available to the middle class, most particularly to men. Education, she asserts, must 'play a very important part in a writer's work' (168). The decades after the Second World War were marked, as is well known, by the broadening of educational opportunities that had a transformative and democratising effect upon British culture generally. In the introduction to one of the most important anthologies of the 1990s, *The New Poetry* (1993), Michael Hulse, David Kennedy and David Morley stress that 'the new poetry emphasises accessibility, democracy and responsiveness, humour and seriousness, and reaffirms the art's significance as public utterance' (16). The following year the Poetry Society launched an initiative that celebrated poets who were young, or youngish (many were in their late thirties) and who, an *Independent* article pronounced, 'are more likely to be Scottish, working class, and holding down a day job in the social services'.[2] These developments also reflected the existence of a wider base of well-educated readers, but the oft-quoted and oft-mocked claim that poetry was the new rock 'n' roll or stand-up comedy signifies the conscious attempt by younger poets to extend poetry's appeal beyond established coteries. This attempt was not initiated in the 1990s – works such as Tony Harrison's controversial 1980s television poem, V, being an obvious precursor in the previous decade – but the fact that the anthology's editors foreground accessibility and democracy promotes work that strives to speak across class boundaries, to connect with a general public that need not fear that poetry, primarily because it *is* poetry, had nothing to say to those outside the middle class audience.

Yet the poetry in the anthology itself at times betrays an awareness of uneasy class distinctions, as in Sean O'Brien's 'Cousin Coat':

> You are my secret coat. You're never dry.
> You wear the weight and stink of black canals.
> Malodorous companion, we know why
> It's taken me so long to see we're pals,
> To learn why my acquaintance [*sic*] never sniff
> Or send me notes to say I stink of stiff.
>
> But you don't talk, historical bespoke.
> You must be worn, be intimate as skin,
> And though I never lived what you invoke,
> At birth I was already buttoned in.
> Your clammy itch became my atmosphere,
> An air made half of anger, half of fear.
>
> (O'Brien, in Hulse et al. 1993: 199)

A problematic interplay between association and differentiation invigorates 'Cousin Coat', the speaker slightly embarrassed in the following stanza about trying to shed the coat's legacy 'in libraries with Donne and Henry James'. O'Brien, from a working class family, studied English at Cambridge, not a unique résumé among writers from that background who came to maturity in the 1990s. Woolf's point about the importance of education for writers and writing, while never universally applicable, remains pertinent in this instance. In 'Cousin Coat', the speaker probes gaps between rhetoric, memory and reality, the coat a symbol, but no mere stage prop.

> No comfort there for comfy meliorists
> Grown weepy over Jarrow photographs.
> No comfort when the poor the state enlists

> Parade before their fathers' cenotaphs.
> No comfort when the strikers all go back
> To see which 20,000 get the sack.
>
> (199)

The representative historical instances of class betrayal fuse present and past, requiring contemporary recognition and engaged and considered poetic response from the speaker. Ultimately, the secret coat is invoked both as a call to testify and as a guide to keep the speaker 'cold and honest', to prevent the self-deceptive lie; or, if inevitably, it is committed, to expose that lie.

Where O'Brien concerns himself with a personal attitude or relationship to the working class, Duffy's 'Making Money' explores in detail the ways in which making money defines and somewhat defiles those who undertake those acts, part of a verbal economy where the sheer variety of terms for money register its ubiquitous, malevolent power. So, the poem begins with a staccato roll call:

> Turnover. Profit. Readies. Cash. Loot. Dough. Income.
>   Stash.
> Dosh. Bread. Finance. Brass. I give my tongue over
> To money; The taste of warm rust in a chipped mug
> of tap-water. Drink some yourself.
>
> (Duffy 1994: 72)

The language employed to talk about money is varied and energetic, insinuating itself via ambiguities and double meanings – 'Loot'; 'Bread'; 'Brass' – into daily life, into the very activities of making. For a poet, especially, the subservience of words to commerce, the servile and perverse giving over of the tongue to money, resounds strongly. Money conveys power globally, as in the follow-up image of Salaamat, 'an Indian man in Delhi', whose job requires squatting 'by an open drain for hours, sifting shit / for the price of a chapati'. Or Kim, the sex worker mentioned in the opening epigraph, a dehumanised sex toy 'only in it for the money', as though she had chosen physical humiliation as a canny business plan. Or, again, Ahmat, rushing on to a target range to find spent cartridges for scrap, knowing that 'Some shells don't explode', and that consequently 'bomb-collectors die young. But the money's good' (73). Bob Dylan famously declared that 'money doesn't talk, it swears'; Duffy examines a thesaurus of terms that camouflage money's dirty work, ending by incorporating the contemporary British reader:

> ... We leave
> our places of work, tired, in the shortening hours, in
>   the time

> of night our town could be anywhere, and some of us
>   pause
> in the square, where a clown makes money swallowing
>   fire.
>
> (73)

This surreal, gothic finale reiterates the links between quotidian slog and the prospect of self-harm, foolhardiness and finance, graft and danger.

The economist Will Hutton considers the parlous state of Britain in his bestselling argument for Keynesian political economy, *The State We're In* (1996). Hutton notes peculiarly local elements within a globalised capitalist environment, arguing that 'The individualist, *laissez-faire* values which imbue the economic and political elite have been found wanting – but with the decline of socialism there seems to be no coherent alternative in the wings' (23–4). He adds that

> what binds together the disorders of the British system is a fundamental amorality. It is amoral to run a society founded on the exclusion of so many people from decent living standards and opportunities; it is amoral to run an economy in which the only admissible objective is the maximization of shareholder value; it is amoral to run a political system in which power is held exclusively and exercised in a discretionary, authoritarian fashion. (24)

A serious fallout from this amorality, Hutton later contends, is increasing inequality, something built into the dominant economic arguments of the age. Without inequality, the arguments run, 'a capitalist society simply loses its dynamism', and that 'unless there is a penalty for being out of work, workers will not seek employment. There needs to be fear and greed in the system in order to make it tick' (173). The consequences are that 'to be born poor means to stay poor and ill-qualified; while to be born rich brings with it educational attainment and career achievement' (176). Hutton continues, that 'Class hardens subtly into caste – and economies did not prosper in caste societies' (176). This mid-1990s report card charts a bleak narrative begun in the late 1970s by certain austerity policies under Labour, but turbo-charged under Thatcher's monetarist policies, with chapter titles in *The State We're In* such as 'The Conservative Supremacy', 'Finance Unbound', 'The Revolution Founders' and 'Why Inequality Doesn't Work' fleshing out Hutton's counter-position to nineties orthodoxy.

Writers presented a wealth of report cards. As well as the provocative take on sexuality examined in the previous chapter, Mark Ravenhill's *Shopping and Fucking* deals confrontationally with economic amorality, without offering the sorts of solutions proposed by Hutton. The play's title boldly challenges prevailing social norms of propriety but also of hypocrisy, fusing rampant consumerism and primal human desire into a compound designed to confuse moral certainties. In the opening scene, Robbie and Lulu ask Mark, who at the outset they have been attempting to feed, to tell them once again 'the shopping story' that functions as a combination of foundational myth, fairy tale and bedtime horror story. Mark relates how, in a supermarket, he had watched a couple (whom he comes to know as Lulu and Robbie):

> Mark: you see me and you know sort of straight away that I'm going to have you. You know you don't have a choice. No control. Now this guy comes up to me. He's a fat man . . .
> ...
> Well, says fat guy, they're both mine. I own them. I own them but I don't want them – because you know something? – they're trash. And I hate them. Wanna buy them?
> ...
> So, I do the deal. I hand it over. I fetch you. I don't have to say anything because you know. You've seen the transaction.
> ...
> And I've been keeping a room for you and I take you into this room. And there's food. And it's warm. And we live out our days fat and content and happy. (Ravenhill 2001: 5)

Blending the contemporary slave trade with domestic bliss, Mark's story first reduces the others to tokens, before conjuring up an economic Stockholm syndrome. He instantly destroys that cosily deviant atmosphere by announcing that he is leaving to receive treatment at a centre for his addictions. But 'the shopping story' establishes some of the grim power dynamics of a world in which individuals and interpersonal relationships are commodities traded to the highest bidder, or sometimes simply to the nearest available bidder. Lulu openly challenges the pretence that those purchased are completely in thrall to those with money, telling Mark that, in his current reduced financial state he has no power, and that, in any case, 'You don't own us. We exist. We're people. We can get by. Go' (7). Despite her confidence in her agency, though, Lulu and Robbie repeatedly are shown as vulnerable, exploited and exploitable. If, by play's end, they find some freedom, it is because Brian presents them with a potentially liberating economic windfall.

Repeatedly, sex is the commodity traded for cash or other forms of security. Mark, for instance, is expelled from the treatment centre for infringing the rules against forming personal attachments when he pays someone to lick the arsehole of one of the other inmates. Importantly, for Mark, the act of paying dislocates the sexual act from emotional meaningfulness. He tells Robbie that it was a 'transaction. I paid him.

I gave him money. And when you're paying you can't call it a personal relationship, can you?' (18); and again: 'We did a deal. We confined ourselves to the lavatory. It didn't mean anything' (19). He protests slightly too much, and will repeat this argument to Gary, the rent boy he meets in Scene 4. The audience might interpret this as once again confusing or undermining the confidently expressed power trip of 'the shopping story', with Mark paying without gaining dominance. In fact, with Gary he stays beyond the initial transaction and begins to protect the streetwise, but damaged, boy. 'I used to know what I felt', Mark admits in Scene 6: 'I traded. Tic Tac. And when I made money I was happy, when I lost money I was unhappy' (33). While coins symbolically clatter from an arcade downstairs, Mark asks almost rhetorically, 'are there any feelings left?', declaring, 'I want to find out, want to know if there are any feelings left' (34). Gary's offering of 'Beef' or 'Nice and Spicy' Hot Noodles (an act that recalls Robbie's and Lulu's attempts to feed Mark in Scene 1), suggests the potential for feeling separated from money, or other forms of economic domination; but it only suggests.

A rather different challenge to the money economy comes when Robbie, in a burst of liberating anarchy, gives away 300 E tablets that he was supposed to be selling in a nightclub. As he explains to Lulu:

> I was looking down on this planet. Spacemen over this earth. And I see this kid in Rwanda, crying, but he doesn't know why. And this granny in Kiev, selling everything she's ever owned . . . And I see this suffering. And the wars. And the grab, grab, grab.
> And I think: Fuck Money. Fuck it. Fuck this selling. This buying. This system. Fuck the bitching world and let's be . . . beautiful. Beautiful. And happy. You see? (39)

Unfortunately, this moment of transcendent humanity clashes with the reality of an aggressive nightclub habitué, so furious that Robbie's supply of free Es has run out that he beats Robbie up. Nor does Lulu, comforting Robbie in an accident and emergency waiting room, respond positively to the slowly revealed news that the drugs he was supposed to sell have been given away: 'Fucking fucker arsehole. Fuck. Pillowbiter. (Hit)'. She quickly undertakes a crude cost/benefit analysis, understanding that 'suffering is going to be handed out' for Robbie's momentary disavowal of the profit motive, and that it will be meted out by Brian to 'both of us' (39). As members of the new underclass, Robbie and Lulu as a consequence are forced into a form of prostitution with a contemporary twist, staffing phone sex lines, the modish form of sexual commodification. This is preferable, nonetheless, to the threatened torture by Black and Decker power tool that Brian shows them on video, with the added economics lesson that 'I have to keep the cash flow flowing you see? Which is why I can't let people FUCK. ME. AROUND. You understand?' (49) They understand.

Brian epitomises the violence underpinning economic power. He also lauds money and possessions as inherently positive, as he explains to Lulu in Scene 2, when she auditions for a part holding up merchandise on a television sales channel: 'Our viewers', he tells her, 'they have to believe that what we hold up to them is special.' In this case, the object held aloft is a plate. 'For the right sum – life is easier, richer, more fulfilling. And you have to believe that too. Do you think you can do that?' (10). He then pressures her into stripping off her jacket and blouse, which she does. On the verge of humiliation or worse she declares:

> One day people will know what all this is for. All this suffering. There will be no more mysteries. But until then we have to carry on living. We must work. That's all we can do. I'm leaving by myself tomorrow. (13)

This lyrical riposte undermines Brian briefly, and through his tears and sobs he asks her did she 'make it up?' She replies that she learnt it from a book. Those words, and her next speech, in fact are cribbed from the ending of Anton Chekhov's *Three Sisters*, where they provide a tentatively positive ending to the search for meaning. Here, though, they might be read as a cynical rejection of apparent meaning, or as a means of calibrating the philosophical and cultural distance between early twentieth-century Russia and late twentieth-century Britain. Chekhov's words contrast with Brian's own deeply felt insight about fathers given earlier in the scene, where Brian draws on the Disney animation, *The Lion King*. Fathers are problematic figures in *Shopping and Fucking*, although Brian's own father had presented him with what he took to be a revelatory question: 'what are the first few words in the Bible?' Denying the young Brian's reply, 'In the beginning', his father insists that, in fact, the first words are: 'get the money first. Get. The Money. First' (87). To which Brian adds his commentary:

> It's not perfect, I don't deny it. We haven't reached perfection. But it's the closest we've come to meaning. Civilisation is money. Money is civilisation. And civilisation – how did we get here? By war, by struggle, kill or be killed. And money – it's the same thing, you understand? The getting is cruel, is hard, but the having is civilisation. Then we are civilised. Say it. Say it with me. (87)

This stripped back paean to money records with brutal certainty a Hobbesian economic world Will Hutton might take as indicative of the nineties. Brian will reiterate this view, believing that Lulu and Robbie have learnt the lesson he has taught, and leaves the stage predicting

'That's the future, isn't it. Shopping, Television' (89). But Mark then gives his picture of the future, via a version of 'the shopping story' set on a benighted Earth in the year 'three thousand AD. Or something.' There, a 'fat sort of ape-thing' tries to sell a "mutant" with a three foot long dick' (89). With postmodern flippancy, Robbie had earlier dismissed the old world of 'big stories' – 'The Powerful Hands of the Gods and Fate. The Journey to Enlightenment. The March of Socialism' (66) – so Mark's futuristic update on the framing story is not meant to be definitive. As he admits, it is simply 'the best I can do' (90). For all that, while the play starts with Lulu and Robbie failing to feed Mark, it ends in a tableau that recalls *Blasted*, with about as much optimism as can be mustered, the three '[taking] it in turns to feed each other as the lights fade to black' (91), their small acts of mutual nurturing less nihilistic than the surrounding environment marked by selfish acquisition.

The deliberate excesses of *Shopping and Fucking* set the plight of the underclass in high relief. Other nineties texts paint that class, and the struggling working class in general, in more realistic colours and tones, especially in novels from that most anti-Thatcherite nation in the United Kingdom: Scotland. In *Morvern Callar*, considered in Chapter 1, for example, the eponymous main character scrapes out a forlorn existence at a 'superstore' in a small coastal town in the west of Scotland, harassed by the supervisor she nicknames 'Creeping Jesus'. Her unfulfilling job entails mindless activities such as stacking shelves, filling plastic bags with goods, sweeping and 'tipping the buckets down the drain in the meat-cutting room. You could see the pale yellow maggots still there under the grate' (Warner 1995: 10). Morvern understands the level of manipulation involved, having started part-time at thirteen, working for a manager who 'has you working all hours cash in hand, no insurance, so when fifteen or sixteen you go back full-time at the start of that summer and never go back to school' (9). She must also take class-based insults from customers, such as a 'woman with a well-to-do south voice who told me to wash my soily hands before touching her messages. They all paid with these credit cards. I put the bags in the trolleys and pushed them to the Volvos' (9). Her hard-earned awareness of class division and exploitation is muted by a generational ennui fuelled by alcohol, drugs, sex, parties and music. The novel's gothic opening lines provide her the means to escape to this anomic existence, for in the lead-up to Christmas she finds her boyfriend's body on the floor of their flat. As explained in Chapter 1, the never-named boyfriend supplies a Walkman she finds is her Christmas present. Because she rarely takes it off subsequently, it provides a soundtrack to her life. He also provides the bank account Morvern will plunder to finance a rave trip to Europe, and a book manuscript that she will claim as her own and from which she will reap financial benefits. While she does weep for him initially, her state of mind remains ambiguous, so that she walks past the phone box she was going to use to report the death, reflecting that 'It was the feeling the music gave that made me' (5). This dull thought approximates a similar post-emotional, affectless response that characterises the figures in *Shopping and Fucking*. For all her drifting through Europe and eventually back to Scotland, though, what distinguishes Morvern is that she retains an energy and a mordant independence that allow her to deal with setbacks, engage critically with the world (including the rather tainted world of fiction publishing) and take advantage of emerging economic opportunities.

Something similar might be said of Mark Renton in *Trainspotting*, although he is altogether more aggressive, manipulative and cynical. In the putative post-politics world of the 1990s, where the 'big stories' like 'The March to Socialism' go unheeded and untold, Renton's gleeful descent into the drug underclass constitutes a middle-finger rejection of materialism and careerism, his confident reaction to the overhyped ideology of consumption being to reject it:

> The fact is that ye simply choose tae reject what they have tae offer. Choose us. Choose life. Choose mortgage payments, choose washing machines; choose cars; Choose sitting oan a couch watching mind-numbing and spirit crushing game shows, stuffing fuckin' junk food intae yir mooth. Choose rotting away, pishing an sheiting yerself in a home, a total fuckin' embarrassment tae the selfish, backed up brats ye've produced. Choose life. Well, ah choose no tae choose life. (Welsh 1993: 187–8)

Renton, like Morvern, exemplifies demotivated youth and the rejection of Thatcherite tenets. Unlike others, though, he is intelligent enough to construct an incisive and dismissive analysis of those social norms and inducements, while feeling no compulsion to change the state of things. He takes advantage of the circumstances; easier to rip off the system than to change it. Renton criticises his drug agency counsellor, Tom Curzon, for Tom's refusal 'tae accept ma view that society cannae be changed tae make it significantly better, or that ah can change tae accommodate it' (186). Renton openly admits to alienation that he replaces with the quick and stratospheric uplift heroin supplies, while also recognising how 'society invents a spurious convoluted logic tae absorb and change people's behaviour whae's outside its mainstream' (187). Still, he cannily distinguishes himself from the indelibly underclass Spud at their court appearance for stealing books from Waterstones for drug money. Where Spud instantly admits the charge, Renton pleads that he wanted the books to read, including work by the Danish philosopher Soren Kierkegaard. This surprise gambit activates the magistrate's innate sense of class superiority: 'So you read Kierkegaard. Tell us about him, Mr Renton, the patronising cunt sais' (165). Reminding himself to 'Think deference, Renton, think deference', Mark launches into another riff on choice, this time with a philosophical bent and in an accent bleached of class-ridden Scottishness:

> I'm interested in his concepts of subjectivity and truth, and particularly his ideas concerning choice; the notion that genuine choice is made of doubt and uncertainty, and without recourse to the experience of others. It could be argued, with some justification, that it's primarily a bourgeois, existential philosophy and would therefore seek to undermine collective social wisdom. (165–6)

Strategically playing the middle class card of intellectual competence with this improvised mash of philosophy and class analysis earns Renton a suspended sentence and a fine, where the lumpenproletarian Spud gets ten months in prison. In the novel's finale, Renton makes a more consequential and perhaps existential choice, choosing betrayal over friendship, ripping off his putative pals in a London drug deal. This immoral or amoral act provides the means for his escape to Amsterdam. He is no working class hero, then, being at times a giro scammer, thief, ex-Aberdeen University student (albeit for less than a year), and 'Mr Suit en Tie' and a 'nine to five arsehole' (300) during escapades in London. Renton navigates shrewdly between class categories, protean, self-serving and alert, contemplating 'life in Amsterdam' at the novel's end, where 'he could be what he wanted to be', even as this thought 'terrified and excited him' (344). Renton remains the selfish, atomised individual on the make, a criminal parody of the system he rejects. Welsh's point is not so much political as sociological, recording reality without caring to provide any sustained critique of the system, beyond Renton's cynical appraisal.

Renton's capacity to manipulate the class system to his advantage places him at odds with one of the more memorable characters of nineties literature, Glaswegian ex-con Sammy Samuels, the sometimes builder's labourer, ex-con, social security beneficiary protagonist of James Kelman's Booker Prize-winning novel *How Late It Was, How Late* (1994). Kelman tracks the life of someone permanently consigned to the underclass, a man who wakes up against some railings after a night 'on the bevy'. Sammy tries to inveigle two plainclothes policemen, or 'sodjers', to give him a pound. When they refuse, he starts a fight that ends in him being thrown into a police cell overnight. Waking, he soon realises that

> it was his eyes, that was the main fucking problem like he had gone blind but the black [darkness of the cell] had stopped him appreciating the fact. But it felt like morning. He tried some manoeuvres. But naw, he couldnae see a thing. Nothing. Fuck all. (10)

Comic awareness of his own absurdity and a growing despair at the larger absurdity of existence get woven into the practicalities of coming to terms with his condition, of trying to understand the breakdown of his relationship with his girlfriend, Helen. He immediately and unceasingly must deal with a social world that actively excludes or ignores him and those like him. Kelman presents Sammy as a fully realised individual, the novel coming to us through Sammy's sense (at different times bewildered, aggressive, mocking and amused) of a life in which he is constantly running very hard to stay in the same spot. He understands himself as 'A battler man that's what he was. One thing about the Sammy fellow, a fucking battler. If ye had asked him he would have telt ye: nay brains but he would aye battle like fuck' (47). This doggedness allows him to see positives, to believe, for instance, in the fact that the blindness – 'through no fault of his own cause the fucking sodjers did it man and they were a Government Department' – should mean the end to state-funded community programmes he has been forced to undertake; these have required him to climb 'a ladder with a bucket of fucking concrete'. Instead, he projects a rosier future in which he was 'only gony be fit for special blind jobs' (68). The intricacies and absurdities of government bureaucracy frustrate those hopes. The novel maps the short period in Sammy's life as he tries to make sense of an immediate past, half-lost in the mists of alcohol, and a permanent present in the mean streets of Glasgow. Like Renton, he is no working class hero, but his pinched individual circumstances, his blindness and the impoverished and put-upon world he and others like him inhabit make him far more vulnerable than Irvine Welsh's young heroin addict. He, too, has done wrong, even if, as his relationship with Helen (who never returns) reveals, regular drunkenness means that he cannot quite remember what he has done. What Sammy retains, though, is a gritty, self-deprecating resilience that propels him on. In the finale, he evades those he suspects want to harm him, and, like Renton, flees Scotland, in Sammy's case for England. His future is massively uncertain, but it is one that he is brave enough to face.

If Welsh introduces readers to the rather limited subgroup of Edinburgh heroin users, Kelman does something similar for the far larger underclass many readers might have little or no experience of in real life. Not that some readers would want to experience them. Although the novel won the Booker Prize, word that some of the judges were avidly antagonistic to *How Late It Was, How Late* reached across the Atlantic, *The New York Times* reporting that one of the judges, Rabbi Julia Neuberger, had 'declared the book was unreadably bad and said that the awarding of the prize, Britain's most important, was a "disgrace"'. The paper also noted that 'Simon Jenkins, a conservative columnist for *The Times* of London, called the award '"literary vandalism"', and described the novel as 'the ramblings of a Glaswegian drunk'.³ Neuberger reportedly threatened to resign from the panel if the book won. Kelman added to the controversy with his passionate acceptance speech at the awards ceremony. Dispensing with the expected pieties, Kelman used his oration to berate British writers, publishers and critics for ignoring the significant part of the population not likely to be interested in the topics or approaches expected of Booker Prize winners. He argued the worth of the speech and thoughts of ordinary folk, declaiming that no one had the authority to dismiss his language and his culture. Written in a demotic voice, *How Late It Was, How Late* was Kelman's demonstration of the type of novel he clearly thought needed to be more regularly published, read and rewarded. The world beyond that of the middle classes was a serious and genuine concern of much 1990s literature. Yet a power imbalance clearly remained as to what was deemed valuable by those who traditionally acted as the gatekeepers of value. *How Late It Was, How Late* sold fewer copies than any Booker winner of the period, but Kelman, the first Scottish writer to win the prize, opened the eyes of many readers to a world in which the notion of a classless society made no sense, spoke to no actual experiences or reality.

As already shown, Kelman's Glasgow was not the only place where class was still a tangible and forceful component of daily existence in the nineties. In Robert McLiam Wilson's *Eureka Street*, Jake Jackson roams the streets of Belfast in a large van with his work colleagues, musing as he drives that he

> weltered in sentiment. And it was briefly good to be doing what I was doing. Driving to my hard day's toil. In my big boots, my artisan's shirt and my rough trousers I felt dignified, I felt worthy, I felt like the nineteen thirties.
> Then I remembered what I did for a living. (Wilson 2015: 61)

What Jake does for a living is repossess furniture and other items from Belfast working class and underclass families behind on their credit payments. With two burly companions not prone to empathy, he is a stand over man to those living beyond the dreams of instant gratification promoted by a culture founded on all-too-easily-available credit. 'Some would say the working-class aspiration always ends like this – ', he muses, 'hard-faced hoodlums taking all the gaudy baubles away. I still felt like a criminal' (8). These conflicts might seem to be complicated further by the city's religious divides, but Jake notes breezily that 'We were thrillingly ecumenical and we raided Protestant estates with all the *élan* and grace with which we raided Catholic ones. I could never see the difference', adding that

> They could paint their walls any colour they wanted, they could fly a hundred flags and they still couldn't pay the rent and we would still come and take their stuff away from them. It was Povertyland. It was the land where the bad things happened.' (63)

Far more than simply a paid thug, he understands the ruinous effect of compulsive consumerism on people with the socially sanctioned desires but not the money. Still,

> they bought on, unsurprisingly. There were still allowed to purchase, to consume. They shored themselves up with comfort goods. They'd committed the crime of wanting what they could not have and they all came quietly. I had not had to hit anyone since I'd started working in repo again. I hadn't needed to. I would never need to. They were already beaten, these people. There was nothing more that I could do to them. (64)

While his response to the plight of such people might seem purely cynical, his shame at remembering 'what I did for a living' exposes his own qualms: he eventually leaves his job after one of his fellow repo men viciously throws a sick old woman with a medical condition out of the expensive bed she requires but cannot continue to pay off. Jake later buys the woman a replacement.

Where Jake from the outset understands the corrupting effect of nineties consumerism, the novel's other protagonist, Chuckie Lurgan, is a man on the make, plotting to escape the working class Eureka Street where he lives with his 'archetypal working-class Protestant Belfast mother'. He comments dryly that

> Not an inch of her headscarf or fibre of the slippers in which she shopped departed from what would have been expected. She had *doppelgängers* all along Eureka Street and all the other baleful streets around Sandy Row. It was absurd. (47)

Chuckie is dismissive of his background and keen to absorb and prosper from the decade's approved ideology:

> He needed money. He needed much money. But Chuckie was not foolish enough to consider looking for a job. Employment was the goal of fools. Chuckie had decided he would set up in business for himself. He felt that only self-employment would entirely satisfy his independent instincts. Chuckie knew that he had some way to go, but phrases like start-up capital, overheads and profit margins peppered his thoughts and felt quite as good as money in the bank. (24)

His first commercial venture involves a massive scam, a comic affair involving people buying giant dildos by mail order, and then, having found the poorly made product deficient, being too embarrassed to cash the reimbursement cheque that had 'Giant Dildo Refund' stamped in large letters across it. Armed with the approved vocabulary and mindset, Chuckie then fronts a grants committee eager to promote commercial expansion in Belfast, and through a combination of chutzpah, lies and the innate corruption of such bodies, secures himself huge sums of money and instant wealth. Wilson deftly skewers the venality and superficiality of an exploitative culture that Chuckie understands rests on a simple premise: 'Good business was getting paid as much as possible for as little as possible. That was capitalism in essence. Something for nothing' (57). While not as violent or extreme as *Shopping and Fucking*'s Brian, the affable Chuckie nevertheless colludes with a system that maintains essential class distinctions and intensified inequalities, while professing to enhance social mobility. As Adonis and Pollard declare in 1998,

> the separation of classes remains one of the key facts about modern Britain. And segregation has become more, not less, marked in the last generation as a large and distinct lower class has separated from the old working class, while a smaller but equally distinct and immensely powerful Super Class has taken off at the top. (33)

Despite the rhetoric of classless meritocracy, Chuckie's quick rise shows how this might be done with nothing more than shameless exploitation and chutzpah.

Given the eternal funding difficulties faced by the British film industry, and the reality that films reflecting heritage themes and texts, or the foibles of the English middle class, tended to appeal to the vital American audience, a surprising number of films captured the realities of working class and unemployed life in the nineties. They also celebrated working class resilience in the aftermath of Thatcherite policies. Key directors such as Mike Leigh and Ken Loach (neither lured by Hollywood's lucrative siren call) produced tough studies of working class life, or of those betrayed by the new arrangements. These mostly centred on men made redundant or put under extreme pressure socially and economically, the title of Loach's *Raining Stones* (1993) emblematic of an environment of unyielding hardship. His *Riff-Raff* (1991) presented a more comically inflected take on the lives of workers on a building site trying to make ends meet, while *Ladybird, Ladybird* (1994) foregrounded the life of an unmarried working class woman, Maggie Conlan, struggling to keep her head above water and custody of her children in the face of the Social Security belief that she is a negligent mother. *My Name is Joe* (1998) tracks the life of the eponymous Glaswegian, a recovering alcoholic trying to piece his life together, who meets the lower middle class Sarah. But while their romance promises Joe a new life, his own class loyalty leads him back to his darker past, something Sarah cannot easily accept. As he explains to her, 'we don't live in this nice, tidy world of yours', adding that while the economic system protects and benefits the middle classes, 'Some of us don't have a choice.' Those who do choose sometimes choose a self-destructive route, as with the nihilistic Johnny in Mike Leigh's *Naked* (1993), who believes that 'I don't have a future' and indeed that 'Nobody has a future.' Something similar might be true in an even grimmer way in Gary Oldman's harrowing and partly autobiographical *Nil By Mouth* (1997), about an underclass family in a south-east London high-rise estate tormented by a tyrannical and incestuous father, played with terrifying force by Ray Winstone. Against these unapologetically frank accounts of ordinary life, two comedies, *Brassed Off* (1996) and *The Full Monty* (1997), celebrated working class hardiness in the face of what they portrayed as a Thatcherite war against coal and steel in the north of England. Both films trace a narrative arc from initial social and economic depression resulting from the crippling of traditional working class industries that gave structure and purpose to whole communities and cities. Both use humour and pathos to applaud the solidarity of such communities, and to suggest the great cultural loss entailed by the breakup or the denigration of such social forces. Ultimately, both end in triumph against potentially overwhelming odds, and in the validation of working class camaraderie and values. Perhaps this more optimistic, if somewhat nostalgic, take on contemporary British life (no doubt aided by stellar casts) contributed to the surprising local and international acclaim enjoyed by both films. *The Full Monty* made a remarkable $45 million at the US box office and gained three Oscar nominations, winning one Oscar for best score. They and films like them challenged the soothing and self-serving myth of a classless society.

One way for those in the working class to escape their situation was associated with a far older, more romantic myth, that of Camelot. This myth was reworked for the 1990s, though, Camelot being the name of the company that would administer one of the signal innovations of social life in the decade, the National Lottery. In a time when the National Health Service appeared under constant threat, the National Lottery, introduced by the Major government in 1994, won instant and widespread support. Adonis and Pollard (1998) provide a useful summary of its neat fit with the decade's tenor:

> The passion for easy wealth and undemanding pleasure. Vicarious engagement in a national sport, mobilizing every dimension of the electronic media. Shiny, modern presentation, buttressed by classless rhetoric. Vociferous insistence by those in charge that all sections of society participate and benefit equally, packaged in soundbites ... that disguised the reality. (259)

The reality was that the working classes spent more per person than those in the middle classes, which, accounting for inbuilt economic discrepancies, meant that a higher percentage of the smaller working class income was being 'invested' in the weekly 'flutter' broadcast live on BBC2. Though the first draw did not produce the hoped-for millionaires, the Lottery quickly became embedded in the national culture. A government White Paper cynically called it 'The People's Lottery', and 'gambling was soon the fastest area of growth in consumer spending' (Adonis and Pollard 1998: 269). While Camelot was making huge profits from the surprisingly high weekly outlays, public qualms about where its money was going were mollified by the justification that, apart from most of the money being returned in prizes, 28 per cent would go to what the Conservative government labelled 'good causes': arts; heritage; sport; charities; and a Millennial Fund to support projects and festivals pertinent to the new century approaching. While these causes were (as intended) largely uncontroversial, and provoked relatively little public discussion, they hid inherent biases. Their foci tended to satisfy largely middle class interests, and three of the five funding bodies (for arts, sports and heritage) were already established, so that traditional bodies were given control of massive amounts of money, with little oversight. As Ken Worpole suggests, the reliance on established bodies meant that 'many of the old patterns of metropolitan, patrician administration' were reinforced. Rather than distribute money evenly across the nation, as a National Lottery might be expected to do, Worpole notes a bias towards London-based institutions such as the Tate Gallery and the Royal Opera House. 'Heritage awards', he adds, 'by definition, largely go to the preservation of historic artefacts, monuments, landscapes and buildings, principally taking advice from already existing bodies such as English Heritage which has always had a cultural agenda of its own' (Worple 2001: 240). An early controversy was the £13 million paid to the Churchill family for the state papers of the former prime minister, something those in charge of the money thought an uncontroversial act to preserve what they considered an obvious piece of national heritage. The average punter, though, reviled the idea as a handout to an already privileged aristocracy. While there were clear benefits from the distribution of money, notably to the film industry, critics of the National Lottery condemned it as a barely disguised vehicle for the struggling working class to subsidise the cultural norms and organisations of their supposed betters.

John Godber's tragi-comic play *Lucky Sods* (1995) addresses some of these concerns from the perspective of Jean and Morris, a working class couple from Yorkshire. Godber was the driving force behind the Hull

Truck Company, since the 1980s one of the most successful and enduring regional theatre companies, specialising in the lives of ordinary folk, primarily those in the region. John Prescott, the member for Hull East, might well have attended such plays. In *Lucky Sods*, Jean, in her early forties, works in a video shop, while Morris is a nightwatchman. Both live lives of quiet desperation and tedium briefly dispelled each week by dreams of winning the National Lottery. They have just failed to win it again as the play opens, but the second scene, presumably a week later, finds Morris furious that Jean has changed his lottery numbers. Just as the tension mounts, as more of her lottery numbers come up, the power goes out. Godber uses the blackout for comic and dramatic effect, for when the lighting is restored the time frame has moved on and Jean and Morris are telling their brother- and sister-in-law, Norman and Annie, that on that night they won £2 million. Jean wants to spend some of the winnings on a conservatory, to go with the bathroom renovation (complete with spa bath) that they've already had done. Annie and Norman urge them to move to a more salubrious neighbourhood, to shuck off their working class surroundings for something grander, more befitting their new economic status. Jean and Morris demur, at this point equating self-identify with their old home. Godber handles their small dreams delicately, gently mocking their circumscribed imaginations while introducing complicating elements: the economic jealousy of others; different expectations about the transformations money can bring; and larger questions about chance, fate and death. He contrasts the optimistic and more adventurous Jean with the morbid, uninspired Morris, who likens adventure to unnecessary risk and disruption. His idea of a holiday for fifteen years had been fishing at the Yorkshire seaside town of Bridlington. Their subsequent trip to Los Angeles prompts a frustrated Jean to demand more than just guilt-laden travel. Given the tedium they have had to endure in their working lives, she feels that they deserve more than Morris keeping watch on a scrapyard. Scene 4 ends with her proposing that they go immediately to Venice.

The audience never gets to see that potentially liberating adventure, for Scene 5 begins at their newly renovated house (which now has a massive conservatory) at the end of a Christmas dinner with Annie and Norman. Initially encountered by the audience on their own, Annie and Norman criticise the waste of money of the subsequent trip back on the Orient Express, complain about their own meagre presents – Norman only having received his usual 'soap-on-a-rope' – while sifting through the deluge of mail Jean and Morris have been receiving since their win. These include one from Connie Wilde, the singer in the band Morris had been drummer for years earlier. When Morris appears, Annie uses the letters and cards to probe whether he and Jean are using the money to help the terminally ill or the destitute. He dodges the loaded question by querying whether the requests are genuine. In a spontaneous pincer movement, Norman pointedly suggests that whoever had helped a young girl with leukaemia probably 'was a lottery winner', before upping the ante in declaring 'I think all the lottery winners should put sommat in a hospital fund, instead of all them bloody holidays' (1.5). Tensions skyrocket, Morris replying that hospitals are a government responsibility. This prompts Norman to question the rationale for the National Lottery itself, noting that the Major government 'aren't interested, are they?' Referencing the Churchill papers controversy, he adds 'I tell you sommat I bet we wouldn't get thirteen million for my grandad's letters', before broadening his attack further: 'Bloody opera, fifty-five million? Robbing the poor to pay the rich, that's what it is' (1.5). Godber's dexterous intertwining of the personal and the political, the financial and the social, give this scene a telling authenticity, the arrival of Jean, who chooses to ignore the mail, providing a further sign of the National Lottery's problematic impact on individuals and on society. Annie and Norman storm out, Jean suspects Connie Wilde's motives, and perhaps Morris's, and he sees bad portents in a series of near accidents he attributes to their win. Jean, though, cannot resist the lure of the lottery, and at the frenetic end to the first Act, while the instinctively panicked Morris predicts 'a plague on our bloody house' (1.5), she wins for a second time.

In fact, Jean wins the lottery four times over the course of *Lucky Sods*. That unlikely, although not impossible, scenario supplies a satirical dig at the faith of lottery ticket buyers of a win against the odds, and at the corrosive effects of such wealth. The second Act opens at the funeral of Morris's mother, with him commenting slightly morbidly that death is 'a safe bet', one of 'the few certainties'. Fundamental questions still apply despite their wealth, and are merely muffled by occasional lottery 'luck'. Godber's comic touch means that the poor vicar who officiates at the ceremony fishes unsuccessfully for a donation on the probably dubious premise that Morris's mother was 'quite a supporter of the church', and then asks Jean if there are any lottery numbers that she feels might be lucky that week; she suggests 'six and forty-two'. We find out later that he wins, and then quits the church. Godber also presents a vision of the afterlife not entirely removed from the world of Mark Ravenhill, Morris telling Jean at the funeral: 'I hope there's a Marks and Spencer's on the other side or you'll be lost', prompting the interchange:

Morris: . . . Just think, shopping in Marks and Debenhams for the rest of eternity?

Jean: Yeh, sounds good.
Morris: I think I'd rather stay on this side come to think of it. (Godber 1995: 59)

These differences in attitudes to shopping and death expose deeper problems within their stagnant marriage that the second win only intensifies. Morris announces to Jean his need to 'find himself' by travelling on his own to Europe. In fact, his trip to Amsterdam will allow him to indulge in an affair with Connie Wilde. Money proves liberating, but only in allowing Morris to indulge in a poorly repressed fantasy that accelerates the disintegration of a marriage held together for him by routine. Money does not transform him from working class to middle class, a £600 meal with Connie causing him to observe that he would prefer 'Fish and chips in the paper, a carton of mushy peas' (90). More significantly, while he naïvely believes that his young dreams of a life with Connie are materialising, the audience understands that her attention is dependent on the money Morris has received from Jean's winnings. By the final scene, he has come to his senses.

The interaction of luck and fate is central to the focus of a play in which the National Lottery might change the established order of things, and via the instant, almost alchemically, transformative power of money, provide a 'new life'. Yet the colloquial title, *Lucky Sods*, mixes envy with a clear implication of the unworthiness of those lucky individuals. 'Sod' is never a term of personal approval, and its associations with the earth underline that negativity. Darker elements are at work throughout the play, including from the outset Jean's and Morris's judgement that in their forties their lives have been wasted, Morris lamenting: 'Forty-one in August and my life's just going' (3). Jean replies that 'my life's going as well, in fact I sit in that chair and wonder where the bloody hell the last twenty years have gone' (4). While his inbuilt self-pity and negativity cannot really believe that he might win the lottery, she has a desperate faith that, essentially, it will furnish her with a future, will help arrest or in any case retard the inevitable procession to the grave. More immediately, it will relieve the interminable boredom of their marriage. But the negative circumstances of their lives are hardly unique: Morris's mother is terminally ill (although even after they have won the lottery, he is too mean to pay to upgrade her treatment); their daughter has died in a crash; Annie eventually contracts cancer. Morris feels that they barely escape accidents while in Venice and Los Angeles. And his elopement with Connie draws from Jean the despairing realisation that she loved Morris. The play's final scene opens with the prospect of reconciliation, Morris returning home, chastened by the collapse of his relationship with Connie, and keen, as he hints to Norman, to remake his marriage with Jean. But Norman reveals that Jean has been killed in an accident coming back from the video shop, having just returned *Deathwish* (97). That grimly comic moment of terminally bad luck for the repeatedly lucky Jean precedes the entrance of the sick Annie, who declares 'I can't believe it after all this time' (98). As Morris tries to find comforting words to soothe Annie's grief, it becomes apparent that they are talking at cross-purposes. Annie's repeated protestations of disbelief do not refer to the tragic death of her sister, but to the fact that she has won £80,000 in the lottery. *Lucky Sods* might easily have concluded with a chastened Morris contemplating what he had lost in leaving Jean for a brief fling, and being comforted by Norman and Annie. Instead, it ends with Annie, shaking with glee, and exultant that none of Jean's numbers have come up, while Norman can't stop smiling over their good fortune. Underlining the warping effect of the lottery and the consumerist mentality of the decade more generally, where nothing is ever enough, Norman complains, as he fails to contain his smile, that 'Mind you, eighty thousand is nowt with you, is it' (100). His final, ambiguous 'we're lucky sods, aren't we?' (100) prompts Morris's bitter 'That's right, Norman. That's dead right!' (101) as he rips up Jean's unsuccessful lottery ticket. The fusion of luck and death, coupled – as the lights fade to black – with Hot Chocolate's seventies hit about lost love, 'So You Win Again', sum up a world in which moral, emotional and social norms have been discarded or become worryingly distorted. Godber discloses through multi-faceted comedy about ordinary folk how the National Lottery reflected and contributed to those changes.

By the end of *Lucky Sods* Morris briefly has experienced the economic power that the middle class and aristocracy had enjoyed traditionally. His unchanged love of fish and chips and mushy peas underline the reality that despite the massively changed financial circumstances, he retains his essential class allegiance. The same to some degree was true of one of the people Alwyn Turner singled out as indicative of the anti-elitist flavour of the decade: David Beckham. For though Beckham would become rich and famous in the 1990s by an astute and crafted publicity campaign in tune with much of the decade's zeitgeist, as Turner notes, he and his wife, Victoria Beckham, though extremely wealthy, retained their appeal because they were 'so essentially ordinary'. This was part of a trend Turner detects, whereby 'the popular icons of the age were those who most conveyed the impression of normality'. The nuanced words 'conveyed' and 'impression' expose the potential for 'normality' to be performed for effect, something Turner detects in Tony Blair's 'habit of slipping a hint of the now ubiquitous Estuary English into his public school accent' (7). Margaret Thatcher famously had taken voice lessons to give her voice more authority, but Blair's efforts at relevant times to downplay his quintessentially middle class accent, perhaps to ingratiate himself with people who did not talk 'posh', reveal a canny operator programmed to exploit the times. Ironically, Victoria Beckham, one of the chief public representatives of Estuary English, an accent geographically proximate to her husband's Cockney accent, was nicknamed Posh Spice. The possibility that Blair himself might adopt aspects of Estuary English for political gain, that he might perform the accent associated with another social class challenges his own view on the reality of classlessness. His support for Newcastle United was seen by some as a calculated manoeuvre to endear himself to working class voters, given that he was educated at Fettes College and Oxford, both known for their concentration on the quintessentially middle class sport of rugby union. This might be too cynical a view, for while football has remained the domain of the working class in terms of players (notable among them in the 1990s David Beckham, of course), it has a massive middle class following.

Interestingly, in choosing sport as the arena for his 1992 poem about class conflict, 'Great Sporting Moments: The Treble', the Huddersfield Town fan Simon Armitage does not choose football, where the classes rarely clash on the field, but two sports associated with the middle and upper classes: tennis and golf. Rather than team affairs, these sports require expensive equipment and facilities less available to the working class (golf clubs and courses, tennis courts), carry associations with leisure than purely with competition, and tend towards restrictive membership policies. For all these reasons, they are the perfect choice for the wily, multi-talented speaker of 'Great Sporting Moments', its title a mocking if somewhat vainglorious register of prowess. From the off, the speaker declares, in a tone that is aggressive and patronising, his contempt for what he terms 'The rich' (the definite article inclusive in its exclusivity) based on that group's long-held certainty about its superiority.

> The rich! I love them. Trust them to suppose
> the gift of tennis is deep in their bones.
> Those chaps from the coast with all their own gear
> from electric eyes to the umpire's chair,
> like him whose arse I whipped with five choice strokes
> perfected on West Yorkshire's threadbare courts.
>
> (Armitage 2001: 43)

This certainty, from deep in their bones, a nod to the supposed genetic superiority that goes with 'good breeding', supplemented by the advantages expected by those with their own expensive gear, make the rich spectacularly susceptible to the arse-whipping the speaker is only too happy to administer. We might read into the slightly vulgar term both the joy in a version of northern, Lawrentian plain speaking about the body, as well as a gesture to the sadomasochism sometimes associated with public schools. But the blend of pain and superiority sets up the second moment of the sporting treble, the even more exclusive activity of golf. Here, the speaker enjoys playing the fool for comic effect, drawing the slightly rattled but still profoundly confident opponent towards defeat

> Smarting in the locker rooms he offered
> double or quits; he was a born golfer
> and round the links he'd wipe the floor with me.
> I played the ignoramus to a tee:
> the pleb in the gag who asked the viscount
> what those eggcup-like things were all about---
> 'They're to rest my balls on when I'm driving.'
> 'Blimey, guv, Rolls-Royce think of everything'---
>
> (43)

The music hall payoff demonstrates the speaker's verbal mastery, social superiority here being undercut by faux naïvety. This beautifully withheld derision, coupled with actual sporting dexterity, draws the victim on, so that 'at the fifth when I hadn't faltered / He lost his rag and threw down the gauntlet: / we'd settle this like men with the gloves on'. The neat combination of the colloquial ('he lost his rag') and a traditional signal of nobility ('threw down the gauntlet'), sets up the final gloved, class-based contest, one where physical brutality meets the Marquis of Queensbury. Unlike tennis or golf, the contest itself is not described, the speaker's pretend reluctance to engage disguising the final *coup de grâce*. 'I said no, no, no, no, no, no, no. OK, come on, then' (43). Given the speaker's dominance at tennis and golf, and the great eagerness with which he finally agrees to partake in the gentleman's sport of boxing, we safely assume that he achieves the sporting treble, with the visceral rewriting of class hierarchies.

Class hostility also irradiates Don Paterson's 'An Elliptical Stylus', from his 1993 collection, *Nil Nil*. This book came with the imprimatur of the Poetry Book Society, which made it a Society Choice, and the Forward Poetry Prize, which chose *Nil Nil* as its Best First Collection. Paterson was also among 1994's New Generation poets. 'An Elliptical Stylus' recounts a sequence of events and thoughts after the speaker's father is told by the speaker's uncle about the superior qualities of the said stylus: 'Aye, yer elliptical stylus – / fairly brings out a' the wee details'. Buoyed by this information, the father and son go to Largs (a small town near Glasgow) to buy the stylus for their 'ancient, Beat-up Phillips turntable'. The man in the hi-fi shop ridicules the father for the poverty of his equipment. 'Still smirking', he dismissed the father and son from the shop with a box of styluses reinforcing the father's low-quality gear. This humiliation is rendered with such poignant force in the poem's first two stanzas that it might have stood sufficiently as a testament to the imbalance of class power. But Paterson then performs two bold manoeuvres in the following two stanzas that wrench the poem into new territory and insight. In the first, the speaker supposes himself to be son of the dismissive man in the shop:

> (Supposing I'd been *his* son: eavesdrop
> on 'Fidelities', the poem I'm writing now:
> *The day my father died, he showed me how*
> *He'd prime the deck for optimum performance*: [sic].
>
> (Paterson 1993: 20)

The stanza continues in this vein, conjuring up a middle class tale of a filial relationship built around subtle parallels between the fidelity of sound and aspects of fidelity (faithfulness, trust), before petering out via an ellipsis. Paterson adjusts tone, vocabulary, setting and perception throughout this section, presenting a beautiful piece of ventriloquism that rams home the different universes the two father and son pairs inhabit. This could be read as a form of rebuke for the main speaker and his father, a form of brutal self-analysis that exposes their deficiencies. Except that the final stanza thrusts the reader back into the initial narrative, of class-based humiliation:

> We drove back slowly, as if we had a puncture:
> my dad trying not to blink, and that man's laugh
> stuck in my head, which is where this story sticks,
> and any attempt to cauterize this fable
> with something axiomatic on the nature
> of articulacy and inheritance
>
> (20)

With barely repressed anger, the speaker launches into a higher order reading of the incident. He simultaneously denies that reading's 'truth' as just intellectual pyrotechnics, compared to the punishing personal and social indignity his father endured. Not allowing the meta-reading, by insinuation the sanctioned or usual reading of such an incident by the average (middle class) poetry reader, the speaker retains control, and immediately throws down a challenge

> But if you still insist on resonance –
> I'd swing for him, and every other cunt

happy to let my father know his station,
which probably includes yourself. To be blunt.

(21)

Blunt, raw, this uncompromising finale functions as a rhetorical staring down, the speaker proudly validating his life and that of his father, repulsing the real or subterranean middle class ridicule of them, and those like them.

'Great Sporting Moments' and 'An Elliptical Stylus' neatly demonstrate how long-held and not easily discarded class antipathies were unlikely to disappear in the course of a decade. The social and economic reality of the 1990s – in which the conditions for many working class people worsened, and when an underclass continued to develop that a decade later would be vilified as 'chavs' – articulated with the harsher historical narrative of the 1980s when Thatcherism waged a form of proxy class warfare. The social and political landscape cleared was reshaped over the two decades, with rare exceptions such as David Beckham 'rising' in an anti-elite climate. But many more did not move from their established class backgrounds, nor aspired to move. Arthur Marwick observes that the traditional British class structure had changed over the previous half-century, as would be expected. He makes the point, though, that

> when two thirds of the sample of the general public interviewed in a MORI poll in August 2002 declared themselves 'working class', they were using that label in a very different way from the accepted usage of 1939, and were in fact cocking a snook at the traditional connotations of class categories. (Marwick 2007: 89)

Implicit in this observation is the truth that the sample was still using 'working class' as a label for something meaningful about themselves. Presumably, for that group, the term retained its power to connect them with something larger and more inclusive than simply individual or family units. It also distinguished them from others they felt did not experience their realities and the determining forces at play. Despite the hopes, disingenuous or not, for a classless society, the term 'working class' retained a historical resilience that projected both into the past they and their forbears had lived, and into the future in which they would persist and flourish.

Notes

1. Available at <http://news.bbc.co.uk/2/hi/uk_news/politics/6636565.stm> (last accessed 12 May 2017).

2. Available at <http://www.independent.co.uk/news/uk/new-generation-of-writers-presents-poetry-in-motion-some-of-todays-best-poetic-talents-tend-to-1399610.html> (last accessed 21 January 2017).
3. Available at <http://www.nytimes.com/1994/11/29/books/in-furor-over-prize-novelist-speaks-up-for-his-language.html> (last accessed 18 August 2016).

Chapter Five

Celebrity Culture

> She was the People's Princess and that is how she will stay, how she will remain in our hearts and in our memory forever. (McArthur 1998: 19)

The nineties was a decade in thrall to the tremendous cultural and commercial attractions of celebrity. If, in hindsight, the seventies seem forever marked by memories of the Winter of Discontent, and the eighties by the dominating presence of Margaret Thatcher, perhaps the signature cultural moment of the nineties was the extravagant national response to the unexpected death of Diana, Princess of Wales. Diana embodied the glamour, beauty and charisma associated with celebrity, and enjoyed the capacity to furnish people with dreams that took them outside their workaday existence. Diana's alluring public persona was founded on the fabricated fairy tale princess narrative constructed for her by the Royal Family, a compliant and sometimes complicit media, and by herself. The truth was murkier and far more complex. In the aftermath of her divorce from Prince Charles, just over a year before her death, Diana's personal life (especially her relationship with Dodi Al Fayed, another celebrity, but one whose millionaire playboy lifestyle was far less endearing to the general public) threatened to sully her reputation. In the lead-up to her violent demise, some sections of the media had begun to criticise Diana's indulgent lifestyle with Al Fayed, chiding her performance as mother to her young sons, Princes William and Harry. As Salman Rushdie noted in a 1997 *New Yorker* essay, her car crash death fused glamour and horror in a manner reminiscent of J. G. Ballard's novel *Crash*.[1] David Cronenberg's controversial film adaptation had appeared the previous year. The crash almost instantly and totally erased criticism of Diana. The very public national and international outpouring of grief was lengthy and itself newsworthy, an odd moment where a celebrity's fans briefly became the story. The new Prime Minister Tony Blair quickly caught the public mood, and in an impromptu speech outside his local church in Sedgefield declared:

> I feel like everyone else in this country today. Utterly devastated. Our thoughts and prayers are with Princess Diana's family ... We are today in Britain in a state of shock. In mourning. In grief ... She was a wonderful and warm human being ... She was the People's Princess and that is how she will stay, how she will remain in our hearts and in our memories forever. (McArthur 1998: 18–19)

A plaque would later be erected where Blair gave the speech. The conservative paper *The Daily Telegraph* later commented that 'even his critics agree – [the speech] marks Tony Blair's finest hour'.[2] By contrast, the Royal Family was slow to respond, its tardiness drawing massive public criticism, until the Queen publically broadcast a tribute on national television that noted the extent and depth of the public's reaction. The speech did not quell public criticism of the Queen or the Royal Family, itself a measure of Diana's unique celebrity status. One of the few dissenting voices was the satirical magazine *Private Eye*, which in its first issue after Diana's death published many of the sharp attacks on her by journalists just before her death, alongside their effusive posthumous praise of her, sometimes only a few days later.

No one in Britain (not even David Beckham) or perhaps globally approached the celebrity level achieved by Diana in the 1980s and 1990s. But her very public life and death exemplify ways in which celebrity in the nineties was a critical aspect of public culture generally. A vital element that had been building at least since the innovation in 1980 of US billionaire Ted Turner's CNN was a more obviously and ubiquitous global media system, with multinational media businesses, the most notable of which in Britain was Rupert Murdoch's News Corporation. Murdoch had constructed a substantial newspaper empire in Britain from the late 1960s, and by the 1990s *The Sun* was the world's most successful tabloid, selling 4.5 million copies daily. Along with other News Corporation papers such as *The Times*, the empire gave Murdoch papers substantial cultural impact and political clout. In the aftermath of the Conservatives somewhat surprising 1992 general election victory, *The Sun*'s famous front page boast, 'It's the Sun Wot Won It', had enough plausibility to appear more than merely hyperbolic. *The Sun*'s 1997 backing of Tony Blair and New Labour showed that it could gauge, as well as influence, the public mood. The Australian-born Murdoch had become an American citizen in order to expand his operation in the United States, acquiring businesses in a variety of related industries, including the film studio Twentieth Century Fox, and the publisher Harper Collins. He retained major interests in the UK, though, and in 1989 launched Sky TV, which would controversially merge with the equally financially troubled British Satellite Broadcasting to form BSkyB in 1990 as a digital subscription television company. Murdoch's endeavours exemplified the strategy of vertically integrated media companies that sought to control and connect various media operations.

The impact of such global changes on book publishing and retailing was profound: the consolidation of publishing under fewer, more powerful corporations, decreasing the number of the smaller, independent publishers who might be keen to take a chance on unknown, experimental or otherwise difficult writers. As Randall Stevenson records, the process had begun before the 1990s, but 'by the end of the century, the greater part of Britain's publishing output was controlled by large media/publishing conglomerates' (Stevenson 2004: 146). The reduction of independent booksellers and the increasing domination by larger bookselling chains accelerated the rise of the blockbuster novel. This trend was enhanced in 1991 when the Waterstones chain abandoned the Net Book Agreement (NBA), which since 1904 had meant that retailers sold books at the price determined by publishers. The NBA would eventually be outlawed, allowing supermarkets into the book selling trade. Waterstones benefitted massively from this change, but nearly 500 independent retailers closed, Stevenson registering from The Booksellers Association's figures 'that as many as 10 percent of its members had been forced to close by the end of 2000' (149). Bulk sales created the need for bestsellers to subsidise the drop in prices per book, which elevated certain writers, including 'serious' writers like Martin Amis, to star status. Yet this sort of author celebrity had its price, as Amis would find out in his protracted, very public, if highly lucrative move from his former agent, Pat Kavanagh, to the high-powered American agent Andrew Wylie in 1995. While Amis's bank balance benefitted, his reputation took a beating from the unwanted publicity the controversy prompted. A vital element of the literary uproar was that the massive advance Amis would receive as a result of what some took as his betrayal of his agent went partly towards expensive dental work. Adding to the orthodontic scandal was the personal rift the move caused with Pat Kavanagh's husband (and Amis's long-time friend) Julian Barnes. The rift between Amis and Barnes was not repaired during the 1990s.

Celebrity, money and controversy are no strangers, and this especially was the case in a decade still responsive to the type of philosophy espoused in Oliver Stone's 1987 hit film, *Wall Street*, in which the venture capitalist Gordon Gekko liberates ostentation and materialism from any shameful associations with the idea that 'greed is good'. That mantra would become a maxim for the 1980s and 1990s in many

Western democracies, especially after the collapse of the supposedly viable socialist option, the Soviet Union. Gekko is completely unrepentant about the benefits and transformative nature of greed, and while this vaunting of greed was perhaps too extreme for British tastes, it presaged Brian's similarly excessive and impenitent views in *Shopping and Fucking*. In the same period comedian Harry Enfield reinterpreted this amoral vitality in his satirical television character, 'Loadsamoney', a mouthy working class plumber incessantly bragging about his wealth and praising Margaret Thatcher. Revealingly, while the crassly exhibitionist Loadsamoney waves a handful of bills about as a taunt, Gekko callously strip-mines companies for millions in quick profit, ignoring the human damage incurred. Eventually, Gekko is jailed for illegal deals, *Wall Street* being Stone's attempt to expose the venality of 1980s American venture capitalism. Nick Leeson would represent a real life British version of this form of enterprise, fleeing the Singapore office of Barings Bank in 1995, where he had lost £827 million in financial speculations. Barings, the world's oldest merchant bank, and illustrious enough to count the Queen among its customers, was sold to the Dutch firm ING for £1. Many investors were ruined, but not before the bank's directors were awarded record bonuses. In line with the mantra that any publicity is good publicity, Leeson penned his autobiography, *Rogue Trader* (1997) from the gaol where he spent four years. He would profit handsomely from the book, its serialisation and from the 1999 film adaptation. Ironically, Ewan McGregor, who had also played Mark Renton in *Trainspotting*, stars as Leeson. He had only recently starred as Obi-Wan Kenobi in the aptly titled blockbuster, *The Phantom Menace*. The crossover between the worlds of finance and fantasy seemed entirely appropriate in a celebrity-obsessed decade.

The cult of celebrity that could attach even to economic criminals whose actions ruined the lives of many others was not restricted to the nineties, of course, but the lauding of conspicuous consumption and media-enhanced glamour reflected some of the decade's tenor. Creative literature, too, was captive to the allure and complex value of celebrity, which James English and John Frow argue 'has lodged itself so firmly at the heart of the scene that we cannot hope to take the measure either of the stakes or the forces in contemporary British literature unless we can reckon with its unique and expanding role' (English and Frow 2006: 55). They explain that literary celebrity 'has more to do with intensified media conglomeration and conscious brand management, expanding intellectual property rights and at bottom a massification of capital, than it does to literary practices (reading, writing, criticism) or literary values "as such"' (41). They understand J. K. Rowling, for example, one of the great success stories of the 1990s, as exemplifying the forces at work, but also treat Salman Rushdie as a figure of 'resonant celebrity' because of *The Satanic Verses* affair, focusing not on money, but on Rushdie's 'symbolic power'. That power, they reckon,

> is determined by the relative strengths and values of all kinds of currency that participants bring to a cultural transaction: the currency of academic credentials, political office, religious rank, a jail record: or of bestseller status, good reviews, honours and reward, social connections, street cred, physical attractiveness or photogeneity. (55)

Rushdie's blend of currencies, those that gave him a particular celebrity in the 1990s, derived from a unique fusion of forces. He was a celebrated author and provocative cultural commentator being protected by British security forces from the call by a leader of a global religion to have him assassinated. He was also a cause célèbre for those defending freedom of speech, for those antagonistic to religious intolerance, and for those (like himself) championing the cultural value, the cultural necessity, of imaginative literature free from control. Although in hiding, Rushdie in the 1990s occasionally would appear publically or commentate in person or on the page, to show that he would not be cowed by his oppressors, even as he strove to keep open lines of communication with tolerant Muslims. And he continued to publish nonfiction, short stories and novels such as *The Moor's Last Sigh* (1995) and *The Ground beneath Her Feet* (1999), works that maintained his name in public and cultural discourse, even as the actual author remained publicly invisible.

As already suggested, Diana, the Princess of Wales, was the most powerful and most visible symbol of nineties celebrity, a figure who blended more traditional fame with contemporary notions of acclaim. In the early 1990s she appeared willing and at times desperate to utilise the media to manipulate how she and her deteriorating relationship to Prince Charles might be presented. A classic example was a 1992 photo in which she posed alone at the Taj Mahal, symbol of the love of the seventeenth-century Mughal Emperor Shah Jahan for his wife, Mumtaz Mahal. The symbolic contrast between the original loving relationship and the already strained dealings between Diana and her husband was obvious and intended, for although the photograph might suggest Diana was alone with a single photographer, she in fact posed before thirty or forty cameramen. The intended effect was achieved, the pic being published in newspapers around the world, revealing her as an astute media manipulator. Diana's photogeneity enhanced the undoubted glamour of her position within the Royal Family, as putative future Queen of

England and mother of a future king. Her public work for charities such as leprosy and HIV/AIDS kept her in the public eye, the latter a brave and genuine move given the enduring public stigma, something that Diana's involvement helped partly allay. As her marriage to Prince Charles disintegrated under the crushing public expectations visited upon an initially shy woman, and her husband openly renewed his relationship with the married Camilla Parker Bowles, the slow-moving disaster played out in the tabloid press and in the 'posh' newspapers in Britain and around the world. Royal infidelity itself was nothing new, but the carefully fashioned fairy tale romance that had culminated in a globally broadcast wedding, along with the birth of two sons, had primed public interest, as it was meant to do. That positive interest boomeranged harmfully back once the rapid collapse of the marriage became obvious.

Diana, easily the better loved of the pair, became the cannier player of media power, providing information and briefings for tabloid journalist Andrew Morton's *Diana: Her True Story*, published in 1992. The book, previously serialised in the *Sunday Times*, was a global bestseller. It detailed Charles' and Camilla's affair, Diana's own sorrow and self-harm, along with her own affairs, presented as desperate acts of a woman deprived of love. The squalid release of taped phone calls through the press in the latter part of 1992 sullied both Diana and Charles, the couple separating at the end of that year. Interviews and counter-interviews by both camps followed over the next few years as the warring individuals and their supporters attempted to garner public sympathy, or to undermine the claims of the other. Charles gave a highly personal interview to BBC stalwart David Dimbleby in *Charles: The Private Man, The Public Role*, broadcast in June 1994. While the two hour-plus documentary, produced to coincide with the twenty-fifth anniversary of his investiture as the Prince of Wales, was meant as a form of public rehabilitation, the effort backfired badly, Charles's public admission of his infidelity even leading to questions regarding his eligibility to be king. Diana's 1995 televised interview with Martin Bashir on the BBC's *Panorama* programme was a far more successful public relations exercise, Diana presenting herself as someone whose own admitted infidelity resulted from her husband's continuing affair with Camilla Parker Bowles. She famously summed this up in the phrase: 'there were three of us in this marriage, so it was a bit crowded'. A month later, Buckingham Palace announced that the Queen had advised the couple to divorce, which they did officially in August 1996. These events would have been sensational enough, but Diana's death in a car crash, alongside her lover Dodi Al Fayed, son of Harrod's owner Mohammed Al Fayed, the heartfelt grief of much of the nation captured in Blair's sobriquet for her as 'the People's Princess', and the Royal Family's fall in favour, including public criticism of the normally sacrosanct Queen, spoke to the fickle nature of celebrity.

In the creative world, celebrity was calculatedly evoked in several characteristic and partly integrated elements: Cool Britannia, Britpop and the Young British Artists (YBAs) phenomenon. Each to some degree represented a distinctive aspect of the 1990s' cultural habitat, and although literature was not central to either Britpop or the YBAs, it did partake of the general spirit of Cool Britannia. The conscious attempt in 1994 by the Poetry Society to foreground so-called 'New Generation' poets reflected a culture where associations with the energy and popularity of Britpop mattered.[3] The promotion followed the second iteration of *Granta*'s highly successful 'Best Young British Novelists' list. The inaugural list, in 1983, had highlighted twenty then relatively unknown young writers, such as Salman Rushdie, Kazuo Ishiguro, Pat Barker, Martin Amis and Julian Barnes, who eventually would enter the British literary elite. The 1993 list foregrounded Hanif Kureishi, A. L. Kennedy, Jeanette Winterson and Caryl Philips, among others, inevitably snaring publicity (some of it sneering) for the chosen, as well as for *Granta* magazine itself, which acquired the position of de facto gatekeeper for emerging fiction talent. The Poetry Society's attempt to garner similar interest highlighted twenty young poets in its journal, *The Poetry Review*. These writers included many who would establish themselves through the decade as among the best new talent. Poets such Moniza Alvi, Simon Armitage, Carol Ann Duffy and Don Paterson were given a *Vogue* photo shoot. Melvin Bragg, who headed the panel that chose the poets, hosted a special programme dedicated to them on the BBC's leading arts programme *The South Bank Show*. A month-long nationwide festival in May 1994 celebrated their work, an *Independent* article quoting the Poetry Society's Bill Swainson on their novelty and energy:

> Poetry now is not London. It's Glasgow and Birmingham. Poetry has gone regional. The only thing that every poet here has in common is confidence in his or her voice. The influence of rock music is among them, and the influence of the great poets of the past.[4]

The allusion to rock music was somewhat dated, but the inference was clear: the new poets were unstuffy, energetic performers responsive to the vitality of the decade's mood and striving to connect to a new, young audience.

The larger umbrella term of Cool Britannia was the more obvious place for popular writers such as Helen Fielding, Nick Hornby and J. K. Rowling. Rowling was unknown before the publication of *Harry*

Potter and the Philosopher's Stone in 1997, but became famous at light speed as the decade concluded, by which time *Harry Potter and The Chamber of Secrets* (1998) and *Harry Potter and The Prisoner of Azkaban* (1999) had also been published. Rowling quickly achieved equal success and greater sales in the United States, *The Prisoner of Azkaban* selling 68,000 copies in one day in Britain, while the American publisher ordered an initial run of half a million copies, the first three books at one point filling the first three spots on the *New York Times* bestseller list, including books for adults. Rowling's ever-increasing popularity, which promoted Britain through the thoroughly British setting and characters of the Potter books, quickly showed itself to be more durable than the Cool Britannia brand. By the late 1990s, when her books were dominating bestseller lists globally, Cool Britannia was largely redundant as a brand and as an exercise in advertising British innovation and dynamism. Back in March 1998, *The Economist*, not obviously at the cutting-edge of cultural studies, already was decrying the ersatz quality of Cool Britannia and the rather contrived efforts by Tony Blair to fuse culture and economics. 'Many people are already sick of the phrase "Cool Britannia"', an *Economist* article ran, adding tartly: 'but they should brace themselves – they are about to be subjected to a barrage of self-conscious hipness from the happening Blair government.' The re-treaded sixties word 'happening' clearly was inserted as a rebuke, the article going on to warn that the government was about to 'launch a committee of ministers and cultural luminaries, to come up with other ideas to help "rebrand" Britain'.[5]

Treating Britain as a brand, let alone pushing for a rejuvenated rebrand, exposes some of the decade's superficiality, something heralded by the rebranded 'New Labour' government under its young, energetic leader, and later prime minister, Tony Blair. John Major's government over the first two thirds of the decade was inherently and perhaps terminally reticent about promoting edgy art, music and literature, to the point where many of the zestiest cultural ventures, such as In-Yer-Face Theatre, consciously strove to shock the establishment out of its lassitude. Even before taking office, Blair, by obvious contrast, cultivated associations with the vivacity and youthfulness of Cool Britannia. The active nurturing of this section of society employed Blair's own, admittedly tenuous, 'cool' (he had once played electric guitar in the band Ugly Rumours while at Oxford). This contrasted with Major, a prime minister ridiculed for revealing that he tucked his shirt into his underpants. Blair cashed in politically and culturally on the self-confidence that grew slowly through the latter part of Major's rule (although not in any noticeable way activated by the inherently backward looking Major).

The term Cool Britannia fused, with a canny blending of nineties insouciance and nostalgia, the glory days of cultural and imperial British rule, gaining Britain, and especially London, the kind of cultural cachet it had not enjoyed since the Swinging Sixties. As Chris Rojek explains, Oasis's Noel Gallagher, designer Vivian Westwood, and alternative comedian Eddie Izzard, among others, were invited to the celebratory Downing Street reception for New Labour's 1997 election victory. More generally, he continues

> Pop groups like Blur, Pulp, Elastica and Oasis, fashion designers like [Paul] Boateng, John Galliano, Richard James and Timothy Everest, restaurateurs and culinary entrepreneurs like Oliver Peyton and Marco Pierre White, artists such as Damien Hirst, Tracey Emin and art collectors like Charles Saatchi were fêted for capturing the spirit of Cool Britannia, radiating national confidence, classlessness and turbo-charged international cultural cachet. (Rojek 2007: 27)

Noticeably, Rojek includes no writers in this list of Cool Britannia cultural icons, although his list of Swinging Sixties equivalents in the same study includes Philip Larkin, Harold Pinter, Joe Orton, Kingsley Amis and Iris Murdoch, among others (28). The decade's most internationally famous British writer, Salman Rushdie, and certainly the one who had enjoyed the greatest cultural cachet in the past, was hiding in fear of his life. His brief appearance onstage with U2 at Wembley in 1993 marked a form of cultural anointing that transcended anything Britpop had to offer.

The Britpop phenomenon was in part a reaction to the import of American grunge, and partly an assertion of the ongoing influence of the highpoint of contemporary British music, the 1960s. Key bands such as Blur, Oasis, Pulp and Suede, the so-called 'Big Four' of Britpop, provided variations on the guitar band with charismatic lead singers that produced bright, witty and often darkly satirical songs about contemporary British life. Pulp's trio of songs: 'Common People', which lampoons a posh girl wanting to do some slumming among the eponymous normal folk; 'Sorted out for E's and Whizz', which celebrates the increasingly popular drug culture; and 'Mile End', which records and to some degree celebrates the vitality and dangerous energy of the working class London East End suburb, create small vignettes of everyday life filtered through the mocking consciousness of front man Jarvis Cocker. Oasis, built around Liam Gallagher's arresting voice and stage presence and his brother Noel's inspired if often too-overt sampling of sixties icons like The Beatles, projected a more obviously macho, working class Manchester sound. Their first two albums, *Definitely Maybe* (1994; for a time, the highest selling debut album ever) and (*What's the Story*)

Morning Glory? (1995), came replete with hit songs and propelled them to the top of the British music scene, eventually securing Noel Gallagher his invitation to the Labour Party's victory party in 1997. The image of Gallagher in Downing Street was improbable at any other moment.

Oasis spent much of the mid-1990s in open competition with their lower middle class Essex rivals Blur, a lighter, more sparkling version of sixties British pop, that perhaps reached its apogee in its 1994 album, *Parklife*. The *New Musical Express* (*NME*) called *Parklife* the 'defining artefact' of Britpop, 'the point where the archness and artiness of the British grunge rebellion merged with the lager-funnelling, Mykonos-ruining masses'.[6] The paper also noted a loftier influence on the Blur frontman Damon Albarn – Martin Amis's dark 1989 novel, *London Fields*, a work that projects forward to a bleak 1999 London. Albarn was reading *London Fields* around the time the band made *Parklife*.[7] The album rejoiced in working class and lower middle class life, on its cover a photo of two racing greyhounds, their faces (to anthropomorphise) masks of struggle and fear that capture the desperate acquisitiveness of the period. The inner photos on the album feature the group enjoying a night at the Walthamstow Greyhound track, while the video accompanying the title track presents Albarn as a gormless sidekick to actor Phil Daniels, whose 'cheeky chappy' working class turn as a double-glazing salesman on the make infuses the song with an extra dimension of wry humour. The press elevated the rivalry between Blur and Oasis to the level of The Beatles and The Rolling Stones. This culminated in the release on the same day in 1995 of the singles 'Country House' (Blur), a dream of flight from working class estates to grand houses, and 'Roll with It' (Oasis), a 1995 anthem to resilience. Hyperbolically billed in *NME* as the 'British Heavyweight Championship', itself a sign of the confected quality of much of the Britpop label and the attendant narrative, the match was 'won', in terms of record sales, by Blur. Both bands achieved success in the American market, the quality control measure for popular music, but Oasis's follow-up album, *Be Here Now*, was pilloried as overblown and overproduced. Blur's video to accompany their hit single 'Country House', from their next album, *The Great Escape*, was another lacklustre affair, with little of the energy and wit of the 'Parklife' video. Damien Hirst, the most famous of the Young British Artists (YBAs), and its most commercially successful and commercially oriented figure, directed the video, a sign of the interwoven or tangled strands that made up Cool Britannia.

By far the most successful British pop group of the 1990s was the Spice Girls. Not strictly part of the male-dominated Britpop phenomenon, but definitely a key element of Cool Britannia, from the outset the group was a conscious commercial attempt to create a British girl group to rival the successful boy bands. This effort proved more than effective, the band far excelling any male rivals. Between 1996 and 1999 they became the highest selling girl group of all time, with album sales in the tens of millions and earnings in the hundreds of millions of pounds. With nicknames loosely linked to their personalities – Sporty, Scary, Baby, Posh and Ginger – the Spice Girls attained a group identity akin to the Fab Four in the early 1960s, fusing 1990s Girl Power with older personifications of female desirability. As Chapter 3 explored, the Spice Girls played a culturally significant (if somewhat regressive) role in the sexual politics of the decade, feeding on, and massively feeding into, the materialist celebrity culture of the time. Their embrace of a particularly media-savvy and commercially oriented sense of Girl Power, one that melded personal empowerment with mass consumption, meant that the Spice Girls and their management shrewdly deployed the established celebrity culture. The group aggressively, and often shamelessly, endorsed scores of products, from cameras to crisps to a hugely successful campaign for Pepsi. The video for their 1997 single, 'Spice up Your Life', drew on the imagery of Ridley Scott's *Blade Runner* to imagine a future world where dulled, trapped people look out at huge floating advertisements trumpeting Spice Girl products. Part self-indulgence, part self-parody, the song and the video project the group as playful and energising, the lyrics 'When you're feeling sad and low / We will take you where you want to go / Smiling, dancing, everything is free / All you need is positivity' providing a provocatively shallow manifesto. Channelling the zeitgeist, it reached number one in the UK charts.

More than other new British groups of the decade, the Spice Girls had a substantial international presence, being popular in Europe and being accepted as part of a British invasion of the American pop scene to rival that of the sixties. Their centrality to the Cool Britannia hype was ensured when Ginger Spice, Geri Halliwell, wore a union jack minidress to the 1997 BRIT awards, producing one of the icons of the decade. The band won two awards, but the dress attracted more attention, almost immediately seen as emblematic of British cultural verve and confidence more generally. Other Cool Britannia alumni were less enthusiastic, Liam Gallagher stating that he would not attend the awards because if he 'met the Spice Girls, he would slap them'. The suitably athletic Sporty Spice challenged him to 'have a go if you think you're hard enough', an offer the somewhat slight Gallagher refused. This moment perhaps marked the Spice Girl's highpoint, for although they remained extraordinarily popular by ordinary standards through 1998, their second album, *Spiceworld* (released late in 1997) sold 'only' 30 million copies, far fewer than the 50 million for their debut, *Spice*. Halliwell left the group in May 1998, and that year Victoria Adams (Posh) and Melanie Brown (Scary) announced that they were pregnant, both giving birth the following year. These and other circumstances slowed the group's momentum, and although they would release *Forever* in 2000, the Spice phenomenon essentially was over. Even before they embarked on a long-term break in 1999, though, members were already attracting and creating media attention beyond the group identity. Victoria Adams, who began dating English football superstar David Beckham in 1998, was the most conspicuously successful. Quickly branded 'Posh and Becks', the pair married in 1999, quickly becoming tabloid fodder. By then, though, Britpop was over.

The label Britpop was something of a misnomer, all the key bands being from parts of England, with London still easily the most attractive cultural magnet. Yet cities such as Edinburgh and Glasgow provided alternatives to the music of the south, bands such as Del Amitri, Texas, and Primal Scream gaining national and international recognition during the decade. Tellingly, though, the music referenced in Irvine Welsh's novel *Trainspotting* included no contemporary Scottish bands. Iggy Pop's lifestyle and songs provided more parallels, and the concentration on the club music scene decreased the opportunity to highlight local bands. The soundtrack of Danny Boyle's film adaptation, *Trainspotting* (1996), however, did include Primal Scream's title track, and the Welsh group Underworld's 'Born Slippy. NUXX.' But it also incorporated songs from Blur, Suede, Pulp and Damon Albarn, as well as older artists such as Iggy Pop, Brian Eno and Lou Reed. These choices come partially determined by the storyline and partly by commercial concerns, but the absence (bar Primal Scream) of Scottish bands and the inclusion of more 1990s English bands underscores the dominance of London-based music, especially.

London was also the point of origin and first site of success for the artists who would come to define contemporary art in nineties Britain, the Young British Artists. The catalyst for this group was Goldsmith's Art College at the University of London, where a group of students with independent aesthetic and commercial concerns established themselves as provocateurs and entrepreneurs in the Thatcherite eighties. Chief among these was Damien Hirst, who would not only become the publicity-seeking *enfant terrible* of British art, but was also someone completely at ease with the materialist culture of the time. Hirst set up edgy exhibitions of work by young artists like himself while still a student at Goldsmith's. His enterprise came partly out of a need for exposure in an environment hit by Thatcher's cutting of public funding of the arts, but also as a means of circumventing the traditional controllers of Britain's contemporary art world. Hirst organised the Docklands exhibition, 'Freeze', in 1988, something that caught the eye of the advertising impresario Charles Saatchi, head of the firm Saatchi & Saatchi. That company was responsible for the iconic 1978 Conservative poster, 'Labour Isn't Working', an advertisement credited with helping the Conservatives into power the following year. (It was later voted 'Poster Advertisement of the Century' by the trade magazine *Campaign*.) Saatchi himself already was a considerable collector of contemporary art from overseas, but refocused his attention and promotional skills on the new wave of British talent, becoming a key backer of Hirst and his ilk. The first of a series of YBAs' exhibitions opened at his Saatchi Gallery in 1992, a display case for his wealth and aesthetic adventure. Perhaps the key early exhibit was Hirst's iconic thirteen-foot tiger shark in a tank of formaldehyde, 'The Physical Impossibility of Death in the Mind of Someone Living' (1991). Hirst would later say that every artwork that ever interested him was about death, but 'The Physical Impossibility of Death', while clearly about that, was simultaneously visually powerful, shocking and also oddly serene, almost sublime. Whatever else it was, it created the sort of controversy that, fused with Saatchi's own celebrity and publicity skill, drew immediate and massive attention to Hirst and those associated with him. Hirst would become the decade's most controversial artist, and one of its richest, revelling in and working consciously to generate his celebrity. Not that all of Hirst's works were shocking. His dot paintings (separated coloured circles on a white canvas) or 'Medicine Cabinet' series (recreations of what might be seen at a pharmacy) were restrained, and retained a contemplative elegance. 'The Acquired Inability to Escape' reconstructed an office worker's desk and chair within a black three-dimensional frame that suggested a prisoner under surveillance. Hirst would also create 'Mother and Child Divided', four glass-walled containers in which a cow and a calf were bisected from front to rear, and arranged so that viewers could walk between the separated halves. Even this macabre piece (reminiscent of his shark, but more clinical and morbid) was eclipsed by the installation 'Thousand Years'. In this work, a cow's head in an enclosure is slowly stripped of its meat by blowflies, which in time reproduce and then are themselves eventually electrocuted by an ultraviolet insect killer.

The rise of this new, commercially aware and sometimes viscerally challenging art reached its apogee in the 1997 exhibition 'Sensation'. The group exhibition of YBAs at the Royal Academy of Arts showcased forty-four artists, including Hirst, Gavin Turk, Tracey Emin and Rachel Whiteread, four of the most acclaimed and widely known young artists in the country. The venue was a clear sign that by 1997 YBAs was a marketable brand, worth the financial investment of one of the nation's most prestigious galleries, and likely to draw large, if at times bewildered or bemused, audiences. The exhibition also displayed the group's diversity, the reality that the YBA's logo itself was always something of a sleight of hand, or an alluring advertising slogan beneath which stood no single approaches. Equally importantly, by being displayed at the Royal Academy of Art, such works received an important cultural imprimatur, being now deemed significant enough to be incorporated (even if tentatively) into the mainstream. YBAs on their part had conferred upon Britain their own glamour and panache, advertising London in particular as a metropolitan art centre for multicultural, multi-media innovation in a way that it had seldom enjoyed. 'Sensation', with implications of physical and emotional stimulation, as well as of public reaction and excitement, was designed to command attention and prompt responses, not all of them positive, and it did that. Hirst's shark in a tank still had the power to impinge itself upon the viewer, even if, by 1997, its centrality to the iconography of the period meant that its power lay less in its ability to shock than to impress. But other works could still provoke outrage, as in the case of Chris Ofili's 'The Holy Virgin Mary', an image in which quasi-religious iconography is integrated with elephant dung, or Marcus Harvey's 'Myra', depicting Moors Murderer Myra Hindley through an image made up of children's handprints. Two other artists, in separate incidents, would deface that work.

Hirst's capacity to provoke outrage jibed with what appeared to be the modus operandi for the key prize for contemporary art, the Turner Prize. Hirst would win the prize himself in 1995 for 'Mother and Child Divided', but other YBAs such as Whiteread were successful as well: she, in 1993, for her uncanny 'House', made by casting the inside of a soon-to-be-demolished house in concrete and then taking away the original structure to reveal a concrete form of death mask for the building. While thought-provoking, 'House' was not in any way controversial in the manner of Chris Ofili's 1998 'No Woman No Cry', which not only paid homage to Stephen Lawrence, victim of a race hate crime, but also used elephant dung on the canvas and (in two large balls) to hold the canvas off the floor. As the avant-garde had done at the start of the century, these artists in varying ways challenged the nature of what constituted art and art appreciation. Their personal affiliations and confidence in their own worth (in several senses) gave them a group identity, partly constructed by Saatchi branding as YBAs. Norman Rosenthal, previewing the 'Sensation' exhibition, observed that

As far as international reputation is concerned, it appears that this latest generation of artists is having considerably more impact than its predecessors and perhaps one of the questions this exhibition will answer is whether art in Britain, never quite central to the European cultural experience nor quite radical in terms of the great American art experiment, can now hold its own as second to none.[8]

The critical and commercial success of 'Sensation' indicated that Young British art could hold its own.

An important aspect of this celebrity derived from the annual fevered publicity surrounding the nominations and the winners for the Turner Prize. In the nineties, the link between celebrity and prizes was emphatically endorsed as a means of attracting public interest and the economic payoff that often entailed. The Turner Prize held a privileged and controversial place in the cultural firmament, winning and losing finalists regularly garnering lurid or contemptuous media coverage. Such publicity ensured that the prize was a launching pad for careers, or a consolidation of cultural capital that might also translate into capital of a more tangible kind. Literature was not immune to such forces, even if Britain's literature's most famous literary prize, the Booker Prize, seemed almost prissy by comparison with the Turner. Interestingly, there is a familial relationship between the two, Virginia Button arguing that the Turner Prize was established in 1984 in 'conscious emulat[ion]' of the Booker (Button 1997: 19), and James English discussing 'annual prizes in other fields in Britain (notably the Turner, aka. "The Booker Prize for Artists")' (English 2005: 66). Established in 1969 by the food multinational Booker McConnell, the Booker itself was a conscious emulation of France's prestigious Prix Goncourt (established in 1903), which had honoured writers as revered as Marcel Proust. Booker plc had, as Graham Huggan points out, a dubious history, formed in the 1800s to profit from the West Indian sugar industry. In the early 1960s, Huggan records, 'it established its book division, primarily designed to buy up copyrights of famous popular fiction authors (Agatha Christie, Ian Fleming, etc.). This proved a lucrative business' (Huggan 1997: 415) enabling the setting up of the prize. From these relatively lowbrow and somewhat problematic beginnings, the Booker, partly by virtue of its initially generous £5,000 prize, rose to pre-eminence, quickly entering into what Huggan, after Pierre Bourdieu, labels the 'legitimizing machinery of the literary *award* or *prize*' (413). Huggan quotes Bourdieu, who writes in Th*e Field of Cultural Production* (1993) that

> The fundamental stake in literary struggles is the monopoly of literary legitimacy ... the monopoly of power to say with authority who are authorized to call themselves writers; or to put it another way ... the monopoly

of the power to consecrate producers or products (we are dealing with the world of belief and the consecrated writer is the one who has the power to consecrate and to win assent when he or she consecrates an author or work). (quoted in Huggan 1997: 413)

The prize aimed to reward the best novel written in English by authors from the United Kingdom, the Republic of Northern Ireland and the Commonwealth. British authors won it overwhelmingly in its first decade. The 1980s, however, was the decade in which the empire struck back, most notably with Salman Rushdie's *Midnight Children* in 1981. Rushdie provided many British readers with their first sense of Indian culture not conveyed through the eyes of 'white' British writers such as E. M. Forster, George Orwell or Paul Scott. Wins by Australians Thomas Keneally and Peter Carey, New Zealander Keri Hulme and South African J. M. Coetzee during the 1980s widened the prize's catchment area, and this expansion increased in the 1990s. Wins by Nigerian-born (then England-domiciled) Ben Okri for *The Famished Road* (1991), Canadian Michael Ondaatje's *The English Patient* (1992), Ireland's Roddy Doyle for *Paddy Clarke Ha Ha Ha* (1993), India's Arundhati Roy's *The God of Small Things* (1997) and J. M. Coetzee's *Disgrace* (1999) disclosed simultaneously the quality of literature being produced beyond British shores and the broadening of British literary tastes. And, as mentioned earlier, James Kelman's *How Late It Was, How Late* expanded the field of British winners beyond the usual suspects.

James English argues that cultural prizes generally are part of an 'economy of prestige', the term clearly evoking the business aspect of financial reward, but more importantly, also following Bourdieu, notions of 'cultural capital' and prestige. 'And of all the rituals and practices of culture', English suggests,

> none is more frequently attacked for its compromising convergence with the dynamic of the marketplace than is the prize, which seems constantly to oscillate between a genuinely cultural event (whose participants only have the interests of art at stake) and a sordid display of competitiveness and greed (whose participants are brazenly pursuing their own professional and financial self-interests). (English 2005: 7)

The literary prize, then, brings together writers, publishers, readers and reviewers, along with the necessary media, interested in the newsworthiness of the works and their authors, especially if there is a hint of scandal or contestation. The commercially focused and celebrity-driven culture of the nineties neatly fitted this established model, with many (though certainly not all) of the key players willing to succumb to the demands of publicity and the attendant scrutiny. The Booker in the 1980s was a worthy, if somewhat staid, affair, but in the more media-dominated 1990s it was more obviously an 'event'. The prize ceremony, held in the magnificent fifteenth-century London Guildhall, was broadcast on the BBC with engaging English Literature academics such as Tom Paulin, Germaine Greer and Howard Jacobsen, who might make trenchant comments about the authors and their works. The telecast would later move to Channel 4, in an attempt to widen its appeal. The actual prize money, which had increased since the inaugural prize, was not extravagant at £21,000, but James English recognises that prestige is more valuable culturally, and 'that the prize money is understood simply to accompany an award, never to stand for it' (156). The more obvious and longer lasting economic benefits came to authors through increased sales for the Booker entry, with both previous releases and subsequent works benefitting from the flow-on effect. In the 1990s the increasing status of the Booker meant a different form of prestige and financial reward was possible: five of the prize-winners (*Possession*, *The English Patient*, *The Ghost Road* [or the *Regeneration* trilogy from which it derived], *Last Orders* and *Disgrace*) were eventually made into films. It is impossible to say, of course, that these adaptations would not have been made without the Booker imprimatur, given film's historical reliance on adaptations (of novels, especially) for much of its source material. But it seems reasonable to assume that the Booker's impact on reader numbers was sufficiently international to warrant consideration by film producers.

An obvious difference between the sustained radical verve of the Turner Prize and the usually more restrained and carefully constructed Booker Prize winners was that where many of the Turner winners in the 1990s were young, some still in their twenties, the majority of Booker winners were at least in their late forties. Only three of the eleven winners in the decade (Michael Ondaatje and Barry Unsworth shared the prize in 1992) were even in their thirties. The Booker appeared more to confirm mastery of the novel form on its respective winners than to encourage bold experimentation, or the type of shock tactics that characterised Turner entrants. The judging panels were predominantly middle class, perhaps with a senior literary academic, a publically acceptable intellectual and someone from the media. There were, nonetheless, controversies, most notably about the composition of the judging panel, or internal wrangling between judges. The Booker operated to publicise contemporary literature, and, by doing so, encouraged a type of celebrity that raised the profiles of writers and increased sales. James English remarks, in terms of the Booker's model, that the '"prestige" of the Goncourt is generally explained in terms of the tremendous increase in sales it effects: the Goncourt winner becomes an instant millionaire' (English 2005: 231). The effect on the winner of the Booker was nothing like as impressive, although Richard Todd notes that 'The Booker Prize exercises a more substantial effect on sales patterns than any other kind of award' (Todd 1996: 12).

Booker winners provide a short guide to the concerns and trends of British and English language literature during the decade, and while more than half of the winners were from outside the United Kingdom, as already mentioned, that in itself indicates a more inclusive response to cultures beyond Britain itself. Two British winners show an inclusiveness within Britain itself. A. S. Byatt's *Possession: A Romance* (the 1990 winner, assessed in more detail in the following chapter) is in many ways the most conventionally 'Bookerish' Booker novel, an intellectually serious, yet sometimes comic and always eloquent work that takes literary history as its theme and material. *Possession* tells of a modern-day literature PhD researcher who by chance discovers secret papers that ultimately solve a suite of Victorian literary mysteries. Its complex plot shifts back and forth between time periods as discovered documents reveal previously unknown connections and deceptions. *Possession* employs and parodies conventions of the detective novel fed through its campus equivalent. Byatt's own life as a university lecturer underpins the novel's erudition, particularly in the confecting of faux-Victorian poems and letters, while providing an insider's view of the jealousies, rivalries and pettiness of academic life. It would be hard to imagine any of the contemporary characters in *Possession* having anything to do with those from *How Late It Was, How Late*, discussed in the previous chapter. And there was a similar disconnect between the reception of the two novels. Where Kelman's drew bitter criticism from some (including Booker judges), *Possession* was an international hit, adapted later with American finance into a film starring Gwyneth Paltrow. Kelman's novel was never adapted. Despite Byatt being a well-considered novelist with four books before *Possession*, her Booker success substantially boosted her international profile. In a commercial sense, it 'made' her.

Two other British winners of the Booker Prize in the 1990s are worth attention in relation to celebrity, each suffering for different reasons from criticism that accompanied their win. These criticisms might not have occurred but for the added publicity attending any Booker winner. Graham Swift's *Last Orders* (the 1996 winner) confirmed his reputation as a slow-burning but high-achieving writer. *Last Orders* gives an account of a group of friends taking the ashes of their dead friend, Jack Dodds, a butcher, to Margate, where he has requested that his remains be cast into the sea. Consecutive chapters are narrated from the perspective, and in the voice, of the men; one of their wives; Jack's widow; and the dead man himself. Those carrying his ashes travel from Jack's home in Bermondsey to the sea, stopping at significant places on the way, such as Old Kent Road, New Cross, Graves End and Canterbury Cathedral. The progress towards Canterbury, along with the tale-telling motif, initially drew some comparisons with the *Canterbury Tales*, but the literary academic John Frow suggested unacknowledged and 'substantial' borrowing in terms of plot and formal structure from William Faulkner's *As I Lay Dying*.[9] Swift had earlier admitted that he admired Faulkner, and that 'there is a little homage at work'. He stressed key differences, however, and argued that the 'very primitive subject' of death is 'perennially told', so that it is possible to go back past Faulkner 'to Homer, and find this funeral narrative. It's an archetypal thing.'[10] Frow accepted that 'These are tricky issues', while not retreating. *The Independent*, in an article with the suitably Faulknerian title 'The Sound and the Fury' (itself, of course, taken from *Macbeth*) gathered together Swift, Frow, the Booker judge A. N. Wilson, and the novelists Kazuo Ishiguro and A. L. Kennedy (among others) to state their positions.[11] No definitive conclusion was reached, and, given the admittedly tricky questions raised, perhaps nothing definitive could ever be established, but the controversy illustrated complications that might derive from the cachet afforded literary prize winners. Swift's reputation took a substantial, if temporary, hit.

A later controversy had less to do with the earlier works of another writer than with the earlier work of the same writer. Ian McEwan's *Amsterdam* won the 1998 Booker, but only to suspiciously polite applause. McEwan, long acknowledged as one of Britain's finest novelists, had failed to make the Booker shortlist for his previous novel, *Enduring Love* (1997), which some critics thought a superior book to *Amsterdam*, a short and somewhat thin and forced effort that hung on the euthanasia pact between two classic McEwan middle class characters, friends Clive Linley (a composer) and Vernon Halliday (a reporter). *The Guardian* critic Nicholas Lezard began his review by declaring that 'Will Self was right, on that live TV commentary on the Booker, to do his nut when this won the award; it really is meant to go to novels, not five finger exercises.'[12] The judging panel, consisting of, among others, the noted literary Oxford don Valentine Cunningham, celebrity cook Nigella Lawson, and former Foreign Secretary and failed Thatcher-successor Douglas Hurd, clearly thought differently. Hurd described *Amsterdam* as 'a sardonic and wise examination of the morals and culture of our time'.[13] While the process of judging was normally a relatively secret affair (Julia Neuberger's attack on *How Late It Was,*

How Late a rare exception), the suggestion was that awarding the prize to *Amsterdam* was a form of compensation for the failure to honour *Enduring Love* the previous year. The win perhaps had a negative flow-on effect, in that McEwan's 2001 novel, *Atonement*, seen by many critics as his best novel to date, did not win the Booker. Some felt that he had already received the award for an inferior work. McEwan himself would later say that it was *Amsterdam*'s '(as opposed to my) misfortune, to win the Booker, at which point some people began to dismiss it'.[14] McEwan would continue to be chosen for Booker longlists and shortlists well into the twenty-first century, so the long-term effects were minimal.

Criticism of the Booker Prize in and of itself also came from the literary and academic community. Huggan quotes from David Dabydeen's 'Song of the Creole Gang Women', which suggests the historical link mentioned earlier between the company's original trade in the West Indies, colonial oppression and modern literary arrangements of power:

> Wuk, nuttin bu wuk
> Maan noon an night nuttin bu wuk
> Booker own me patacake
> Booker own me pickni.
>
> (quoted in Huggan 1997: 414)

Huggan's point was that the Booker Prize might function in similar ways to the original colonial position the company held, determining who and what can be said and not said, and how. 'The Booker might be seen', he argues 'as being bound to an Anglocentric discourse of benevolent paternalism' (418). The makeup of judging panels could provide evidence for this thesis, the judges tending to be white, British and middle class. Four of the ten chairs had been, or still were, Conservative MPs. And while in the nineties there was relative gender balance in terms of the panels (although only three of the ten chairs were women), it was the 1991 shortlist, which included no novels by women, that provided a catalyst for a different sort of prize: the Orange Prize for women's fiction.

Over the previous two-and-a-half decades, women had written only 10 per cent of all Booker shortlisted works, something at odds with the acknowledged productivity of women writers and the quality of the work they published. Establishing a prize specifically for women writers was seen by its proponents as a way of publicising writing by women, encouraging women writers and providing an open challenge to the dominance of the Booker in the realm of cultural prestige. The resulting Orange Prize was inaugurated in 1996 (after an earlier false start) to reward the best novel written in English by a woman published in the previous year in the UK. Unlike the Booker, at that time, the prize allowed for American entrants, a significant point of brand distinction from its rival, as well as a canny way of drawing in the important American market. An anonymous donor put up £30,000 prize money for the winner, higher than the Booker Prize at the time. The prize's sponsor, the European mobile network company Orange UK, whose slogan 'The Future's Bright, The Future's Orange', was one of the decade's advertising success stories, clearly saw possibilities in the prize for promoting itself as modern, cultivated and female-friendly at a time when mobile phone usage in Britain was in its early stages. The selection criteria required that the winning entry display 'excellence, originality and accessibility', the third criterion showing an awareness of the importance of broad popularity with its attendant publicity that the Booker chose to ignore. Another distinctive and contentious aspect of the prize was that all the judges were women.

Those behind the Orange Prize were in no doubt as to its purpose, maintaining that it was 'meant to promote women writers to as wide a range of male and female readers as possible', and recognising in a more abstract way that 'prizes are a crucial and effective way of promoting the arts' (cited in Zangen 2003: 281). Yet in post-feminist times the idea of a prize solely for women could smack of something patronising or reductive, as though women were unable to compete with male writers, or that there existed such a category as 'female writer'. As Chapter 3 suggested, some women at the time rejected what they took to be a reductive label, wanting to be acknowledged simply as writers. Anita Brookner, who had won the Booker Prize, declared that

> I am against positive discrimination. If women want equality, which they do, and which they have largely achieved, they shouldn't ask for special treatment. If a book is good, it will get published. If it is good, it will get reviewed.[15]

Auberon Waugh nicknamed the award the Lemon Prize, and Germaine Greer wondered mockingly if someone would establish a prize for writers with red hair. Despite the attacks, the Orange Prize quickly established itself as a viable and credible prize, sales figures for the first winner, Helen Dunmore's *A Spell of Winter*, quadrupling after the award (Zangen 2003: 281), while the inclusion of American writers such as Marianne Wiggins, Anne Tyler and Amy Tan on the first shortlist activated interest on the far side of the Atlantic. As with other prizes, the publication of a longlist generated extended public and media interest, even if, in the first instance, the question of reverse sexism was the one most frequently asked. Yet publishers and booksellers quickly took advantage of the prize in the usual ways, emblazoning the cover of the winning entry with the banner announcing its triumph, or foregrounding its place on the shortlist.

As well as the Booker and the Orange prizes, a range of established – though, in the public imagination, less prestigious – literary prizes existed, including the Hawthornden Prize (established in 1919) and the James Tait Black Memorial Prize (inaugurated in the same year). These far less media-oriented prizes had their idiosyncrasies: the Hawthornden was for writers under forty-one, the separate James Tait Black Prize for literature and for biography was chosen by the Regius Chair of Literature and literature postgraduates of the University of Edinburgh. These judges were canny enough to realise James Kelman's qualities back in 1989, awarding the prize to his novel, *A Disaffection*. In 1994, while *How Late It Was, How Late* was shortlisted, as mentioned earlier, the James Tait Black Prize went to Hollinghurst's *The Folding Star*, also on the Booker shortlist that year. Other prizes established in the 1990s signalled the potential cultural impact and value put on such awards as means of publicising and consequently popularising particular literary zones. Two such prizes with instructively different provenances were the Wales Book of the Year award established in 1992 (dealt with in Chapter 1), and the Forward Prizes for Poetry, begun in the same year. Underpinned by the philanthropist William Sieghart, to award excellence in poetry and to expand the audience for poetry generally, the Forward Prizes had three categories: Best Single Poem, Best First Collection and Best Collection. The three-pronged approach had the advantage of focusing sharply on a single work, rewarding up-and-coming poets and announcing their arrival to the larger world, as well as acknowledging substantial collections: Thom Gunn's *The Man with Night Sweats* (1992), for example, along with Carol Ann Duffy's *Mean Times* (1993) and Ted Hughes's *Birthday Letters* (1999). And while many of the collections came from established publishing houses such as Oxford University Press (OUP), Faber & Faber, and Picador, the prizes also publicised smaller presses, such as Enitharmon, which published Jane Duran's *Breathe Now, Breathe* (1995), and Peepal Tree, which published Kwame Dawes' *Progeny of Air* (1994). Peepal Tree offers an instructive example of the positive effect prizes might have, not simply on writers, but also on publishers. An independent Leeds-based publisher, Peepal Tree was established on an extremely tentative basis in 1984, surviving hand to mouth for many years. Its website states that 'Our focus is on what George Lamming called the Caribbean nation, wherever it is in the world, though we are also concerned with Black British writing of different heritages.'[16] The award for *Progeny of Air* reflected as well on Peepal Tree as on Dawes, providing both much needed publicity and recognition. Just as the Wales Book of the Year prize drew attention to otherwise obscure publishers, maintaining the important but fragile ecology between them and their writers, on a smaller scale the Forward Prize encouraged and rewarded small publishers such as Enitharmon and Peepal Tree, culturally vital enterprises that often ran only on the fuel of enthusiasm.

Martin Amis had far less need for encouragement or recognition, having been one of the most successful serious authors since his debut novel, *The Rachel Papers* (1973). By the 1980s Amis was acknowledged as being in the forefront of British writing, along with friends such as Ian McEwan, Julian Barnes and Salman Rushdie, all of whom continued to cast meaningful shadows over the literary landscape. Amis's 1980s novels, especially *Money: A Suicide Note* (1984) and *London Fields* (1989), read by Damon Albarn and many others, were seen as emblematic of the writer's capacity to capture and represent particular aspects of contemporary Britain, especially that of London. *London Fields*' failure to make the shortlist for that year's Booker Prize was itself controversial, part of the reason being that two of the judging panel, Maggie Gee and Helen McNeil, disliked Amis's treatment of female characters (including Nicola Six, a femme fatale who wants to be murdered). Amis's next piece of fiction, *Time's Arrow: Or the Nature of the Offence* (1991a), dealt with in the following chapter, was shortlisted for the Booker. But it was his following novel, titled *The Information* (1995), that created the great scandal of Amis's stellar career. A tale of literary rivals – the highly successful, middlebrow Gwyn Barry, who has won a prestigious literary prize, and the stifled, if more talented, Richard Tull – the novel for some spoke to Amis's jealousy at the literary success of his long-time friend, Julian Barnes. In 1994 Jonathan Cape declined to pay Martin Amis a £480,000 advance for *The Information* and a collection of short stories. Amis sidelined his British agent, Pat Kavanagh (Julian Barnes's partner), and in early 1995 his new American agent, Andrew Wylie, secured a contract from HarperCollins for approximately £505,000. Amis was not the first 'serious' writer to receive a large amount of money, Ben Okri receiving a £250,000 advance for his post-*The Famished Road* 1993 novel *Songs of Enchantment* (Todd 1996: 113), and Ian McEwan the same amount for his 1990 novel, *The Innocent*. Even so, the substantially larger amount for a work by Amis, a writer who, for all his reputation, was hardly a commercial monolith along the lines of Jeffrey Archer or Helen Fielding, stunned the insular world of the British literary elite. A *New York Times* article on the story was titled 'How Amis Signed up the Demon King'.[17] Amis's change of agent was interpreted as a form of transatlantic betrayal. As it happens, Kavanagh had finalised a deal fairly close to that secured by Wylie, but Amis changed agents anyway, Wylie being the agent for both Salman Rushdie and for Isabella Fonseca. Her name was unknown to most people, but, to add to the celebrity-level titillation, Amis had recently left his first wife for Fonseca.

If the amount of money involved, the whiff of infidelity, the betrayal of an agent and her revered author husband (who terminated his friendship with Amis as a result) were not enough, the Amis Affair gained an extra dimension of absurdity and tittle-tattle when it became known that Amis had required the advance to have important surgical work done on his teeth, to repair long-standing and extremely uncomfortable problems. This was not how the information was communicated in the press, however, and Amis was ridiculed for the combination of venality and vanity. The size of the advance continued to offend, including other writers. A. S. Byatt, who had won the Booker Prize for *Possession*, accused Amis of a 'folie de grandeur', adding, 'he must believe his name is so extraordinary that anyone will pay an extra £250,000 – about $397,250 – to have him on the list'. She also wrote scathingly, as reported in the *New York Times*, 'that Amis's approach was a kind of male Turkey cocking', adding that 'I always earn out my advances and I don't see why I should subsidise his greed simply because he has a divorce to pay for and has just had his teeth redone.'[18] Amis argued in his autobiography, *Experience* (2000), that, rather than some vanity piece of cosmetic surgery, the dental intervention was extended, intensive, painful, necessary and expensive, a 'dystopia of scrape and grind – and stitching, with the yarn like bloodied dental floss' (204). But that was private pain; the public type (by way of damage to his reputation) was more lasting, and ironic in an individualistic environment where conspicuous consumption was more allowable than ever before. In purely economic terms, the deal – which was based on the assumption that Amis's celebrity (and perhaps, viewed cynically, the publicity the scandal itself generated) – required that *The Information* sell double what Amis's biggest hits of the 1980s, such as *Money*, had sold. Again ironically, it failed to outperform *Money*. Richard Todd suggests that *The Information*, which was 'promoted as a bestseller by a publisher anxious to establish its literary credentials, actually became a loss leader. A fair estimate suggests that by the end of 1995 it had earned out not much more than 10% of the advance' (Todd 1996: 18–19). The celebrity power of the Amis brand clearly had its limits.

Amis was also involved, though more tangentially, in another literary scandal that did much to diminish the reputation of another British writer, in this case Philip Larkin, a close friend of Amis's own famous father, Kingsley. Philip Larkin had died in 1985, seen by his supporters (who were very much in the majority) as one of the best English poets of the twentieth century. His accessible style also made him far more read, taught and quoted than most twentieth-century English poets. Despite, if not because of, his curmudgeonly persona, he was also revered. The publication in 1992 of *Selected Letters of Philip Larkin 1940–1985* revealed that the curmudgeonly mask concealed a more than curmudgeonly interior, one that harboured dark thoughts that were expressed with a gleeful vigour to a range of close friends over four decades. Those friends included Kingsley Amis. Racist, misogynist and displaying an extreme Little Englander sentiment, coupled with his own reverence for Margaret Thatcher, the letters painted a far more damning portrait of Larkin than had previously come to light. While most people did not read the letters themselves, the scandal that played out across the media did substantial damage to Larkin's reputation. The situation was not improved the following year with Andrew Motion's biography, *Larkin: A Writer's Life*, which unwittingly added to the damage by noting Larkin's father's support of the Nazis in the 1930s, Larkin's own repressed homosexuality and his often-scathing opinion of, and callous treatment of, an assortment of often devoted women. Then there was his racist streak (at an odd angle to his lifelong love of jazz) and his unapologetic right-wing political views. Defending him against a line-up of celebrity literary detractors, including media dons Lisa Jardine, Terry Eagleton and Tom Paulin, Martin Amis observed:

> In 1985, the year of his death, Philip Larkin was unquestionably English's official laureate, our best-loved poet since the war: better poet, *qua* poet, than John Betjeman, who was loved also for his harm, his famous giggle, his bohemianism, and his televisual charm, all of which Larkin notably lacked. Now, in 1993, Larkin is something of a pariah, an untouchable. He who was beautiful is found to be ugly. (Amis 2000: 153)

Despite the support of Amis and others, Larkin's posthumous standing plunged dramatically.

Another of the great literary controversies of the decade swirled around another celebrity poet, Ted Hughes, whom Larkin himself openly disparaged in his letters. Hughes had succeeded Betjeman as Poet Laureate, after Larkin turned down the honorary post. Hughes's own reputation had for decades been under attack, particularly, though not solely, by feminists, who held him personally responsible for the suicide of his first wife, the gifted American poet Sylvia Plath, in 1963, and the woman for whom he left Plath, and whom he subsequently married, Assia Weevil. Weevil killed herself and her child in 1969. Hughes's position as Laureate advertised his powerful position in the literary elite, while his editing of Plath's work after her death, which included selecting and suppressing work, dismayed and angered some champions of

Plath. Just before his death in 1998, he published his account of their relationship, the book-length poetry sequence, *Birthday Letters*. Plath had only published one collection of poems during her life, but her posthumously published poetry, and her novel *The Bell Jar*, had increased her reputation enormously – she was awarded a posthumous Pulitzer Prize in 1981 for her *Collected Poems*, chosen and edited by Hughes. To his detractors, *Birthday Letters* only confirmed Hughes's malevolent control of the real and perceived relationship between him and Plath, and while there was undoubtedly a confessional element to *Birthday Letters*, those detractors felt that Hughes was reworking the circumstances of their life together for his purposes and to her detriment. That he died soon after the publication of the book only added to the sense of frustration of Plath advocates, one played out in newspaper articles. No doubt that frustration was intensified by the lavish praise accorded *Birthday Letters*. Larkin's biographer, Andrew Motion, in a move that did nothing to soothe Hughes's critics, described reading it as 'like being hit by a thunderbolt'.[19] Perhaps in part because of the celebrity status of the poets individually, and as a one-time couple, *Birthday Letters* was a surprise bestseller, and went on to receive a clutch of prizes, including the Forward Prize for Poetry and the T. S. Eliot Prize for Poetry (the latter inaugurated in 1993 by the Poetry Book Society).

The complexities and ambiguities surrounding the Amis, Larkin and Hughes controversies, as well as the Kelman, McEwan and Swift situations, reflect the fickle quality of celebrity in any age, but also the peculiar circumstances in the 1990s. It seems undeniable that some of these problems stemmed from a new cultural climate that revered celebrity in a way not seen, as the Cool Britannia brand brashly advertised, since the Swinging Sixties. One obvious difference between the decades was the move from the dominance of counterculture values, which meant that, for all their wealth, The Beatles could plausibly present themselves as psychedelic hippies, to the far more ostentatiously wealthy celebrities of the 1990s. Not all the scandals were money driven, as the very different scenarios of Kelman, Larkin and Swift reveal, but in a decade of career-defining prizes and potentially massive advances, money was often a contributing factor. These pressures were increased by the general significance given to celebrity and celebrities across the social and cultural world in the 1990s, illustrated in cultural brands such as Britpop and (at a much lower intensity) of New Generation poets. While some writers in the 1990s suffered from the radioactive fallout from celebrity, others (for instance, James Kelman) used even fleeting celebrity to establish themselves in a larger cultural habitat. Cool Britannia was more hype than reality, a fleeting and superficial branding exercise, but the quality and quantity of literature produced in the nineties proved far more substantial and enduring than celebrity culture's temporary and sometimes dangerous allure.

Notes

1. Available at <http://www.newyorker.com/magazine/1997/09/15/crash-3> (last accessed 21 January 2017).
2. Available at <http://www.telegraph.co.uk/news/politics/tony-blair/10454599/Tony-Blairs-peoples-princess-speech-honoured.html> (last accessed 16 August 2016).
3. Available at <http://www.independent.co.uk/news/uk/new-generation-of-writers-presents-poetry-in-motion-some-of-todays-best-poetic-talents-tend-to-1399610.html> (last accessed 21 January 2017).
4. Available at <http://www.independent.co.uk/news/uk/new-generation-of-writers-presents-poetry-in-motion-some-of-todays-best-poetic-talents-tend-to-1399610.html> (last accessed 21 January 2017).
5. Available at <http://www.economist.com/node/370877> (last accessed 12 August 2016).
6. Available at <http://www.nme.com/infographic/blur/> (last accessed 12 May 2017).
7. Available at <http://www.nme.com/infographic/blur?recache=1> (last accessed 8 August 2016).
8. Available at <http://www.artdesigncafe.com/Norman-Rosenthal-Sensation-Royal-Academy-of-Arts-London-1997> (last accessed 8 August 2016).
9. Available at <https://www.theguardian.com/books/2012/jul/24/booker-club-graham-swift-last-orders> (last accessed 18 August 2016).
10. Available at <http://www.salon.com/1996/05/06/swift_2/> (last accessed 18 August 2016).
11. Available at <http://www.independent.co.uk/news/the-sound-and-the-fury-1273239.html> (last accessed 18 August 2016).
12. Available at <https://www.theguardian.com/books/1999/apr/24/fiction.ianmcewan> (last accessed 18 August 2016).
13. Available at <http://partners.nytimes.com/library/books/102898booker-mcewan.html> (last accessed 18 August 2016).
14. Available at <http://www.theparisreview.org/interviews/393/the-art-of-fiction-no-173–ian-mcewan> (last accessed 18 August 2016).
15. Available at <https://www.theguardian.com/books/2005/mar/06/orangeprizeforfiction2004.orangeprizeforfiction> (last accessed 20 August 2016).
16. Available at <http://www.peepaltreepress.com/about-us> (last accessed 20 August 2016).
17. Available at <http://www.martinamisweb.com/works.shtml> (last accessed 1 October 2016).
18. Available at <http://www.nytimes.com/books/98/02/01/home/amis-bigdeal.html> (last accessed 12 February 2017).
19. Available at <http://articles.latimes.com/1998/oct/30/news/mn-37648> (last accessed 12 May 2017).

Chapter Six

Rewriting the Past

> Fact and fiction are so interwoven in this book that it may help the reader to know what is historical and what is not. (Barker 1991: 251)

Historian David Cannadine claimed in 2004 that the Britain of the late 1990s and early 2000s was interested in history to an unprecedented level. Cannadine judged that this interest was widely dispersed 'among publishers, in the newspapers, on radio and in film, and (especially) on television; and from the general public who, it seemed, could not get enough of it'. Translating this interest to 'the market-oriented language of our day, it looked as though more history was being produced and consumed than ever before' (quoted in Korte and Pirker 2011: 11). Yet history itself was not the only growth area, literary historian Jerome de Groot noting in 2010 that 'at present the Historical Novel is in robust health, critically, formally and economically'. De Groot adds that 'in particular the last two decades [from 1990] have seen an explosion in the sales and popularity of novels set in the past' (de Groot 2010: 1). The reasons for the detectable upsurge in history and in the historical novel particularly in the 1990s were many, but in some measure that interest was activated by the almost unique confluence of the end of the decade, century and millennium. Allowing that these were Christian artificial historical markers, such a treble had only happened once before, and never, of course, with the global interest it received through the last decade of the second millennium. With the historical novel, though, it was sometimes difficult to delineate the historical from the fictive, illustrated by the epigraph above, from the final 'Author's Note' in Pat Barker's acclaimed novel *Regeneration*. Implicit in Barker's statement, appended to a narrative in which real and imagined characters interact, is the question of the complex purpose and effect of historical fiction in general, and its relation to historical reality. In what, if any, sense is historical fiction 'history'? This type of question became even more multi-faceted and controversial in the 1990s, when the academic centres of History themselves were under assault from postmodern thinking on, and rendering of, the topic. Historical provocateurs such as the American academic Hayden White, for instance, in 1995 promoted the argument for 'The Historical Text as Literary Artefact'. White criticised mainstream historians for their reluctance

> to consider historical narratives as they most manifestly are: verbal fictions, the contents of which are as much *invented* as found and the forms of which have more in common with their counterparts in literature than they have with those of the sciences. (White 2002: 192)

For creative writers and historians, the lines between history and fiction in the 1990s were blurring dangerously, or – depending on your inclination – promisingly.

Of the three historical markers of decade, century and millennium, the end of century appealed as the most important. The end of the millennium, though clearly significant in terms of Christianity and Western narratives, was simply too extended an historical period to come to terms with in any profound or even useful sense. All adult Britons, necessarily, had lived through more than one decade, and possibly took their bearings from whichever decade in which they were born or grew to maturity. The end of the century, though, was suitably momentous, something most adults knew they would likely never experience again. Contemplating that interplay of personal and societal narrative encouraged a revealing and educative awareness of possibly the most transformative century in human history. Among countless important events could be counted two world wars, a global economic depression and a Cold War whose aftershocks still unsettled the international scene. Britain had been a central player in global power politics for much of that time, but the difference between Britain's influence in 1900 and in 1999 was all too apparent. The oldest Britons might still recall the glory days of Empire, when much of the globe's population and its surface, all the way to New Zealand, were under the control of small islands off the European coast no larger than New Zealand itself. The loss of imperial holdings over the century, especially after the Second World War, was extensive and extended, reducing Britain's position from the major global player to a second-tier nation – still an important European power (even if Europe was sometimes excoriated for political purposes by Britain's political leaders) but not a 'superpower', a term that postdated British imperial rule. While much of this territorial loss took place in the first decade after the end of the Second World War (India's independence in 1947 being a particular blow), as Chapter 1 noted, Britain was still losing former possessions into the 1990s, most symbolically with the handover of Hong Kong. The United Kingdom itself literally was a smaller place than it had been in 1900, with the establishment of the Irish Free State in 1922. Indeed, at the start of the twentieth century, Britain had a different name, the United Kingdom of Great Britain and Ireland. From 1922, it was the geographically smaller United Kingdom of Great Britain and Northern Ireland. History's narrative was one in which Britain's place as a global protagonist was over; not yet merely a Prufrockian attendant lord, but certainly not Prince Hamlet.

In purely literary terms, though, Britain and plays like *Hamlet* still mattered. As Chapter 3 showed, the rise of the so-called 'New Jacobean' theatre, led by figures such as Sarah Kane and Mark Ravenhill, productively unsettled British theatre by returning to the sort of energy, physicality and shock of Shakespeare's *Titus Andronicus* or Kyd's *The Spanish Tragedy*. The nineties also witnessed one impressive example of the enduring power of such early plays, and of the cultural influence of history, through Shakespeare himself: the completion and opening in 1997 of a plausible replica of Shakespeare's Globe Theatre. The long-term project of the American actor and director Sam Wanamaker, Shakespeare's Globe married the enduring heritage value enjoyed by classics exemplified in the Bard's plays, with staging that took account of some of the original conditions and conventions enlivening such performances. The most obvious aspect was the incorporation of the modern-day version of the 'groundlings' into the action, a means of giving theatregoers the feeling (or illusion) of being part of the play in an Elizabethan or Jacobean sense. Rather oddly, its first Artistic Director, Mark Rylance, did not believe that Shakespeare wrote the plays attributed to him. But this subversive view certainly prevented any po-faced reverence for the Swan of Avon, while foregrounding the plays themselves. In a different way, Tom Stoppard subverted the mythical Bard in his screenplay for one of the most successful 'British' films of the 1990s, *Shakespeare in Love* (Madden 1998). (The scare quotes around British acknowledge the film's American vital financial backing.) The film both draws on and plays with the film audience's knowledge and/or ignorance about the nation's most revered and historically significant cultural figure. In it, as with other texts, including critically acclaimed novels such as *Birdsong*, *Possession* and *Ulverton*, readers are actively pushed to consider how they interpret the past, or misinterpret it. They are asked to review the status of any text, fictional or factual, as historical evidence. Each novel adopts a distinct approach to these questions and problems. *Birdsong* creates a pivotal interplay between generations. *Possession* constructs a plausibly three-dimensional Victorian world through fabricated versions of Victorian poems and letters, which are then interpreted by contemporary (if fictional) literary scholars. *Ulverton* playfully fashions a series of texts, supposedly drawn from different centuries, to construct an historical narrative of the eponymous town, the people who have lived in it, and the ways in which a past other than what might be found in historical records continues to impinge on the present.

Poetry also paid its respects to the classics, in two unlikely bestsellers in the nineties: Ted Hughes's *Tales from Ovid* (1997), which adapted some of Ovid's *Metamorphoses* for a contemporary audience, and Seamus Heaney's 2000 translation of the Old English epic, *Beowulf*. Both won the respective Whitbread Book of the Year award, the overarching prize that selects from the best novel, first novel, biography, poetry and children's book of that year. In his introduction to *Tales from Ovid*, Hughes makes the case that the *Metamorphoses* reflect a Roman Empire in turmoil, 'at sea in hysteria and despair', while 'searching higher for a spiritual transcendence'. He suggests that the 'tension between these extremes' establishes 'a rough register of what it feels like to live in the psychological gulf that opens up at the end of an era. Among everything else we see in them, we certainly recognize this' (Hughes 1997: xi). The valedictory note about the end of an era captured some of the tone of the nineties, although Hughes sensibly was vague about quite *what* that era encompassed, and, therefore, what was at an end. Heaney provided a different, more conventional, rationale for the value of *Beowulf*, not only for the late twentieth century, but for all time, writing that 'what we are dealing with is a work of the greatest imaginative vitality, a masterpiece where the structuring of the tale is as elaborate as the beautiful contrivances of its language' (Heaney 2000: ix). A foundation text of English Literature, Heaney contends that while the poem's 'narrative elements may belong to a previous age', nonetheless 'it is a work of art that lives in its own continuous present, equal to our knowledge of reality in the present time' (ix). Elsewhere, he argues for its contemporary relevance to the situation in Ireland, and to that nation's contested past, declaring it 'one way for an Irish poet to come to terms with that complex history of conquest and colony, absorption and resistance, integrity and antagonism' (xxx). Heaney's suggestion is that the historical distancing the poem creates provides an instructive perspective from which to assess the present. Yet Heaney's position also whispers the possibility that Britain's separate nations might draw on different pasts, or differently inflected, and sometimes disputed, pasts.

James Joyce, an Irishman who left for Europe when the United Kingdom of Great Britain and Ireland still existed, famously had his alter ego Stephen Dedalus declare in *Ulysses* that history was a nightmare from which he was trying to awake. To some degree Stephen means Irish history up to 1904, the year in which *Ulysses* is set, but Joyce's larger point is that history in the broadest sense can be a trap for all, a retarding mesh of traditions and prejudices. In this vein, Britain in the 1990s at times seemed hampered and haunted by a past some could not, or did not wish to, escape. For those like John Major, the past supplied a comforting idyll, and a return to that world, with its long-established traditions, was preferable to the frenetic lived existence of the 1990s. That wish for the past exposed the harsher possibility already intimated: that the best of Britain might be behind it. Major's success in the 1992 election showed that he was not alone in finding comfort in nostalgia – something unexceptional in a Conservative, naturally. Major differed from Margaret Thatcher, though, the latter's historical familiars more likely to be Boadicea than Orwell's old maids, a bulldoggish Churchill rather than Orwell's dog lovers. History was a comforting dream, one from which Major was unwilling to wake.

New Labour, by contrast, presented itself as centrally and energetically future-oriented. The 'New' part of its rebranding was a rather crude attempt to signify a break from its own recent and somewhat moribund past. In real terms, the most salient example of the party's reconfiguration was the dropping from its constitution of Clause IV, its totemic 1918 commitment to nationalisation. Michael White suggested in an October 1994 *Guardian* article that Tony Blair was about to pull off the 'most sensational political coup for a generation as the Labour conference embraced his unexpected call for an overhaul of the party's time-honoured aims and objectives'. White continued that 'Labour strategists believe that such an achievement would decisively convince the electorate that Labour has had a fundamental breach with its discredited past, if not with what Mr Blair called the community values of modern "socialism".'[1] The scare quotes around 'socialism' indicate the slightly problematic quality of the term in the post-Cold War period, while the title of the article, 'Blair defines the new Labour', seems odd only because, in late 1994, with Blair still a new leader, the signage for the fully capitalised version of 'New Labour' had not been updated. While the modifications to constitution and name activated rancour, Blair quickly set about making himself and the party the champions of innovation and change. The past could be invoked, as in the linking of New Labour to the cultural vitality and putative savvy of Cool Britannia, but primarily New Labour was fashioning the New Britain.

As the revived Scottish nationalism in the 1990s associated with *Braveheart* exposed, the past was still potent, even if historical accuracy might be one of the first casualties of creative works with historical concerns. Historians immediately pointed out *Braveheart*'s numerous inaccuracies, undermining its claim to depict history in any academically acceptable sense. Mel Gibson played William Wallace, the eponymous hero, with a mix of nobility, humility and twentieth-century knowingness and cockiness. Gibson's Wallace was a buff, handsome, blue-faced, bum-exposing guerrilla warrior. The film's anachronisms were many, but the idea of Wallace as a thirteenth-century proto-nationalist appealed to many twentieth-century Scots. *Braveheart* had its European premiere in Stirling (where Wallace had defeated the English at the Battle of Stirling Bridge in 1297). The Scottish National Party cannily or cravenly adopted the film as part of its unofficial advertising. *Braveheart*'s tremendous success improved Scottish cultural stocks beyond its borders and self-perception within them, even if (as Chapter 1 showed) less heroic counter-narratives of Scottish heritage were also being propagated. Such failings did nothing to impede the film's international box office triumph, and gilding (or gelding) the truth possibly did something to improve its appeal. The film was a prime example of the 'invention of tradition', to quote the title of the provocative collection of historical studies that the young Cannadine and others, including towering figures, such as Eric Hobsbawm and Hugh Trevor-Roper, had contributed in 1983 (for Cannadine's contribution, see Ranger and Hobsbawm 1983: 101–64). Cannadine and his illustrious colleagues probed how much that passes for ancient and (for its defenders) unchangeable tradition in fact resulted from historically specific acts that often had the clear intention of constructing a history for ideological purposes. Particularly pertinent in the case of *Braveheart* was the reality that the rise of tartan to the position of Scottish national cloth was the invention of Scottish cloth merchants of the eighteenth and nineteenth centuries, who cannily, if fallaciously (and profitably), fused the myth of Scottish clans with that of specific individualised patterns. Cannadine and his fellow historians understood that historical inaccuracy was no barrier to powerful and sustained cultural resonance.

Scotland's spiky independence movement was more energised in the 1990s than that in Wales, although the Welsh version also drew on history. Yet the elegiac Welsh film *Hedd Wyn*, considered in Chapter 1, a film set in the lead up to, and beginning of, the First World War, while hardly less lyrical than *Braveheart*, was no match for the 'Scottish' film in terms of political and social ardour or contemporary analogues. Welsh culture did gain sustenance from the past, nevertheless, most obviously in the centuries-old tradition of the Eisteddfod discussed in Chapter 1. As Heaney's comments on the relevance of *Beowulf* suggest, the attitude of those in Northern Ireland to their immediate and longer-term history was more problematic. For much of the 1990s the nightmare of the Troubles remained apparently unsolvable. Michael Longley's 1998 poem 'Ceasefire', which deals with the problematic need for reconciliation in Northern Ireland, employs a different, older parallel from Heaney's *Beowulf*, Homer's *Illiad*, concluding with the words of King Priam:

> I get down on my knees and do what must be done
> And kiss Achilles' hand, the killer of my son.
>
> (Longley 1999: 118)

History, in the form of epics from the distant past, could still speak to, and for, the present. As Chapter 1 also recounted, to the surprise and joy of many, the decade produced a major and genuine advance in the lives of most people in Northern Ireland. The Good Friday Agreement adopted in 1998 came into effect the following year, with the Northern Ireland Assembly being established in 1999, part of a long and tortured process by which those in Northern Ireland worked in difficult and disputed circumstances, to construct a meaningful future. Northern Ireland might not have fully awoken from the nightmare of history in the 1990s, but it showed clear signs of stirring.

These national historical variants, powerful in themselves, were somewhat overridden by a more globally significant series of historical events later grouped together as the end of the Cold War. This almost entirely unexpected sequence was in some ways precipitated by human error, specifically by one human, Günter Schabowski, a member of the East German politburo. Schabowski became temporary spokesperson for the teetering regime late in 1989. In answering a reporter's question on 9 November 1989, about changes to rules for East Germans to get permission to cross borders, Schabowski mistakenly announced that the changes were to take effect immediately. This encouraged thousands of East Berliners, who saw the press conference on television, to demand exit to West Berlin. When overwhelmed and unprepared border guards permitted them, the Berlin Wall was breached. Within days jubilant Germans were dismantling it, marking the start of the collapse of the Eastern Bloc, the reunification of Germany in 1990, and the eventual collapse of the Soviet Union 1991. These startling events, possibly unprecedented in the history of a major power, seemed not just signs of the end of communism and even the more widely accepted socialism, but confirmation of the triumph of capitalism and of Western liberal democracy more generally. The confident belief that there was no ideological alternative for developed nations generated fevered debate.

It also popularised the phrase 'the end of history' used by the American political philosopher Francis Fukuyama in his provocative article and bestselling book. This term would become something of a slogan for the nineties, prompting suggestions that the decade was post-ideological, or even post-historical. The events of 11 September 2001 would crush those always-dubious assertions.

A different sense of the end of history was being played out in universities. As mentioned above, the general postmodernist challenge to academic orthodoxy, embodied in the notion of a 'linguistic turn' that reconfigured subjects as various types of discourse, was in full flow across the Humanities, and especially emphatic in the realm of History. The strategic advances of postmodernism had been slow and sporadic at first, often influenced by different national paradigms. In the United States, Hayden White argued that History as a discipline was closer to literature than many historians understood or might accept. History, he argued,

> has no stipulatable subject matter of its own; it is always written as part of a contest between contending poetic figurations of what the past *might* consist of.
>
> The older distinction between fiction and history, in which fiction is considered as the representation of the imaginable and history as the representation of the actual, must give place to the recognition that we can only know the *actual* by contrasting it or likening it to the *imaginable*. (White 2002: 208)

Such views drew the wrath of Arthur Marwick, a leading British historian, who argued in 'Two Approaches to Historical Study: The Metaphysical (Including "Postmodernism") and the Historical', in an issue of the *Journal of Contemporary History*, that postmodernist ideas were 'a menace to serious historical study' (Marwick 1995: 5). The national and international disputes among academic historians invigorated discussions in the 1990s. White's consciously subversive line of argument exemplifies the sort of attacks postmodernist historians made upon what they dismissed as traditional historiography. One of those traditionalists, Richard J. Evans, in *In Defence of History* (1997), quoted the Dutch postmodernist Frank Ankersmit, who declared (in Evans's term) 'triumphantly' that 'Autumn has come to Western historiography' (8). Evans's own approach accepted the value of the questions postmodernist history raises, but Evans concludes, against the claims of the postmodernists:

> I will look humbly at the past and say despite them all: it really happened, and we really can, if we are very scrupulous and careful and self-critical, find out how it happened and reach some tenable though always less than final conclusions about what it all meant. (253)

For creative writers, these two conceptions of history, one based on playful scepticism of history's 'truth' value, the other committed to allowing readers, in the words of Sebastian Faulks's (1997) novel *Birdsong*, 'to know what this was like', provided distinct and valuable ways of representing the past, and of trying to understand it. Jerome de Groot's positive diagnosis on the health of the Historical Novel since the 1990s promotes the continuing relevance of history to a supposedly post-historical age.

Or rather, the relevance of histories plural, because works in the 1980s such as Rushdie's *Midnight's Children* (1981) and Julian Barnes's *A History of the World in 10½ Chapters* (1989) already had introduced the general public to what the literary theorist Linda Hutcheon in *A Poetics of Postmodernism: History, Theory, Fiction* (1988) had famously named 'historiographic metafictions'. Hutcheon argues that such works incorporate literature, history and theory, and that on the 'awareness of history and fiction as human constructs (historio*graphic meta*fiction) is made the grounds for its rethinking and reworking of the forms and contents of the past' (Hutcheon 1988: 5). The plural forms of 'form' and 'content' are important, allowing, if not requiring, a scepticism towards the easy privileging of one rethinking over another. Historiographic metafictions consciously drew on (or unknowingly reflected) insights produced by the postmodern sections of History departments. Some of these works were experimental in the metafictional sense, as with Caryl Philips's *Crossing the River*, which, as Chapter 2 explained, presents a multi-faceted take on the racial and ethnic complexities of transatlantic negotiations between Britain, the United States and Africa. This novel, with its multiple narratives and historical leaps, or Martin Amis's *Time's Arrow, or the Nature of the Offence* (1991a), where history goes backwards with disturbing implications, all the way to the Holocaust, stand as illuminating examples of the possibilities historiographic metafiction enabled. Not all historical novels of the 1990s were structurally metafictional, so that one of the most powerful and lauded historical fictions of the decade, Pat Barker's First World War *Regeneration* trilogy, has a relatively conventional historical narrative. It does, however, add another dimension, in a sense, blending together the historical and the fictional by integrating a range of 'real people' – including the poets Siegfried Sassoon and Wilfred Owen, and the psychologist W. H. R. Rivers, one of the pioneer researchers on 'shell shock' – along with the genuinely fictional, such as the working class soldier, Billy Prior. Faulks's *Birdsong*, also set predominantly in the First World War, is different again, moving forward and back in time, but, situating the enormity and impact of that war within a larger narrative that both predates and post-dates that far-reaching conflict. A. S. Byatt's *Possession* shifts between the late Victorian period and the contemporary world on a less weighty matter, the relationship between two writers in the first period and two academics in the second, exploring how creativity finds form, while offering a wry and salutary assessment of literary academics. If postmodernism presented new ways of understanding and representing the past, creative writers provided no sanctioned position or approach from which to tackle the past. A hundred flowers bloomed.

The title of Barnes's *A History of the World in 10½ Chapters* gave a knowing wink to the pretensions of history and of traditional fiction. Amis's *Time's Arrow, or the Nature of the Offence* presents a far darker, more troubling comedy about the complications of history and our understanding of it. Amis reverses the clock, or the emblematic arrow of time, replotting the life of American doctor Tod T. Friendly backwards from his death to his activities as a doctor assisting a surgeon modelled on Auschwitz's Josef Mengele. Friendly's name then was Odilo Unverdorben. As always, names matter for Amis, *Todt* being German for death, adding a grim twist to the faux bonhomie of his adopted surname 'Friendly', with its absurdly American positivity. *Unverdorben* is German for uncorrupted. Amis's narrative reversal, while not unique, was adventurous, given that the topic leads inevitably back to the Holocaust, reworking the horrific deaths of the inmates of concentration camps so that they are restored to life and enjoy the happy existences they had before the Second World War. The novel drew from the work of Primo Levi, in writing such as *If This Is a Man* and *The Reawakening*, where Levi recounts his return from Auschwitz to his home city of Turin. Levi observes that those who experienced what he had experienced could never wash their memories or their consciences clean,

> that now nothing could ever happen good and pure enough to rub out our past and that the scars of the outrage would remain with us forever ... no one better than us has ever been able to grasp the incurable nature of the offence, that spreads like a contagion. It is foolish to think that human justice can eradicate it. (Levi 1995: 2)

Against the bravely horrific quality of this honesty about a hellish experience, the consciousness that narrates *Time's Arrow* (when considered in terms of the usual direction in which time's arrow flies) has escaped prosecution for his crimes at Auschwitz, fled to Portugal, where he changes name, and then has travelled on to New York, and another name change, this time to John Young. Whether as Unverdorben, Young or Friendly, the narrator seems largely oblivious to the moral conundrums and dilemmas confronting him. More slyly, he is consciously forgetful of the horrors he and those like him have perpetrated, and the ethical abyss from which he has escaped without apparent damage. The reversal of time allows Friendly to experience consequences before actions, this having the perverse effect that the dead come back to life, the old become young, that those murdered in Auschwitz live again. Readers become the main agents of critique, with the actively disorienting narrative requiring especial concentration to understand not only what has taken place, but also the ethical, political, psychological and historical aspects that might all too easily be folded into an easy interpretation that 'knows' what will happen, precisely because of the historical direction of time's arrow. By reversing the direction of this arrow, Amis requires his readers not simply to follow the narrative to its conclusion, but to contemplate which historical narratives are constructed and potentially adulterated to cover up the past rather than to reveal or restore it. Clearly, this scepticism about the 'truths' that history proffers extends beyond the confines of *Time's Arrow* itself.

At the very least, Amis suggests other historical possibilities, narratives that might not inevitably lead to the Holocaust. But what, the novel seems to ask, would have to have been different? Not surprisingly, in a decade prone to reviewing the century, the 1990s witnessed the flourishing of so-called 'counterfactual' history, examples including Geoffrey Hawthorn's *Plausible Worlds: Possibility and Understanding in History and the Social Sciences* (1991) or *Virtual History: Alternatives and Counterfactuals* (1997), edited by Niall Ferguson. While these were not in any way works of literary 'fiction' – in that they argued from given historical realities towards the possibility of different historical outcomes – their appearance in the 1990s was indicative of a creative approach to historical facts, something that *Time's Arrow* takes to disturbing and absurdist levels that nevertheless require readers to confront historical reality. At a less elevated level, popular counterfactual novels such as Robert Harris's *Fatherland* (1992) provided vivid accounts of worlds in which history had taken an alternative path. In the case of Harris's multimillion selling novel, Germany has won the Second World War, Hitler is still alive in the Nazi Germany of 1964 and due to celebrate his seventy-fifth birthday, and Joseph Kennedy, JFK's father, is US president. With Europe ruled by the Nazis, Princess Elizabeth and Winston Churchill have escaped and live in Canada. HBO made a television film of the novel in 1994, a sign of the hold even fictionalised versions of real people could retain.

While Harris's novel was a highly competent counterfactual, Amis's novel was a particularly challenging take on history, although not specifically British history, because of the nature of the material it dealt with and for the way in which Amis forced the reader to work hard at achieving a satisfactory interpretation. *Time's Arrow*'s interest in characters refashioning their identity in the United States to escape a compromised past connects it coincidentally to one of the decade's great literary and intellectual scandals. This was the revelation that one of the most brilliant and influential literary theorists of the late twentieth century, the Belgian Paul De Man, who had emigrated to the United States in 1948, and had died in 1983 a lauded academic figure, as a young man had written pro-fascist articles for two Belgian papers controlled by the Nazis during the Second World War. He had later tried to erase this past from his history. Some of the major liberal figures of postmodernism, including Roland Barthes, Jacques Derrida and Fredric Jameson, defended De Man. Whatever the merits of the cases for and against him, there was something wildly unsettling about a brilliant literary interpreter – in an era when the authority of the author (let alone his or her actual existence) was under radical scrutiny – being under intense examination about his own primary texts, and especially about his efforts to erase his undeniable connection to them. The De Man controversy was symptomatic of a world in which literature and history were required to justify their existences, their practices and their intersections.

For all its literary and historical difficulties, *Time's Arrow* was shortlisted for the 1991 Booker Prize, although it did not win. But Del Ivan Janik (1995) argues that, in the 1990s, more traditional historical fiction returned, in some ways a reaction to the destabilising impact of the type of postmodernist complexity and self-awareness that Amis employed. Pat Barker's trilogy of First World War novels, published between 1991 and 1995, established itself as one of the most successful and sustained attempts to return to the past and attempt to present and interpret that war in a more traditional way than that taken by Amis. The first in the series, published in 1991, was titled *Regeneration*. That became the overarching name for the trilogy, the other two novels being *The Eye in the Door* (1993) and *The Ghost Road* (1995). Together, they represent the Great War less from the perspective of the battlefield than in terms of its effects upon combatants now hospitalised in Britain. These effects, the trilogy strives to show, ultimately had a far larger and more sustained impact on the national psyche than was understood at the time. *Regeneration* conveys the horror of the actual battles through nightmares that the recuperating soldiers cannot escape, but can barely comprehend. Consequently, as already mentioned, a crucial character is the psychologist W. H. R. Rivers, a real neurologist and social anthropologist conducting pioneering research and treatment on what would later be called post-traumatic distress. Rivers undertakes his research and treatment at the hospital where he worked, Craiglockhart Hydropathic Hospital, in Edinburgh. Much of the action in *Regeneration* takes place there. Rivers provides a point of entry into the hellish psychological world of his patients, while existing within a society in which the mental suffering of his patients is something he is trying to 'cure', in part for the utilitarian reason of replacing the ranks of soldiers available to fight. As he says of Siegfried Sassoon, whom he is treating, 'He's a mentally and physically healthy man. It's *his* duty to go back, and *my* duty to see he does' (73). The fact that Rivers, Sassoon and other characters in the novel, such as Robert Graves and Wilfred Owen, are real people, just as Craiglockhart was a functioning psychiatric hospital, infuses the novel with a degree of reality reinforced by documents, real and otherwise, such as Rivers' reports on patients, army files, letters and citations. Yet these 'factual' elements are set against the 'creative' poetry by Sassoon, Graves, Owen and others. The latter offer a far more subjective, though from Barker's position, a no less 'true', evaluation of the reality of battle and its horrendous consequences.

Regeneration opens, paradoxically, for a novel dealing with the Great War, with a declaration by someone publically finishing with the war. More specifically, and again rather oddly for a piece of fiction, that declaration is a real document: Siegfried Sassoon's 'Finished With the War: A Soldier's Declaration'. Sassoon wrote the declaration while convalescing in Britain from his time in battle, sending it to his commanding officer. He refused to return to fight in the trenches, risking a court martial by his action, as he acknowledged in the declaration, 'in wilful defiance of military authority, because I believe the war is being deliberately prolonged by those who have the power to end it' (1). When the novel was published in 1991, Sassoon's action was well established as a piece of brave defiance, a vivid signal of the pointlessness of a war whose questionable purpose, with the benefit of seventy-five years of hindsight, were acknowledged by many. Sassoon's declaration by then had become a celebrated document, something that had been read in the Houses of Commons, and had appeared in *The Times*, partly as a result of Sassoon's upper middle class connections with anti-war campaigners such as Bertrand Russell. The fact that, as a result of the controversy surrounding the declaration, Sassoon would be sent for psychiatric treatment at Craiglockhart Hospital, is a central element in the narrative and moral thrust of *Regeneration*. The document frames what comes later in the narrative, while simultaneously linking the largely fictional tale to historical reality.

Literature also intrudes, of course, given that several of the key characters are real poets. Early on, Rivers opens an envelope left by Robert Graves that has three works by Sassoon: what appears to be a draft of his poem 'The Rear-Guard'; 'The General'; and 'To the Warmongers'. Barker cleverly integrates these works into the narrative, hinting at the effort necessary to polish drafts into completed poems, teasing out connections between experience and its representation in literature, emphasising the different types of responses, subject matter, attitude and voice, and requiring the reader to engage in some form of literary criticism. The poems can also be read in contrast to or in connection with Sassoon's opening statement. This provocative introduction of a different form of interpretation to the one the reader has been undertaking with the novel gets a further twist with Rivers' own response, that he

> knew so little of poetry that he was almost embarrassed at the thought of having to comment on these. But then he reminded himself they'd been given him as a therapist, not as a literary critic and from that point of view they were certainly interesting, particularly the last. (25)

Rivers' modest reaction presents the reader who does not have literary training with a way of working through the poems from their own perspective – for Rivers, it suggests 'that Sassoon's attitude to his war experience had been the opposite of what one normally encountered' (26), in that while most soldiers struggled to forget their traumas, Rivers suspects that Sassoon is forcing himself to *remember* through his poems, and that this might be therapeutic. The poetry, then, is not ancillary to Sassoon's or to Rivers's experience, but central to it.

Regeneration is not simply populated by 'real' people, nor primarily by poets, however important they are to the novel. A key fictional figure is Billy Prior, a working class Northerner who, while important in *Regeneration*, increasingly becomes the main character in the two later volumes. Tellingly, at the start, Prior has lost his voice, and when he gets it back Rivers acknowledges

> A Northern accent, not ungrammatical, but with the vowel sounds distinctly flattened, and the faintest trace of sibilance. Hearing Prior's voice for the first time had the curious effect of making him look different. Thinner, more defensive. And, at the same time, a whole lot sharper. (49)

Rivers' capacity to interpret patients exceeds his ability to interpret poetry, but Prior also has a perspective, one he propounds in a later interview about snobbery in the army. 'It's made perfectly clear when you arrive', he tells Rivers, 'that some people are more welcome than others. It helps that you've been to the right school. It helps if you hunt, it helps if your shirts are the right colour' (66). Prior's class-based belligerence marks him out from many of the other major characters in *Regeneration*, but while he is distinctive, he is by no measure tokenistic. He is more in line with Barker's writing in the 1980s – including *Union Street* (1982), *Blow Your House Down* (1984) and *Lisa's England* (1986) – which dealt with the lives of ordinary people, especially women. *Regeneration* constituted a major break for her, both in terms of subject matter and setting, but it allowed Barker to incorporate the stories of ordinary men and women into narratives normally reserved for the middle class and upper classes, such as Sassoon. Chapter 4 registered the resilience of class in 1990s literature about the present; Barker makes sure not to neglect the importance of class in representations of the past.

Sebastian Faulks adopts a different strategy in recounting the impact of the First World War in *Birdsong*, his own powerful account of the madness of war and its devastating personal and cultural effect. Where Barker focuses on the psychological effects of war, displacing action away from the actual battlefield, Faulks produces a sustained, harrowing picture of the front line over several hundred pages that fits *Birdsong* more obviously into the genre of war novel. He comes up against an obvious problem for many novelists of that conflict, in that readers feel they know more than its participants about the outcome of the war originally understood primarily as a patriotic adventure. Any writer on the war has to fashion a convincing innocence that dispenses with easy pieties, while opening up the possibility that history might have panned out otherwise. Faulks achieves this by beginning the first of the novel's seven parts in France in 1910, with a measured piece of scene-setting: 'The Boulevard du Cange was a broad, quiet street that marked the eastern flank of the city of Amiens' (Faulks 1997: 3). Only those with sufficient historical knowledge would appreciate the importance of Amiens, but Faulks tightens the focus at the start of the second paragraph: 'Behind the gardens, the River Somme broke up into the small canals that were the picturesque feature of Saint Leu.' The name 'Somme' blazes from this sentence as it would not have done in 1910. But the first section of the novel is not a short opening gambit, before a rapid advance to the battlefield. Instead, it takes up nearly the first quarter of the novel, and sets up the critical relationship of Stephen Wraysford and Isabelle Azaire that resonates through to the novel's end nearly seventy years later. Stephen visits Amiens in 1910 to learn more about the textile trade from his host, Réne Azaire, has an affair with Azaire's wife, Isabelle, and, when she becomes pregnant, flees with her. She later deserts him, eventually returning to her husband, leaving

Stephen at the end of this section bereft, drinking wine to console himself, and still in the year 1910. This section might have formed the basis of a conventional, finely written tale of love and betrayal, but for that word, Somme, which readers know more about than the characters.

Part Two, taking up another quarter of *Birdsong*, fast-forwards to France in 1916, showing the lead-up to the Battle of the Somme, and the horrors of one of the worst battles in human history. Stephen now has a command position in his part of the battalion of the British army. This section traces in detail the inevitable disaster, made moving by the dramatic irony that readers know more about the outcome of the battle than do the British soldiers who expect a swift victory that will prove decisive in ending the war quickly. Jerome de Groot suggests that 'the historical novelist' aims to explore 'the dissonance and displacement between the then and now, making the past recognisable but simultaneously and authentically unfamiliar' (De Groot 2010: 3). Faulks manages this by piling up fine detail and developing a compelling cast of distinctive and plausible characters who feel part of what they assure themselves and each other will be an easy triumph – the section begins with Jack Firebrace, a miner now digging tunnels beneath the Germans in which explosives would be deployed. Readers know differently about the actual timeline, of course, and this disparity between hopes and known result creates an unnerving dissonance. It reaches a particularly tormented crescendo as Faulks constructs letters sent by soldiers on the night before battle, displaying a disquieting level of courage and innocence. This is the Battle of the Somme the modern reader has been primed for from the first page. The start of the battle itself is rendered swiftly in its monstrous brutality, so that within a few pages futility and barbaric destructiveness dominate, no more so than in the description of the courageous soldier, Byrne. Wounded, he rescues others, but, caught in barbed wire that has not been cut as expected, he suffers horrifically: 'Within two hours [the Germans] had blown Byrne's head, bit by bit, off his body so that only a hole remained between his shoulders' (Faulks 1997: 187). When the firing eventually stops, the sound of dying soldiers moaning fills the void. To Stephen's ears it sounds 'as though the earth itself was groaning', a sound he understands as 'the sound of a new world' (192). Only 155 of the 800 men in his battalion survive.

Because the novel has no table of contents, the unexpected start of Part Three roughly halfway through the novel produces further displacement, resituating the novel temporally and geographically in the England of 1978. Faulks introduces Elizabeth Benson, a late thirties single career woman in an ongoing and potentially ruinous affair, who is also Wraysford's granddaughter. A newspaper article marking the sixtieth anniversary of the Armistice, and a photograph of her as a three-year-old child with her grandmother who dies soon after, prompt Elizabeth to wonder about herself, her ancestors and the war. As she tells her mother: 'I feel there is a danger of losing touch with the past. I've never felt it before. I'm sure it *is* something to do with my age' (200). When a friend tells her that it is morbid to dwell on ancient history, she counters: 'I'm not sure it *is* ancient history' (205), later travelling to France to find answers to her questions. This historical shift sets up the novel's historical dynamic, which over the succeeding four parts alternates between First World War France and late 1970s England. Where Pat Barker concentrates on the war period itself, Faulks's strategy encourages readers to reassess the past in the manner Elizabeth adopts. Setting that reassessment itself in the late 1970s, rather than in the 1990s when the novel was published, *Birdsong* asks readers to think through different degrees of distance from the past, and to consider how history itself requires an ongoing process of evaluation and re-evaluation. The process can lead, as it does in Elizabeth's case, to revelations about her own identity. Investigating her grandfather Stephen Wraysford, for example, she finds his old journals, written in code, which, when translated, include his despairing thoughts:

> No child or future generation will ever know what this was like. They will never understand.
> When it is over we will go quietly among the living and we will not tell them.
> We will talk and sleep and go about our business like human beings.
> We will seal what we have seen in the silence of our hearts and no words will reach us. (340)

Yet *Birdsong*, in presenting these fictional musings within an eloquent, complex and multilayered narrative, urges readers towards knowledge and, through it, to some form of limited, though necessary, understanding.

Hugely popular works such as the *Regeneration* trilogy and *Birdsong* fed a public keen in the last decade of the twentieth century to find out more about the war that ushered in, in Stephen's words, 'the sound of a new world' – their world. That success did not please the celebrated historian Niall Ferguson, who in a massive study of the First World War, *The Pity of War* (1998), argues that 'The persistence in the idea that the war was a "bad thing" owes much to the genre of war poetry (usually meaning "anti-war"), which became firmly established in British curriculums in the 1970s' (Ferguson 1998). Rather bizarrely, given that charge, the title of Ferguson's work comes from Wilfred Owen's poem, 'Strange Meeting'. Still, he claimed that novels were performing a similar task and would have a similar influence on 1990s attitudes to a war that, as a historian, he believed had very different motives and logic to those prosecuted by many historians, let alone novelists. 'Nothing illustrates better the persistence of the First World War's reputation as an evil war', he writes, 'than the recent fiction it has inspired such as Pat Barker's 1990s trilogy *Regeneration, The Eye in the Door* and *The Ghost Road*' (Ferguson 1998: xxxi). He includes Sebastian Faulks's *Birdsong* in his attack of such fiction, adding 'It is not from historians that people gain their impressions of the First World War, but from books like these – and of course from newspapers, television, theatre and cinema' (xxxii). It is clear from Ferguson's tart tone, and for the extended argument he fashions over more than 500 pages, that while he sees this state of affairs as understandable, he also finds it regrettable, a falsification of the true history of the war.

Ferguson's stance itself is understandable, especially from his position within what could broadly be described as the historical establishment (he was a fellow at Oxford at the time, and soon after a professor). As mentioned earlier, one of the signal features of the 1990s was how that historical establishment itself was under threat, not primarily from literature, but from historians willing to accept a certain cross-pollination between the fields of history and literature. Ferguson, while he does not dismiss the importance of literary versions of the past as literature, falls squarely on the side of the traditionalists who think that history is best written by historians trained in the methodology of the discipline and with access to the necessary historical documents. Even so, as mentioned above, he is willing to indulge in the counterfactual history presented in *Virtual History: Alternatives and Counterfactuals*, a form of playful conjecture dismissed by many historians. Pat Barker's position, given in a 2003 interview, is that 'History is never a judge but a dialogue between the past and the present. The answers change because the questions change, depending on our preoccupations.'[2] What is also true, and what distinguishes Barker's notion of history from Ferguson's, is that Ferguson understands history primarily from the top down, as the play of massive international forces controlled (or not) by powerful figures, while Barker strives to capture history from the bottom up, to register and comprehend the larger historical narratives from the personal perspective of smaller, individual narratives that combine to create a larger story that is fine-grained and synoptic.

History can be very contested ground, no more so in Britain in the twentieth century than in Northern Ireland. In 1990, the sectarian division within what itself was a disputed nation (some within the Irish Free State refused to accept its legitimacy) was still enormous, despite numerous tortured efforts from various, often mutually suspicious, actors to achieve a lasting peace. One of the older generation of writers, John Montague, presents a different aspect of Northern Irish angst in his 1993 poem, 'A Welcoming Party', from the collection *Time in Armagh*. Here, the speaker reminisces about a childhood that the adult finds almost dangerously, if still poignantly, innocent, one that connects the situation in Northern Ireland to other deadly places and times. It begins with a German phrase that translates as: 'How was that possible?'

> Wie wor das moglich?
>
> That final newsreel of the war:
> A welcoming party of almost shades
> Met us at the cinema door
> Clicking what remained of their heels.
>
> From nest of bodies like hatching eggs
> Flickered insectlike hands and legs
> And rose an ululation, terrible, shy:
> Children conjugating the verb, 'to die'.
>
> ...
>
> To be always at the periphery of incident
> Gave my childhood its Irish dimension; drama of unevent:
> Yet doves of mercy, as doves of air,
> Can falter here as anywhere.
>
> That long dead Sunday in Armagh
> I learned one meaning of total war
> And went to my Christian school
> To kick a football through the air.
>
> (Montague 1993: 49–50)

The poem conjures up other times (Montague was born in 1929) in places far less dangerous than Belfast (although Armagh during the Troubles would earn the soubriquet the Murder Mile). The connection between devastating wars is made clear to the reader, even if the child registers himself and his country as peripheral, uneventful. Not that the child fails to comprehend at all, 'one meaning of total war' simply not being the religious meaning still to be learned fully. The poem carries within it the sense of melancholy education that fuses the guiltless childhood act of kicking a football with the cinematic memorialising of horror. But that is only one meaning of total war; lurking within the reminiscence of childhood is the far older adult's more measured and melancholy sense of other meanings, learned later, and far closer to home.

The long-term history of Irish colonial rule as far back as Cromwell's conquest of Ireland in the mid-1600s provides the starting point for one of the more inventive historical novels of the decade, Adam Thorpe's first novel, *Ulverton* (1992). Where many historical novels place their protagonists at significant temporal moments, investigating the historical through the personal, the title of Thorpe's novel registers not a time, nor a person, but a place, a fictitious rural village in England. *Ulverton*'s twelve chapters move sequentially from 1650 to 1988 through various documents, the first a modern story in a local newspaper recounting the return of a farmer, Gabby, who has been away for five years fighting with Cromwell in Ireland. As he has been presumed dead, his wife Anne has married another man, Thomas Walters. Gabby mysteriously disappears, and the story's narrator, another shepherd named William, suspects Anne, who he thinks is a witch. She then seduces him, something that guarantees his silence. But the initial disappearance begins a myth that the area itself is cursed. Subsequent chapters are presented by different historical voices, often through media that reflect the respective times: the story of Gabby retold in a modern county newspaper; letters, written for an illiterate mother in Ulverton to her gaoled son in London; a book of nineteenth-century photographs of the town and its surroundings, with explanatory text; the transcript of a BBC Home Service programme about one of Ulverton's famous citizens; the post-production script of a contemporary documentary about the ultimate failure of a housing project near the village. One of the key characters in this final chapter is Thomas Walters's descendent Clive, a property developer wanting to exploit the property boom in a Thatcherite Britain. Villagers who feel the new housing will threaten Ulverton's rural isolation, and its National Heritage status as an Area of Natural Beauty, oppose Walters, but his plans start to unravel fully when a skeleton is found in a field that readers alone realise is that of the centuries-dead Gabby. The story of the ancient curse in a local newspaper, that begins the novel and then is resurrected in the final chapter (and is written by 'Adam Thorpe', an author with the same name as the novel's writer), rattles potential buyers, and infuriates Clive Walters, who denounces it as 'Totally invented. Total fiction' (380); which, indeed, it is. But other, more material, contemporary problems such as shoddy workmanship, inferior materials and a downturn in the housing market scupper the project. At least for the time being. At the end of the narrative a bitter, but still hopeful, Clive speaks the last defiant words that unwittingly record a basic historical truth: 'Another year. There's always that. Another year.' The final chapter in the novel is in the form of a documentary script, and *Ulverton* ends with the post-production script notation: SHEPHERD'S PIPE MUSIC. LONG-S [LONG-SHOT] SUN SETTING BEHIND TUMULUS' (382), a sardonic comment on the triumph of the murky bucolic past over the mercantile present.

Ulverton milks the generic properties of the pastoral for comic effect, within an intricate narrative that makes serious comments about history and the capacity of literature to represent and assess it. Thorpe declared in a later interview that his novel

> is about history and the way we record history, a process in which most of humanity (let alone nature) is left out of the picture. Historical fiction does not generally record the loss, it puts history back without the shatter-mark, and *Ulverton* tried to make the reader aware of this illusion, revealing what is left in the ground. (Thorpe 2015: 196)

This allusion to nature and 'the ground' points to his belief that, despite its rural setting, *Ulverton* does not glamorise the countryside. The novel is what he calls a 'counter-pastoral', in that it does not depict a de-historicised, idyllic picture of the countryside. All the different voices in the novel, and the different perspectives they present, are marked by their time, readers undertaking the necessary detective work to link incidents, individuals and families within the larger narrative of the village. Part of the comic fun of the novel comes from the reader making the necessary connections and from understanding how characters in different chapters interpret and misinterpret the past. The past, admittedly, is fictitious, but the interpretive exercise educates readers about the processes through which written history is created and understood. Underpinning *Ulverton* is the truth that written history is not without its deficiencies and biases.

These concerns also invigorate one of the most successful historical novels of the decade, A. S. Byatt's *Possession: A Romance*, which plays comically with the real and fictitious past, with interpretations of that past by characters within the texts, and teasingly with attempts by readers to make sense of the texts themselves. As mentioned, the novel comes inflected with Byatt's own background as a lecturer in English Literature, beginning in the idyllic setting (for such a lecturer) of the London Library. That is the *physical* setting where the novel begins, but the opening lines in the novel are from an 1861 text, *The Garden of Prosperina*, by the major Victorian poet, Randolph Henry Ash. Where Pat Barker begins *Regeneration* with Siegfried Sassoon's declaration finishing with war, by way of establishing the factual underpinnings of her novel, Byatt begins with a piece of poetic 'evidence' to introduce Ash, a central character, and to activate the interpretive skills of her readers in the sophisticatedly creative, but ambiguous, realm of poetry. Barker includes poetry in *Regeneration* too, not surprisingly given that actual poets such as Sassoon and Owen inhabit the fictional text. The critical difference in *Possession* is that Ash himself is fictitious, as are his poems. Or rather, Ash is a fictitious character, while the poems in the novel are actual poems written by Byatt in 'his' voice. Byatt quickly introduces the protagonist, Roland Michell, a part-time research assistant working on Ash for Professor James Blackadder, his former PhD supervisor and a world authority on the famous poet. Examining *The Garden of Prosperina*, Michell discovers two hidden letters from Ash to an unknown female correspondent, which, in a frenzied moment, he steals from the Library. This act of academic theft sets in train a multidimensional plot that brings him into contact with Dr Maud Bailey, who is both a LaMotte scholar and a distant relative to the forgotten figure. Michell and Bailey join forces to establish that LaMotte was the intended recipient of the letters, finding out through new discoveries of secret love letters and journals that Ash and LaMotte had a brief, hitherto unknown, affair that produced a child. These startling revelations are potentially an academic goldmine (valuable for the struggling Michell, though no less useful for Bailey, the more career-wise and far more successful junior academic). But the findings also put both in competition with other scholars of Ash and LaMotte, such as Blackadder, the redoubtable Leonora Stern and the duplicitous American scholar Mortimer Cropper. As revelations continue to fill in details of the hidden, but largely tragic, affair between Ash and LaMotte, Michell and Bailey are drawn inexorably together in a parallel (though, ultimately, not disastrous) relationship while pursuing the literary sleuthing that gives the novel much of its narrative surprise and energy. The many subplots are drawn together in a Gothic graveyard scene where Ash is buried. There, the heroes claim a box from Cropper containing a final unopened letter from LaMotte to Ash that reveals the child, and establishes that Bailey is a direct descendant of that illegitimate child, and therefore the great, great, great-granddaughter of LaMotte and Ash. The box also contains a lock of La Motte's hair, a sign of Ash's continued high regard for her. With these fantastic elements of the romance genre fulfilled, Maud and Roland complete the other definition of the term by consummating a barely submerged love, their passion for each having been in part sublimated by their academic journey of literary discovery.

This rough plot summary barely covers the essentials of an extraordinarily suspenseful and detailed narrative that successfully combines the romantic quest motif with aspects of detective, campus and gothic novels. Through these structuring elements, Byatt displays her capacity to create extremely plausible versions of nineteenth-century texts. *Possession* regularly won plaudits for its convincing ventriloquism, an effect that required Byatt to confect poems, letters and journals for Ash and for LaMotte. This historical 'furniture' functions not merely to create a three-dimensional Victorian world, in contrast to and at times in parallel with the novel's contemporary world, or to advertise the interest in the Victorian period that was so marked in the 1990s. It also sets up questions about the ways in which the modern world understands and misunderstands the past. For, while the assortment of modern scholars are experts on the period, and specifically on Ash and LaMotte, until Roland's totally serendipitous discovery of Ash's letters (which originally were hidden away precisely so that they would not be found) none knew of their existence, or of the crucial relationship they concealed. The expertise of scholars, in the case of Blackadder based on thirty-five years' work, sits, the novel suggests, on shaky foundations, ones held together by academic tradition, duplicity, vanity and a failure to have, or to recognise, historical evidence. *Ulverton*'s creator, Adam Thorpe, considers that much historical truth is concealed 'in the ground'; A. S. Byatt shows how truth concealed 'in the archive' undercuts academic pretence, while also needing careful scrutiny for what it reveals and conceals. This is exposed even further in the novel's 'Postscript', where the narratorial voice reveals something none of the scholars ever finds out in the narrative itself – that Ash, by chance, came across the child he and LaMotte had conceived years before, and that it is the child's lock of hair in the box, not Christabel's. Any academic papers and books based on the 'discoveries' the main characters make in the graveyard will therefore be flawed. By the nature and process of historical and literary scholarship, those flaws will be passed on in turn to future scholars. Scholarship can reveal much about the past, but not all. Perhaps more importantly, what is revealed, even based on the documents traditional historians rely on, might still be misinterpreted, and transmitted, with unsubstantiated confidence, to future generations. As with novels such as *Birdsong* and *Ulverton*, *Possession* explores the importance and attraction of historical events, while arguing for modesty about the historical interpretations writers and historians present. Historians do this as well, of course, but historical novels such as the ones considered here address an audience beyond the academy. Their individual and collective flexibility and acuity supply vivid, challenging historical scenarios that ask readers to engage critically and imaginatively with the mysteries of the past.

Possession was adapted into a 2002 film, the American finance necessary to underpin the film, along with its American director, Neil LaButte, leading to the character of Roland Michell being turned from a bumbling young English literary researcher into a more thrusting American, played, in a serious piece of miscasting, by the dynamic, handsome uber-male Aaron Eckhart. That such an openly 'bookish' film was adapted at all spoke to *Possession*'s success on both sides of the Atlantic, and the suitably mid-Atlantic Gwyneth Paltrow was also miscast as Maud Bailey, the physical attractiveness of both Eckhart and Paltrow inevitably foregrounding their mutual attraction and enhancing their romance, to the detriment of the literary sense of romance linked to fantasies and quests that the novel promoted. Additionally, the literary artefacts in the novel that readers analysed for literary significance, quality and clues, were diminished on screen to the point of stage props. The brilliance with which Byatt had imagined and then successfully constructed the opening poem by Ash, for instance, inevitably was lost in the different medium. *Possession*, essentially, was too 'literary' for it to be adapted with anything like fidelity. Many 1990s films did tap into the more obviously adaptable heritage texts of English literature, including the plays of Shakespeare and the small library of literary classics, with the usual suspects: Jane Austen, E. M. Forster and Virginia Woolf. The enduring power of heritage in British culture was confirmed in 1990 when the National Trust reached two million members, more than the combined membership of all political parties. As *Ulverton* showed, the National Trust also was a formidable organisation in the fictional world. The acclaimed translations by Ted Hughes and Seamus Heaney emphasised how the classics still had important parts to play in the British literary scene and in the culture more generally, as did the instant and continued success of the Globe Theatre, which quickly established itself as a highly successful venture commercially and critically. But the 1990s was far more than a pleasant amble down heritage trails. Perhaps not surprisingly, the last decade of the century activated writers and readers to consider passages of time at least as long as a human life, or to reconsider the intricate and often almost-invisible, if immensely powerful, forces that had produced the present. The general interest in history was not simply a nostalgia trip, for a clear view of the present informed by a knowledgeable view of the past offered the chance to speculate on the mysterious, and potentially fantastic, future.

Notes

1. Available at <https://www.theguardian.com/politics/1994/oct/05/labour.uk> (last accessed 2 October 2016).
2. Available at <https://www.theguardian.com/books/2003/aug/16/fiction.featuresreviews> (last accessed 2 January 2017).

Chapter Seven

Fantasiecle

> Chloë: The future is all programmed like a computer – that's a proper theory, isn't it?
> Valentine: The deterministic universe, yes.
> ...
> Chloë: But it doesn't work, does it?
> Valentine: No. It turns out the maths is different.
> Chloë: No, it's all because of sex
>
> (Stoppard 2000: 103)

An English computer whizz invented the twenty-first century. This, of course, is a fantastic claim, but Tim Berners-Lee rightly gets credited for inventing the World Wide Web, which became operational in the 1990s, and which quickly began to shape the way people around the globe learn, communicate, trade, debate, are manipulated, scrutinised and entertained, fall in and out of love, reinvent their identities, engage in politics, and indulge their fantasies and sexual desires. Such a state of affairs might have seemed impossible, or indeed unthinkable, for much of the twentieth century, the stuff of science fiction, although another Englishman had proposed something similar in the late 1930s. In a series of talks on what he called a World Brain, H. G. Wells, himself one of the pioneers of science fiction in the Victorian Age, with works including *The Time Machine* (1895), speculated that such an entity would 'bring all the scattered and ineffective mental wealth of our world into something like common understanding' (Wells 1938: 17), adding that it would spread

> like a nervous system, a system of mental control about the globe, knitting all the intellectual workers of the world through a common medium of expression into a more conscious cooperating unity and a growing sense of dignity, informing without pressure or propaganda, directing without tyranny. (33)

This seems a remarkably prescient approximation of what Berners-Lee created, although what a relentlessly utopian mind like Wells might think about the actual World Wide Web must itself remain the stuff of speculation. More than a century after *The Time Machine*, Roger Luckhurst notes, in 'British Science Fiction in the 1990s: Politics and Genre', that there was a 'remarkable renaissance ... in different types of genre fiction': 'Detective fiction, fantasy, Gothic, horror and science fiction entered phases of extraordinary vitality in the 1990s, all the more striking for being surrounded by the language of entropic decline and millennial gloom (Luckhurst 2005: 78). Intriguingly, several of these genres first became popular during the late 1880s and 1890s, the previous *fin de siècle*, through writers such as Arthur Conan Doyle, Robert Louis Stevenson, Bram Stoker and Wells himself. The possibility of both renaissance and entropy suggests a tension between aesthetic and scientific orders of thinking, but rather than a perpetuation of the 'two cultures' dichotomy, some of the most creative fantasy and speculative literature of the 1990s productively integrated literature and science. Other fantasy literature veered toward the fairy tale, the narrator of Salman Rushdie's fantastical *The Moor's Last Sigh* (1995) suggesting that 'stories are what's left of us', and that readers go for the darker tales: 'Poisoned apple, bewitched spindle, Black Queen, Wicked Witch, baby stealing goblins, that's the stuff' (110). Creativity in the speculative and fantasy realms thrived, despite the entropy and the gloom. Fantasy also has a ludic quality, a feature of Stoppard's *Arcadia*, from which the epigraph for this chapter is drawn. In that play, Stoppard playfully adapts and illustrates ideas from a range of intellectual sources, wittily knitting together distinct time periods.

Luckhurst's use of the term 'genre fiction' points to the patronised status of this kind of writing, but in the previous chapter of the same collection, Patricia Waugh takes a slightly different perspective. Waugh deals specifically with science, rather than detective fiction, Gothic horror and science fiction, observing the ways in which putatively 'highbrow' works, such as Martin Amis's *Time's Arrow* (considered in the previous chapter), Jeanette Winterson's *Gut Symmetries* (looked at later in this chapter) and David Lodge's 2002 novel *Thinks*, all employ and evaluate scientific discoveries and thoughts. Waugh also quotes from an exasperated section of Cressida Connolly's review of Ian McEwan's *Enduring Love* (1997), which she felt exemplified certain worrying trends in 1990s fiction:

> You can't pick up a novel these days without being bombarded by Heisenberg's Uncertainty Principle, or the latest theories of Darwinism. Popular science now occupies ample shelf-room in every bookshop and a prominent place in bestseller lists. Novelists should tell us stories, not recite particle physics. (quoted in Waugh 2005: 63)

We can assume that Wells, one of the greatest popularisers of science, would have been pleased by this development. Connolly is right to point to the rise of popular science books, especially from the late 1980s onwards. Talented writers such as Stephen J. Gould (*Bully for Brontosaurus*, in 1991) and Richard Dawkins (*The Blind Watchmaker* in 1986, with a documentary film tie-in) were also talented scientists, and compelling media presenters. One of the more esoteric bestsellers of the period was James Gleick's *Chaos: Making a New Science* (1987), which explored the challenge chaos theory posed for contemporary physics – as Gleick put it, 'Where chaos begins, classical science stops' (Gleick 1987: 3). An even more surprising global hit (selling more than 10 million copies) was Stephen Hawking's *A Brief History of Time: From the Big Bang to Black Holes* (1988). Hawking's book proved one of the extraordinary bestsellers of the 1980s, although it was often said sotto voce that the book was more referred to than read from cover to cover.

Connolly's comment about the importation of scientific jargon into 1990s literature is pertinent and telling. McEwan's *Enduring Love* has observations such as the following, observations that might seem to have been beamed in from another, scientific, dimension:

> In physics, say, a small elite of European and American initiates accepted and acclaimed Einstein's General Theory long before the confirming observation of data was in. The theory which Einstein presented to the world in nineteen fifteen and sixteen, made the proposition, offensive to common sense, that gravitation was simply an effect caused by the curvature of space-time wrought by matter and energy. (McEwan 1997: 49)

This explanation by the narrator, Joe Rose, a science journalist, goes on for another sixteen lines, with only the use of words, rather than numbers, to designate 1915 and 1916, suggestive of a literary sensibility. (His wife, Clarissa, by important contrast, is a Keats scholar, with a contrasting take on the interpretation of people and events.) *Enduring Love* comes complete with an Appendix in the form of an academic journal article explaining the 'variant of de Clérambault's syndrome' from which the third major character, the obsessed Jed Parry, suffers. Yet Connolly's criticism of McEwan's novel specifically, and the nineties novel generally, for 'reciting particle physics', could just easily be levelled at Tom Stoppard's *Arcadia*. Sometimes considered Stoppard's masterpiece, this high-minded comedy of ideas deals with the rival claims of Newtonian determinism and chaos theory, and with characters existing in two time periods, the present day and the early nineteenth century. Stoppard was influenced by Gleick's *Chaos* in writing *Arcadia*, although his play also alludes to Fermat's Last Theorem and the heat death of the universe, something captured vividly in Wells's *The Time Machine*. These concerns are integrated with aesthetic discussions about the distinctions between neo-classicism and romanticism, as well as about the poetry and life of Byron, the theories of Thomas Hobbes, and much more, blurring the fantastic reality being uncovered by science with debates that illuminate the value of the Humanities. Stoppard explores the mysterious ways in which, as one of his modern characters, Valentine Coverly, elegantly puts it, 'The unpredictable and the predetermined unfold together to make everything the way it is' (Stoppard 2000: 68). What gives this snapshot of chaos theory peculiar clarity is that, in *Arcadia*, the principle behind chaos theory is 'discovered' by Valentine's nineteenth-century ancestor, Thomasina. She is a fictional, undiscovered teenage genius who inhabits the play's other time period. Her brilliant ideas are too advanced to be understood in her own world, and could only be understood by a 1990's theatre audience with a passing knowledge of chaos theory of the sort popularised by Gleick's book. Everything is connected, Stoppard suggests, if only we knew how to read the connected data.

In a time of considerable advances in, and revisions of, thinking about humanity's place on the planet and in the universe, popular science caught the public's attention. If historical fiction reflected consciously or otherwise on the provocations of postmodern history, it should not surprise that some speculative writing took on aspects of speculative science that challenged common assumptions about the world and the universe (or universes), providing a liberating playground or laboratory for creative thinking. The literature produced in the 1990s illustrated other worlds, times and dimensions, populated by aliens, spirits, wizards, humans and humanoids, in which magic and science might equally be determining forces. Yet the sheer weight of speculative and fantasy writing through the decade would require a full-length study; this chapter cannot connect everything. Instead, it presents samples from an impressively eclectic catalogue, noting the variety and vitality that contributed to the decade's literary exuberance. Such writing is sometimes dismissed as juvenile. It seems appropriate, therefore, to start with the most popular and transformative fantasy character of the decade, one whose escapades directly addressed the open and adventurous minds of juveniles around the globe: Harry Potter.

If *Arcadia* uses chaos theory to explain how order comes out of chaos to produce a fantastically complex reality, fantasy explores the distinctions between the way things are and the way they appear to be. This exploration can begin with entering portals to new realms, whether through wardrobes, as in the case with C. S. Lewis's Narnia books, or via fantastic railway platforms, as in Rowling's Harry Potter. *Harry Potter and the Philosopher's Stone* (1997) was seen (rightly or wrongly) to begin the revival in reading for a generation who came to adolescence in the late 1990s, and who might otherwise have been lost to the world of Berners-Lee's World Wide Web. The Potter Effect would extend well beyond the nineties, as new instalments came out and new sets of young readers raced in their imaginations along platform 9¾ at King's Cross Station, to journey by train to Hogwarts School of Witchcraft and Wizardry. It transformed the international status and popularity of children's, or young adult, fiction. The same impact was true in terms of cinema, where the adaptation of *Harry Potter and the Philosopher's Stone* in 2001 broke box office records around the world. As with the books, the success of the films in the early 2000s had a flow-on effect in cinema, helping to shape what was and was not produced. Three *Chronicles of Narnia* films would be produced from 2005, for example. This was not surprising given the established classic status of the books, although it is hard to imagine that the *Narnia* films would have been made without the immense commercial success of the Harry Potter franchise. One film highly unlikely to have been made without the Potter boost was *The Golden Compass* (2007), based on Philip Pullman's 1995 novel *Northern Lights*. Darker in tone and subject matter than *Harry Potter and the Philosopher's Stone*, *Northern Lights* was the first of Pullman's His Dark Materials trilogy (the other two novels being 1997's *The Subtle Knife* and 2000's *The Amber Spyglass*). While *Northern Lights* appeared before the first Harry Potter novel, it seems undeniable that Rowling's novels were the crucial 1990s texts in creating a new, fertile environment for children's fantasy literature. Rowling's influence was immense and undeniable. And not just for children – from 1998 Harry Potter titles began to appear with alternative adult-oriented covers tailored to an older demographic. These, too, proved popular, indicating both the basic quality of the texts and the broad-based readership for such material.

The reasons for the renaissance in various genres of fantasy and speculative literature in the 1990s are difficult to fathom definitively. Luckhurst, for example, provocatively suggests that in the 1990s, especially under New Labour, where the rhetoric of heritage was replaced by the rhetoric of culture, 'the interpenetration of economic, social and cultural spheres' (Luckhurst 2005: 82) created a new environment of 'cultural governance'. In this new habitat, the 'low value' accorded much genre writing allowed it to 'flourish below the radar of a cultural establishment often complicit with the new methods of governance' (83). Another explanation would point to the importance of the liberating effect of postmodern thought in breaking down delineating boundaries between genres, ideas and types of existence, with a subsequent release of cultural energies. What perhaps is surprising is that this flowering took place in a decade where the new lure of the internet had led cultural doomsayers such as Sven Birkerts to prophesy the inevitable, if not immediate, 'death' of the book, and with it of the reader. The 1990s proved these portents wrong. But the very breadth of writing that might be incorporated under the fantasy and speculative umbrella also works against conclusive explanations that can account for science fiction and Harry Potter, the intellectual gymnastics of Stoppard and the emotional exuberance of Jeanette Winterson, the fairy tale inventiveness of Salman Rushdie, or, as we will encounter, Gwyneth Jones's humanoid aliens.

The story of the Harry Potter phenomenon, of Joanne Rowling's elevation from struggling single mum writing her first book in Edinburgh cafes with her sleeping baby nearby, is the stuff of popular myth and the dreams of unpublished writers. Indeed, the reality itself is fantastic in a workaday sense, with the original manuscript (completed not on the latest 1990s laptop, but on a manual typewriter) being repeatedly rejected before being picked up by the small London publishing house, Bloomsbury. Given the scandal of Martin Amis's massive and ultimately excessive advance for *Time's Arrow*, and the general trend towards the smaller publishing firms being swallowed up or annihilated by the global multimedia giants, Rowling's tiny advance of £1,500 and an initial print run of 1,000 copies for *Harry Potter and the Philosopher's Stone* goes against the trends of the decade, including the belief that the children's book market was in terminal decline. The massive and almost instant global success of all Harry Potter books trashed many certainties, the release to unprecedented sales in 1998 of *Harry Potter and the Chamber of Secrets* and *Harry Potter and the Prisoner of Askaban* in December 1999 transforming the decade into one indelibly associated with the revival of children's fantasy literature. *Harry Potter and the Philosopher's Stone* won the major awards for British children's literature in 1997, including the Smarties Book Prize Gold Medal and the British Book Awards 1997 Children's Book of the Year. Prizes matter both as an encouragement to writers, and as a signal of quality, at all levels. A more startling measure of the novel's larger cultural importance was that it would top and dominate the *New York Times* bestseller list, as would subsequent instalments of the series. *The Times* eventually created a separate children's bestseller list so that sales for books written specifically for adults could still top the main bestseller list. Initially, though, the first Harry Potter book failed to receive substantial reviews in the British 'quality' press, perhaps not surprising for a children's book, but another sign of the marginalised status of genre literature generally. By the time the book was published in the United States, though, it was already a cultural phenomenon, and was reviewed glowingly in the *The New York Review of Books*. Luminaries such as Christopher Hitchens and Stephen King reviewed subsequent volumes.

The Potter series revived, rather than reinvented, children's literature, for in terms of characterisation and narrative the Harry Potter books were highly traditional. Subject matter, tropes and emblems bear comparison with the worlds of Oz and Narnia. This is not to denigrate Rowling's achievement in creating a plausible *Bildungsroman* over multiple volumes that was sufficiently ingenious, textured and engaging to sustain the interests of children and adults over the course of a decade, as Harry and his friends grew to maturity and finally defeated Lord Voldemort and his minions. Yet the world of Harry Potter, despite the occasional flying car, is essentially backward looking and nostalgic, set somewhere in the recent past, rather than in the near future. A key psychological plot is Voldemort's killing of Harry's parents when the teenager was just an infant, and Harry's thwarted desire for reconnection. Transformative power in the novels lies not in cutting-edge science and future-oriented worlds, à la H. G. Wells, but in witchcraft and wizardry that leads at least as far back as Shakespeare's 'weird sisters'. It is instructive that the world Harry Potter enters is one of ancient customs and enmities, and of supposedly timeless forces and clashes between good and evil in the past that threaten the present, and, only by implication, the future. Power emanates not from lasers and laptops but from wands, spells and curses. The title of the first volume, *Harry Potter and the Philosopher's Stone*, references age-old legends of the material that turns base metals into gold. In that novel itself, Harry tries to prevent the ancient stone falling into the hands of Voldemort, and ultimately it is destroyed, saving Harry, his friends and Hogwarts. The novel's dynamic, as it is for most of the series, is recuperative rather than speculative. Beyond its value as a plot device, Rowling clearly understood the enduring cultural power of such ancient myths for younger readers, crafting a fast-paced and inventive narrative with compelling characters and a magical setting that simultaneously combined modern cultural references with traditional motifs and storylines. The world of Hogwarts, particularly, looks back to an earlier era of public school norms, of overbearing, or quirky, or inspirational teachers, with all the trappings of traditional boarding school life. Diagon Alley retains a rough Dickensian charm, while the costuming in the first film primarily referenced the 1950s among the Muggles and earlier fashion references for everyone else. Revealingly, several of the Harry Potter films use parts of Oxford University, especially Christ Church, as background. Undoubtedly one of the cultural touchstones of the 1990s, Harry Potter stands at an oblique angle to the decade, in several senses a child from another, earlier, time.

Pullman's *Northern Lights* also draws on traditional tropes, being initially set at a fictitious Oxford College, Jordan, where the free-spirited young girl Lyra Belacqua lives and roams with her urchin friends. An explanatory note reveals that

> the first volume is set in a universe like ours, but different in many ways. The second volume, *The Subtle Knife*, moves between three universes: the universe of *Northern Lights*; the universe we know; and a third universe, which differs from ours in many ways. The final volume of the trilogy, *The Amber Spyglass*, moves between several universes. (Pullman 1995, no pagination)

Where the Potter books revel in magic, in *Northern Lights* Pullman tends more toward science fiction, not only with multiple universes but also by introducing the concept of a cosmic and conscious 'Dust' that floats in the universe and is important for the development of personal consciousness. Dust strengthens bonds between humans and their 'daemons', animals that embody that person's soul, although there are characters with a religious bent who dispute its existence. Some have read Dust as the equivalent of dark matter, although the 'dark materials' that give the trilogy its overarching name suggest something 'otherworldly' in a different sense. The phrase is taken from Milton's *Paradise Lost*, specifically about the 'almighty maker' and his power to 'ordain/ his dark materials to create more worlds' (Book II, lines 915–6). In *Northern Lights*, Lyra's explorer scientist uncle, Lord Asriel (later revealed as her father) wants to discover the origin of Dust by journeying to the Northern Lights that might give access to a parallel universe. Once her friends start mysteriously to disappear, stolen it seems by the feared Gobblers, Lyra and her daemon, the monkey Pantalaimon, venture to the Arctic to save stolen children, and to find out more about Dust. Ranged against her, Lord Asriel and their various allies (including ancient tribes, angels, polar bears and explorers) are the churchlike Magisterium and their powerful agent, Marisa Coulter (later revealed as Lyra's mother), who want to maintain their sinister control. Pullman creates a dense, coherent fantasy that incorporates elements of religion, developmental psychology and physics, a world that has greater sophistication than the Harry Potter books, and presents more intellectual challenges for readers. Again, this is not to downplay Rowling's achievement, but to note that *Northern Lights* and the other novels in the trilogy ask large questions about identity and free will, as well as integrating different levels of the fantastic and the real more inventively. Like the Potter books, though, the aesthetic often is backward facing, as the originating Oxford University setting illustrates. The steampunk feel of the novel, where people travel in motorised hot air balloons, and its Victorian markers (such as orphaned urchins and a Dickensian metropolis) reference powerful general trends in late twentieth-century British literature that creatively reworked the past. But there are no Wellsian time machines.

As these multi-volume books exemplify, the series is a notable feature of generic fiction, priming the possibility or even the necessity of adventures with the same character and similar situations. Examples in mainstream literature do occur (Anthony Powell's *A Dance to the Music of Time* being a notable English instance), but for its detractors the sequence advertises the formulaic nature of genre fiction, in terms of character and action. For its supporters, a series of linked novels allows, as with the Rowling and Pullman works, for the detailed and measured development of complex concepts and situations. Iain M. Banks' Culture series taps into the benefits in terms of science fiction. The first of the Culture series, *Consider Phlebas*, appeared in 1987, establishing some of the underlying forces at work in the complex and fundamentally utopian world of the Culture, which, as Banks explained in 1994, is 'a group-civilisation formed from seven or eight humanoid species, space-living elements of which established a loose federation approximately nine thousand years ago'. Critically, in the context in which the books appeared, Banks reveals his personal conviction that he favoured a planned economy over a free market version, but that such an economy, to function in the real world, needed the input of all citizens in its design and implementation to bring this about. Banks explains that his fictional Culture has developed far beyond that

> to an economy so much a part of society it is hardly worthy of a separate definition, and which is limited only by imagination, philosophy (and manners), and the idea of minimally wasteful elegance; a kind of galactic ecological awareness allied to a desire to create beauty and good.[1]

'A Few Notes on the Culture', from where this quotation is taken, was published in 1994, with John Major in power, Margaret Thatcher (a Banks bête noire) still vivid in the memory, and Tony Blair's New Labour (which Banks would also come to loathe) yet to emerge. The Culture novels are, in line with the norms of the utopian genre, critiques of their contemporary society and potential calls to arms for readers to consider and potentially work towards different types of society. As predominantly utopian, they push against the prevailing dystopian mood of much recent genre fiction and general thinking. Which is not to say that the novels making up the Culture series represent bland, ideal, 'happy' zones. The benevolent Minds that control the various worlds can be in conflict (as in *Consider Phlebas*, where a Mind is being pursued by the aggressive Indrian Empire) or in *Excession* (1996), one of the major Culture novels of the 1990s, where the Culture is under threat from an 'Outside Context Problem'. The Excession is the name given to the unusual alien artefact, a mysterious sphere that manifests itself in Culture space, and which the antagonistic race The Affront try to capture and control for their own benefit. Against this dire situation, Banks employs his usual inventive wit to conjure up a mesmeric world of political intrigue, social critique and bewilderment, in which the Excession is both threat and opportunity, and in which the actions and intentions of the various parties are regularly reappraised in the light of conflicting and conflicted motivations.

Where Banks' Culture novels creatively remapped the skies, Gwyneth Jones's White Queen trilogy brought science fiction crashing back to an Earth invaded by humanoid aliens. The first novel, *White Queen*, published in 1991, deals with the arrival in 2038 of a race the humans call Aleutians, forced to Earth when their ships crash-landed in the Aleutian Islands, near Alaska, as well as Southeast Asia and in Asabaland. In this fictional African country, the protagonist, Johnny Guglioli, suspects their existence and seeks a meeting. The novel charts various first contact manoeuvres and misreadings of one group by the other. An obvious form of difference and miscomprehension derives from the fact that the so-called Aleutians are hermaphrodites, and so find it difficult to understand the gender relationships they find on Earth. Their fluid identities differ blatantly from the humans they encounter, although such are the relatively benign first interactions that serious clashes are largely avoided. The Aleutians, then, are not akin to H. G. Wells's apocalyptic Martians. While telepathic – their thoughts represented in the text within angle brackets – they are sufficiently human in appearance that the usual hysteria about aliens invading is largely avoided. Indeed, an early problem involves their troubles with a hire car. Earth itself is wracked by geological and political upheaval: earthquakes and volcanoes are violently active, London has summer monsoons, while traditional power in the United States, home of protagonist Johnny Guglioli, has been overthrown by a socialist revolution. In this relatively chaotic political and social world, the Aleutians – who are more powerful and adept than their human counterparts, by dint of their superior intellect, social order and technology – eventually come to dominate the planet.

The differences between humans and Aleutians enable Jones to explore gender distinctions, what the Aleutians call the human 'war between the two broods'. Conflict between the genders differs from the integrated social order deriving from their own non-gendered identities, with the attendant social customs, organisations and circumstances. They find it difficult to comprehend the relationships between human males and females, given that they see the two broods at war. As ever with such speculative texts, the overt distinction between worlds or world views provoke readers to consider new forms of individual existence and social arrangement. How, the Aleutians wonder, can Johnny Guglioli and his partner, the even more subversive Braemar Wilson, be in love. One explanation is that they are in a love suicide pact. This idiosyncratic interpretation of human interaction might not be correct, but it does reflect how questions of gender identity and powerful imbalances within personal relationships continued to intrigue the reading public. *White Queen* also dealt with current and emerging questions such as eco-politics in a world under climate stress, and with the complex legacy of colonialism, given that, in essence, the Aleutians dominate in a manner that resembles the takeover by European powers of Africa. Humans respond variously to the Aleutians, some adopting a cargo cult-like subservience to what they take to be benevolent demi-gods; others, including those in the subversive White Queen group, favouring resistance to the imperial masters. Johnny and Braemar Wilson are part of that resistance, and although ultimately Johnny is executed for his action, in the novel's envoi, the sardonically titled 'Blessed Are the Pure at Heart', Braemar signs off on the failure of her own actions with the Beckettian motto: '*Fail again. Fail better.* "I like that", she murmured. "I'll have that"' (Jones 1992: 304).

The resistance to overwhelming odds lurks between the pages of Salman Rushdie's first novel after the fatwah against him, and possibly his most substantial novel of the decade, *The Moor's Last Sigh* (1995). Unlike the future-oriented *White Queen*, Rushdie's novel ventures into the past; or, rather, as is usual with Rushdie, several pasts. And while Jones's novel incorporates aliens, for all its fantasy elements, Rushdie's novel deals with larger than life figures involved in all-too-human family struggles. The narrative threads the struggles, over several centuries, of real people and the exotically imaginative da Gama-Zogoiby family. The last in the line of this family, Moraes, nicknamed the Moor, narrates the family tale that has versions of poisoned apples, Black Queens and baby stealing goblins throughout. Written while Rushdie was still in deep hiding, the novel deals with the exile of Moraes, who, at the outset has, fantastically enough, escaped from a replica of the Alhambra, the famed Moorish palace and fortress in Granada, Spain. Moraes himself is a suitably fantastic, giant figure with a deformed right hand and a physical condition that means he appears to age at twice the normal speed. As with Saleem Sinai, the narrator hero of Rushdie's *Midnight's Children*, and perhaps for Rushdie himself, time seems to be running out. And, as with Saleem, Moraes is eager to tell his story before his fast approaching death. Banished, as he complains, from his mother Aurora's illustrious cultural salon (she is a great artist, great beauty and a demonically great hater), and on the run, he embraces '*unnaturalism*, the only real ism of these back-to-front jabberwocky days' (Rushdie 1995: 5). Moraes's tale is one of personal estrangement and exile, of familial triumphs and disasters, of colonial and post-colonial power struggles, mostly centred on the spice trade, and a hybrid identity: his mother from a Portuguese Catholic family who made their money in spices; his father, Abraham, a Sephardic Jew who claims to be a descendant of the fifteenth-century Moorish king, Boabdil. Polyphonic stories – some true, some false, some uncertain – run through a complex narrative that traverses centuries and continents. What is clear is that Moraes's telling of the tale, however ambiguous, fantastic or incomplete, is itself the novel's key dynamic, and Moraes's purpose. Having told his tale over 400–plus pages, the final pages are framed by Moraes declaring that 'I went back to my table, and write my story's end' (432). He envisages his tombstone, with the letters RIP upon it. Acknowledging that 'the world is full of sleepers waiting to return', he lists some:

> Arthur sleeps in Avalon, Barbarossa in his cave. Finn MacCool lies in the Irish hillsides and the Worm Ouroboros on the bed of the Sundering Sea. Australia's ancestors, the Wandjina, take their ease underground, and somewhere, in a tangle of thorns, a beauty in a glass coffin awaits a prince's kiss. (433)

Late twentieth-century figure though he be, and entangled in centuries of fantastic family, national and religious politics, Moraes finds a form of solace in fantasy, in myths and fairy tales that foretell his resurrection. These, he argues, plug him into a timeless cultural internet of stories, of other sleepers waiting to wake. It is hard not see Rushdie's unhappy circumstances embedded in such tales of yearned-for solace.

As Chapter 3 detailed, Jeanette Winterson's concerns with questions of gender, sexuality and love enlivened her witty first novel, *Oranges Are Not the Only Fruit*. Later fantasies such as *The Passion* (1987) and *Sexing the Cherry* (1989) forsook continuities of narrative and setting to fashion fanciful characters who inhabited worlds that both approximated and actively broke with reality. *Gut Symmetries* (1997) explores new fields, or perhaps universes. A preliminary 'Author's Note' begins the process of reorientation: 'Until the discovery of the planet Pluto in 1930, the sign of Scorpio was ruled by Mars. Paracelsus assumed Mars as his Ruler. I have used his system where he is concerned.' Paracelsus, proto-scientist and occultist in a time when differences between these fields of enquiry were less obvious or demarcated than at present, provides organising principles for the novel that follows, the 'Prologue' asking 'What do we know of him?' (1), before explaining that Paracelsus 'was a student of Correspondences', recognising pivotal relationships between the heavenly and human bodies. Much of Winterson's exploratory imagination had sought and found unlikely correspondences in her writing, so Paracelsus has obvious attractions. But the focus of the narrative itself is not the Early Modern experimenter, for, important as he is to the design and method of the *Gut Symmetries*, the narrator then asks a central question:

> What is it that you contain?
> The Dead. Time. Light patterns of millennia. The expanding universe opening in your gut. Are you twenty-three feet of intestines loaded with stars?
> The Miracle of the One that the alchemists sought is not so very far from the infant theory of hyperspace, where all the seeming dislocations and separations of the atomic and sub-atomic worlds are unified into a co-operating whole. This is not possible in three spatial dimensions or even four. Ten, at least, lure us out of what we know. (2)

This sounds very much like the recitation of physics, rather than storytelling, that so annoyed Cressida Connolly. The quotation, as with the book's title, plays games with the word 'gut', a term that speaks to the essentially corporeal nature of humans, and is also an acronym in physics for 'Grand Unified Theory', otherwise referred to as the 'Theory of Everything'. Physicists such as Stephen Hawking in the post-war period had at certain points felt on the brink of finalising such a theory, based on advances made by Einstein earlier in the century. Winterson has no such aspirations, but her ambition is not small, either. So, the second section of the Prologue begins: 'Here follows a story of time, universe, love affair and New York. The Ship of Fools, A Jew, a diamond, a dream. A Working-class boy, a baby, a river, the sub-atomic joke of unstable matter' (6). There follows a brief definition of each element in this catalogue, before short individual chapters begin on a boat, the QE2. This functions as an evocative metaphor for change and resistance to change, such a vessel connecting nations, while operating as 'a model of the world in little' (9). Correspondences between the small and the immense play out repeatedly in the book's twelve chapters, their titles ('The Fool', 'The Tower', 'The Page of Swords' and such) taken from tarot cards that offer their own way of interpreting, if not quite structuring, the chaos of existence. In this instance, the focal points are three people connected by another potent and possibly timeless symbol, 'the eternal triangle': Jove, a Princeton physicist; his wife, Stella; and Alice, a British physicist who will have an affair with both. One character narrates each of the chapters, which are themselves broken into fragments, relatively haphazard collections of autobiography, thoughts, action, records of conversations, projections and doubts, most evocatively about the motives behind the search for love and the suspected motives of one's lovers. There are also musings on the innate difficulties in knowing oneself, let alone others, and of divining patterns without which life might appear completely random, and therefore meaningless. These personal aspects are connected to larger questions of matter, reality, time and existence, all elements in a speculative and cosmic kaleidoscope that can be twisted into new startling patterns in an instant. As Alice muses in the final chapter, 'The Lovers',

> Matter is provisional and that includes me. Matter has at best a tendency to exist, and will, it seems divide infinitely because there is no there there. There are vibrations, relationships, possibilities and out of these is formed our real lives. (207)

Soon after, she explains the Schrödinger's cat mental experiment at a length approximating Joe's explanation of Einstein's General Theory in *Enduring Love*. In both novels cutting-edge scientific speculation offers a means into a fantastic reality that is difficult if not impossible to grasp fully. Or, as Alice puts it more for vividly, grafting the physical gut on to the conceptual GUT, 'The new physics belch at the politely seated table of common sense' (207). That said, Winterson's novel is (for better or worse) far more structurally experimental than McEwan's. Each novel reflects the usual approach of its respective author: rational, precise and structured in the case of McEwan; challenging, vivid and risk-taking in the case of Winterson. The new physics, for all its enlivening subversion, does not prescribe how it might be rendered creatively.

A further point of connection between the two novels is how the immensely unsettling assumptions and findings of particle physics are employed to investigate one of the foundational topics of literature: love. Alice, the eponymous narrator of this first chapter, 'The Fool', is giving lectures on the QE2, and after one on Paracelsus meets another lecturer, Jove, who is lecturing on time travel. They have an affair that Jove's wife, Stella, finds out about. Eventually, the two women meet, and also begin an affair. This three-cornered relationship accords, Alice shows, with the new geometry. With Euclid, the lines of an eternal triangle cannot meet, for 'Euclidean theorems work only if the space is flat. In curved space [as theorised by Einstein] the angles over-add themselves and parallel lines always meet. His wife, his mistress, met' (17). *Gut Symmetries* overflows with such parallels between the physics and love, as it does between physics and life, Alice noting elsewhere the 'String paradox of the restless and the formed. If the physics is correct then we are neither alive nor dead as we commonly understand it, but in different states of potentiality' (207). For all the impersonal, theoretical sangfroid of this statement, Alice is vivified by passion, devastated by its absence and hungry for its return. Jove, by contrast, is more practical, less drawn to the fantastic, believing that physics must be evidence-based, or it is not science: 'Call it alchemy, astrology, spoon-bending, wishful thinking' (191). For Jove,

> All of us have fantasies, dreams. A healthy society outlets those things into sport, hero-worship, harmless adultery, rock climbing, the movies. Unhealthy individuals understand their dreams and fantasies as something solid. An alternative world. They do not know how to subordinate their disruptive elements to a regulated order. (191)

For Jove, physics, in explaining what might otherwise seem to be a fantastic universe, imposes necessary order and regulation. 'There is nothing mystical about the universe', he declares. 'There are only things we cannot explain yet. That is all' (191). Ultimately, if the end of the narrative involves some form of summary – something Winterson signals by titling the final chapter after the tarot card, 'Judgement' – Jove's pragmatic view is set aside for Alice's lyricism. She contends that the new physics offers a view of the mystery and poetry of the universe, indeed that it extends and deepens our quotidian understanding of existence and of ourselves. 'The universe hangs here', she declares, 'in this narrow strait, infinity and compression caught in an hour.' Observing that 'They were letting off fireworks down by the waterfront', she concludes, as the novel concludes, that 'Whatever it is . . . that hurls you past the boundaries of your own life into a brief and total beauty, that is enough' (219).

Gut Symmetries explores the great paradoxes of physics, linking them with the interpersonal. Tom Stoppard's *Arcadia* also addresses questions of physical attraction and love, speculating interactively in the scientific, literary and cultural realms, creatively employing a dual time frame to tease out correspondences and differences between the early nineteenth century ('April 1809', in the first instance) and the contemporary world. Crucially, Stoppard explains in the stage directions,

> The play shuttles back and forth between the early nineteenth century and the present day, always in this room. Both periods must share the state of

the room, without the additions and subtractions which would normally be expected. The general appearance of the room should not offend either period. (Stoppard 2000: 26)

In alternating scenes, nineteenth-century characters (including the young Thomasina Coverly and her mother, Lady Croom; her tutor, Septimus Hodge; and the poet Ezra Chater) occupy the same room 'in a very large country house in Derbyshire', with their late twentieth-century counterparts (including Hannah Jarvis, a cultural scholar; Bernard Nightingale, a literary academic; and modern members of the Coverly family, including Valentine, Chloë and Gus). Essentially, this state of affairs enacts theatrically the equivalent of time travel. As Wells had shown in *The Time Machine*, a time traveller does not move spatially at all, only forward or backward temporally in the fourth dimension of time. (It is worth noting that Wells's explanation of time in the novella is reckoned to precede Einstein's theories by a decade.) The two time frame set-up provides Stoppard an ingenious means for his audience to distinguish the Newtonian universe of 1809 and that of the 1990s, in which works such as Gleick's had popularised chaos theory. In the long final scene, characters from both time periods inhabit the room together, although they do not acknowledge the presence of those from the other time. Their interlaced thoughts, dialogue and action alert the audience to fundamental parallels and differences they themselves do not comprehend. The play ends with one couple from each era dancing together, emblems of what Chloë pronounces (in the epigraph to this chapter) is the element of human attraction or sex that undermines the entropic forces of nature. It is not so much that love conquers all, but that reproduction creates immense complexity out of a few interactive cells.

The scientific distinction is complemented by the awareness of some modern characters, such as Hannah, of a radical cultural shift from neoclassicism to romanticism that took place in the eighteenth century, and that can be seen, appropriately enough at a very large country house, in the landscaping. Hannah is researching 'landscape and literature 1750–1840', and has a marked preference for the formal beauty of classicism over what she sees as the chaos of romanticism. As she explains to her sometime-rival Bernard: 'English landscape was invented by gardeners imitating foreign painters who were evoking classical authors ... Arcadia!' (40). This ideal (for her) was supplanted by the fashion for 'untamed nature' that she derides as 'the Gothic novel expressed in landscape', an abomination for her that has 'Everything but vampires' (40–1). She proposes a similar distinction in literature, lampooning the 'whole Romantic sham' that replaced Enlightenment thinking as 'a century of intellectual rigour turned in on itself. A mind in chaos suspected of genius. In a setting of cheap thrills and false emotion.' She writes the change off as 'The decline from thinking to feeling' (43). Her prime example is the so-called Sidley Hermit she is researching, a supposed genius who died having covered hundreds of pages 'with cabalistic proofs that the world was coming to an end' (43). Bernard, as a Romantic scholar, necessarily disagrees with her dismissal of romanticism and genius, but her assessment sketches in the dynamic between order and chaos that powers the play in subtle and sophisticated ways.

The key character from the outset is Thomasina, thirteen years in the first scene and nearly seventeen in later scenes. She is being instructed by her worldly tutor, Septimus, who understands that she is 'far cleverer' than her elders, including himself. Her genius, a term derided by the anti-Romantic Hannah, but applicable to the precociously intelligent girl, is to develop concepts from simple observations that nearly two centuries later will find form in chaos theory. So, for example, thinking about the fact that you can stir jam into rice pudding, making it ever pinker as the jam disperses into the pudding, but that 'if you stir backward, the jam will not come together' (12), she intuits the notion of entropy, ahead of its scientific discovery. Later, she will apply this understanding to the newly invented steam engine, realising that more energy is required to power the engine than it produces. Contemplating Newton's laws of motion, she declares to Septimus:

> If you could stop every atom in its position and direction, and if your mind could comprehend all the actions thus suspended, then if you were really, *really* good at algebra you could write the formula for all the future; and although nobody can be so clever to do it, the formula must exist just as if one could. (13)

Septimus's reaction – '(*pause*). Yes. (*Pause.*) Yes, as far as I know, you are the first person to have thought of this' (13) – conveys his awareness of the insight's revolutionary potential. Implicit in Thomasina's brilliant mental leap of the mind, and recognisable for a modern audience, is that while the maths might be beyond any human to complete in a lifetime, given the immense complexity of the data, a sufficiently powerful mathematical machine (say, a computer) could make such calculations. Thomasina, later as a sixteen year old, begins to 'plot' a 'leaf and deduce its equation', hitting upon the ways in which the apparent 'chaos' of the natural can be plotted and therefore understood using numbers. The point here is that the incipient version of chaos theory that Thomasina 'invents' requires nothing more than the kind of *sui generis* mind she possesses, capable of conducting mental experiments along the lines of an Einstein. The ideas are not beyond the realms of possible thought at the time, but are simply beyond what had then been thought. What seems fantastic might merely require a bold imagination to understand it. The problem is, that if others cannot (or do not) understand the discovery, to all intents and purposes, it remains undiscovered. The dual time frame illustrates this problem, for although Thomasina's modern descendant, Valentine, is shown her treatise 'New Geometry of Irregular Forms' (essentially, an argument for chaos theory), at first he cannot believe that she or anyone is capable of approximating a computer in the early eighteenth century and carrying out the enormous number of calculations required. This despite the fact that he advocates chaos theory and comprehends that the sort of activity Thomasina proposes theoretically could be carried out. Only late in the play, once he has 'pushed her equations through the computer a few million times further than she managed with her pencil' (107), does he understand that 'She saw' how 'everything is mixing the same way, all the time, irreversibly', until 'there's no time left. That's what time means.' Immediately he has said these mournful words Septimus ruefully tells Thomasina: 'When we have found out all the mysteries and lost all the meaning, we are alone, on an empty shore' (132). Her response is to invite him to dance. Near them, their modern equivalents, Hannah and the mute young genius of his time period, Gus Coverly, do the same thing, fuelled by the same timeless human attraction that pushes back against entropy, that creates anew.

Much of the fantastic and speculative aspects of *Arcadia* are worked through science, but Stoppard also explores the mystery of creativity. Or its absence, as is the case with the poet Ezra Chater, whose wife Septimus has seduced the night before the action of the play begins. In this instance, Thomasina, although still perceptive, is too young to fully comprehend the rules of attraction, and so berates Cleopatra as an 'Egyptian noodle' (56) whose promiscuity led to the burning down of the great library of Alexandria, with the loss of hundreds of plays and poems by the great Athenians. Here Septimus's greater experience prevails, his argument being that great literature, indeed all human creativity, will eventually emerge, so that, like travellers, 'We shed as we pick up', and 'what we let fall will be picked up by others' (57). As almost instant proof of this notion, he pretends to translate a piece of Latin from Plutarch about Cleopatra, cribbing from Shakespeare's *Antony and Cleopatra*. Thomasina understands the ruse, and calls Septimus out: 'Cheat!' What the modern audience possibly knows, but that Septimus and Thomasina do not and cannot know, is that T. S. Eliot will later splice these words into his revolutionary poem, *The Wasteland*. As

Septimus had assured Thomasina, even though he will not be alive to acknowledge the fact, what might have been let fall has been picked up by another – in this case, by Eliot. Stoppard also acknowledges the importance of criticism, as well as creativity, and of the dangers of misinterpretation, as when Bernard misunderstands literary evidence and so erroneously claims on breakfast television that Lord Byron shot the poet Chater in a duel. Like the literary scholars in *Possession*, Bernard fashions a reality out of scraps of evidence that create a falsehood he precipitously blurts out to satisfy his ego. Hannah promises, as a matter of academic necessity, to expose the error. But she comes to realise her own error in dismissing the Sidley Hermit as 'off his head' and the 'perfect symbol' for the deficiencies of romanticism. Ultimately, she understands that the mad genius known as the Sidley Hermit, the person she is researching, was most likely the exceptionally brilliant Thomasina, whose ideas were too advanced for the world she inhabited. As a result, those ideas were written off in her own time. The epithet that the hermit was 'off his head' adds a level of sexism to the mistaken dismissal of 'him' – the implication is that women were not capable of the kind of intellectual work required to fashion the cabalistic writing attributed to the hermit, even if the writing was deemed to be the ravings of a lunatic. Hannah's new knowledge simultaneously punctures her own antipathy to romanticism, with its disorder and emphasis on the emotions, as opposed to the intellect that she has championed. Chaos is not disorder so much as an order not yet understood. James Gleick (1997) wrote in *Chaos: Making a New Science* that 'For as long as the world has had physicists inquiring into the laws of nature, it has suffered a special ignorance about disorder' (3), an ignorance that Hannah eventually rectifies. Valentine validates disorder, declaring to Hannah that 'The future is disorder', and that 'It's the best possible time to be alive, when almost everything you thought you knew was wrong' (69), but his initial failure to understand the revolutionary quality of Thomasina's ideas detracts from the status announced in his hard-won scientific credentials. Like Jove in *Gut Symmetries*, access to new if tentative 'truths' does not insulate the mind from error. For Valentine, at least, the nineties was a time alive with possibility. But it is his more intuitive brother, Gus, mute but acutely perceptive, who exemplifies the kind of transformative mind capable of making intellectual leaps that uncover new knowledge, new and fantastic ways of comprehending what might otherwise be dismissed as chaos. For Stoppard, the stage offers the perfect medium to address these dynamic and productive tensions. It is one of the play's singular achievements that it makes highly complex, abstract and counter-intuitive ideas concrete, entertaining and educative in the most arresting way. But the fact that the play exists at all speaks to the popularising of conceptually rich notions and discoveries, and the sense that at the end of the twentieth century the world of science produced understanding that approximated creative fantasy and speculation.

While undoubtedly a brilliant playwright, able in the case of *Arcadia* to bring the fantastic and the speculative together with profound imaginative skill, Stoppard was also adept as an adaptor of material to the screen. His most successful screenplay of the 1990s also happened to be one of the most successful British films of the 1990s, *Shakespeare in Love* (Madden 1998). This film had no pretensions to the kinds of intellectual games, conundrums and insights of *Arcadia*, but in its treatment of creativity, and of theatre's magical capacity to fashion make-believe into a performance that can transfix an audience almost alchemically, it did fall squarely within the realm of fantasy. An unashamedly frothy piece of cod literary history, dealing as it does in an explicitly non-reverential way with the Bard's personality, reputation and creative processes, the film also demonstrates the power of great theatre to move audiences. It simultaneously ridicules the deficiencies of the various individual contributors, while displaying how, out of sometimes unpromising elements, something moving and true about the human condition can be created and understood. *Shakespeare in Love* also deals with the stresses of being Shakespeare, but a Shakespeare taken down from the pedestal of universal genius, a bard for a postmodern age. The brilliance with which these parts are fused explains why the screenplay won an Oscar for Stoppard and his American collaborator, Marc Norman.

The film looks at Shakespeare's fumbling attempts to complete a much-overdue play, whose work-in-progress title is *Ethel, The Pirate's Daughter*. Stoppard's own reputation as one of British theatre's most intelligent and eloquent playwrights was confirmed in 1966 with *Rosencrantz and Guildenstern Are Dead*, which relegated Hamlet to a minor character in his 'own' play. In the film, Stoppard has enormous fun lampooning Shakespeare, as well as the Shakespeare culture industry, and audiences lazily in awe of the Bard myth. The film was a critical and commercial triumph, taking in more than $100 million in the US alone, and winning seven Oscars in total, including (not surprisingly) Best Picture and (more surprisingly) Best Actress in a Leading Role for Gwyneth Paltrow. The latter award, whatever one thought of Paltrow's acting, is apt, in that in the film she plays Viola de Lesseps, a young noble woman who yearns to act on stage in a time when only men and boys could appear. Eventually she will play the part of Juliet to young Will Shakespeare's own performance as Romeo (by this point the play's title and plot have been changed to the more famous version). The film starts with a suitably romantic shot of the Rose Theatre, lyrical music accompanying the camera's slow descent through the open roof of the sixteenth-century theatre. But a caption thrusts the audience back into the 1990s, telling it that while Richard Burbage's company plays on the northern side of the Thames, 'South of the river was the competition, built by Philip Henslowe, a businessman with a cash flow problem.' This importation of neoliberal jargon into Elizabethan times is only one of the many consciously embedded anachronisms in the play: Shakespeare, for example, tells a boat ferryman to 'Follow that boat!'; he visits the Elizabethan version of a psychoanalyst to overcome writer's block; when a tongue-tied Henslowe stammers 'The show must', Shakespeare provides the hoary stage punch line, 'Go on!' Where *Braveheart* rode roughshod over historical niceties, *Shakespeare in Love* revels in historical absurdities and conscious errors. It also brings to the Elizabethan theatre the mentality of the 1990s: when Fennyman the Money Lender works out the production costs for *Ethel, the Pirate's Daughter* in such a way that the actors and author will not get paid, he explains that they will be given 'a share of the profits'. When Henslowe tells him 'There's never any', he replies blithely, 'Of course not.' This interchange exposes the venality and cynicism of the theatre, and, by implication, its contemporary equivalent, the film industry.

The action in the film, especially the blossoming romance between Shakespeare and Viola, increasingly parallels the plot of *Romeo and Juliet*, Stoppard and Norman also playing with the film audience's recognition of this and other pieces of 'Shakespeareiana'. At one point Shakespeare tosses away a screwed-up page that lands next to a skull clearly emblematic of *Hamlet*; another time a rejected piece of paper falls into a casket, suggesting *The Merchant of Venice*, at another moment we see a mug with the logo 'A Present from Stratford Upon Avon'; in the street Shakespeare hears people call out phrases such as 'a plague on both their houses' that he will use in his own plays. This meta-textual playfulness underpins an interchange on creativity between the pragmatic Henslowe and the acquisitive Fennyman:

> Henslowe: The natural condition [of the theatre business] is one of insurmountable obstacles on the road to imminent disaster.
> Fennyman: So what do we do?
> Henslowe: Nothing. Strangely it all works out well.
> Fennyman: How?
> Henslowe: I don't know. It's a mystery.

This timeless verity rings true for *Ethel, The Pirate's Daughter*. Yet, as theatre owner, Henslowe is also under the age-old necessity to turn a profit, advising Shakespeare that he, Henslowe, knows what the audience wants – 'love and a bit with a dog', the Elizabethan equivalent of the genre text.

The film plays fast and loose with Shakespeare's early life, presenting him not as the young literary genius, but as a bumbling, barely competent scribbler and chancer in a London theatre world dominated by the virile creativity of Christopher Marlowe. In a chance meeting with Marlowe that exposes *Ethel, the Pirate's Daughter* for the crock it is, Marlowe casually provides Shakespeare with motivations and plot lines he will incorporate into the final version of the play. Historicising 'Shakespeare' the brand by portraying him through much of the film as flawed and human, *Shakespeare in Love* restores him to the status of timeless genius at the film's end. In the world of the film's action, Viola must do her duty as a rich, young noble women, and marry the deplorable Lord Wessex, who is bound for the new colony of Virginia. Before she does so, she gets to play Juliet to Shakespeare's Romeo in a performance that displays their genuine love and the play's capacity to 'show the very truth and nature of love'. While Viola becomes Wessex's bride and departs for Virginia, in the process of Shakespeare writing the play and falling in love with her she becomes his sought-after muse. Imagining her being shipwrecked on the voyage to Virginia supplies the plot line for *Twelfth Night*. He promises her that she will never age for him, while she pleads: 'Write me well.' The film that begins by undercutting the audience's sense of the loftiness of the Elizabethan theatre and Shakespeare's talent and reputation ends with conscious evocation of a classic Hollywood romantic finale. While *Shakespeare in Love* indulges in postmodern playfulness, the film must also make money, the uplifting payoff being Viola walking into the distance to the sound of trumpets and strings.

Shakespeare in Love exemplifies many of the forces at work in 1990s Britain. Simultaneously historically nostalgic and casually postmodern, it exhibits – in the casting of Gwyneth Paltrow as Viola and Ben Affleck in the minor part of the vainglorious actor Ned Alleyn – a revealing weakness for the celebrity American actors can bring. The film's American financing, its American co-writer and the American market the film clearly aimed at (and successfully charmed), expose where cultural dominance rested in the last decade of the twentieth century, something that had not been the case, in literary terms, until well after the Second World War. The foregrounding of economic imperatives in the exchanges between Henslowe and Fennyman locates the play temporally in the amoral and finance-determined world of the decade. The comic focus on Shakespeare as a potential brand, both within his own time and (more overtly) the time the film was released, emphasises the commodification of culture that the film exposes, mocks and (for all its satirical undertone) partly celebrates. The film is also striking, given all its qualities as unapologetically light entertainment, for ambition and confidence, the scope of its concerns and the verve with which it undertakes and completes the tasks it sets for itself. In this it reflects a broader cultural confidence detectable in the imaginative variety and adventure of fantasy and speculative writing in the 1990s, work that could range from boy wizards to aliens, from fairy tales to particle physics.

Note

1. Available at <http://www.haddonstuff.f9.co.uk/A%20Few%20Notes%20on%20the%20Culture.pdf> (last accessed 12 May 2017).

Conclusion: Endings and Beginnings

Will it work? Of course. Will it be ready on time? Certainly. Probably. Maybe. The Government is prepared to throw as much money into the hole as it takes (around £758 million and rising). They can't fail. This is their Big Idea. The vision thing made manifest. A celebration of that which is to come (with heavily edited highlights of whatever has been achieved in the last thousand years of human history that is not offensive to BT, Manpower, Marks and Spencer, Sky, Tesco, McDonald's and anybody else prepared to chip in £12 million). (Sinclair 1999: 14)

Noam Chomsky declares in *Deterring Democracy* that 'History does not come neatly packaged into distinct periods, but by imposing a structure upon it, we can sometimes gain clarity without doing too much violence to the facts' (Chomsky 1992: 1). Looking back on the 1990s, it seems clear that the Britain Margaret Thatcher led in January 1990 was strikingly different from that which, on 31 December 1999, projected forward with vitality and confidence. There were salient points of difference between Thatcher's Britain and Blair's, in terms of stance towards the outside world, the internal configuration of the nations of Great Britain and Northern Ireland, the perception that, by the end of the decade, Britain was culturally on the rise, and the possibility that chicken tikka masala might have assumed a place as the national dish. With its then still new, young leader, a reasonable simulacrum of the United States' Bill Clinton, Britain economically and politically was a global player. The decade also was a notable period culturally, as this study has attempted to show. It was a time of literary experimentation and innovation, one that built substantially on the advances of the 1980s, so that writers who had emerged and quickly dominated that decade, such as Salman Rushdie, Jeanette Winterson and Martin Amis, were part of a more diverse and broadly activated cultural scene in the 1990s. The decade had its failures and its false dawns ('Cool Britannia'; the 'New Generation Poets', perhaps; and, by 1999, the project of New Labour), but it also heralded genuine new talents and perspectives in fiction, drama and poetry: Sarah Kane, Mark Ravenhill, Simon Armitage, Jackie Kay and Irvine Welsh, among many others. Henry Perowne's early twenty-first-century assessment, in Ian McEwan's *Saturday*, that the nineties was 'an innocent decade' in the post-9/11 world in which *Saturday* is set, itself now seems a tad smug. Perhaps every previous decade looks a little innocent in the light of current experience.

As he left Downing Street to watch the New Year's Day millennium parade in Whitehall on the final day of the 1990s, the profoundly popular Prime Minister Tony Blair commented: 'What struck me both last night and again today is this real sense of confidence and optimism. You just want to bottle it and keep it.'[1] Blair was, in typical fashion, accentuating for effect, but he also was detecting, and to some extent channelling, an atmosphere that was suitably positive and energetic for a nation and indeed a world on the edge of a new century, a new millennium. Cycles of history were ending, which meant the prospect of beginnings, a form of global New Year's Resolution. Not all the signs were positive and energetic – they never are – an ironic example being the structure specifically constructed to assess the past, review the present and project into the future: the purpose-built Millennium Dome, situated on the banks of the nation's greatest river, the Thames. Peter Brooke, the national heritage secretary, had proposed an exhibition to mark the end of the millennium in 1992, a Millennium Commission being set up under John Major in 1994. As noted in Chapter 4, specific money was set aside by the National Lottery to finance the venture. Iain Sinclair's sardonic take (above) on the still incomplete Millennium Dome in the May 1999 number of the *London Review of Books* was one of many attacks on the Dome's empty, self-congratulating symbolism. The Dome, to be opened on 1 January 2000, did not want for detractors, although, for its supporters, including Tony Blair, it was an uplifting statement, a symbol of the history, hopes and dreams of the nation, a nation expanding and improving. The Dome was meant to provide a modern-day exhibition that would foreground British innovation, daring and vitality in the 1990s, qualities aligned with New Britain and Cool Britannia. In sections such as 'Who We Are', 'What We Do' and 'Where We Live', the Dome aspired to tell Britain's story and give a foretaste of where that narrative might lead. It was hoped that, as with other historical exhibitions, the material on display within the Dome would advertise enterprise in its various forms. In the event, the Dome presented a rather lamely branded 'Millennium Experience', one that attracted less than half the expected visitors in 2000.

If the Millennium Dome would prove something of a national flop in 2000, the failure of another Millennium-branded phenomenon to occur was cause for global celebration. The concept of the millennium itself, of course, and with it the division of centuries and decades that help to delineate the 1990s, were determined by Western, Christian calendars. 31 December 1999, was the last night of the 1990s, if we assume that a term such as 'the nineties' only makes sense of the years beginning with 1990 and ending with 1999. But the end of the second millennium technically would not occur until 31 December 2000. The proper dating of the end of the century and the millennium was an occasional point of public discussion and pedantry during the nineties, but in fact the dating had enormous, and unprecedented, implications. This was made clear once a circumstance understood primarily by the cybernetically minded was transmitted more generally: many computer programs had been constructed to register dates in terms of days, months and years, with two figures for each division: DDMMYY. This formulation was adopted to cut costs, as it saved the endless, and it was thought, needless, repetition of the 19 in 1990, 1991, 1992, etc. But such programs theoretically could not distinguish between 1900 and 2000, both being represented in the DDMMYY formulation as 00. The problem had been pointed out as early as the culturally ominous year of 1984, in a book with the suitably ill-omened title *Computers in Crisis: How to Avert the Coming Worldwide Computer Systems Meltdown*. Not wishing to miss out on the revival of interest in the phenomenon, the book was rereleased in 1996 as the *Year 2000 Computing Crisis*. By 1999 the potential dilemma had its own horror movie title, 'The Millennium Bug', and a catchier brand name, 'Y2K' (for Year 2000). The decade's addiction to branding could even incorporate a potential global disaster.

The nightmare scenario was that computer-controlled machinery and systems would fail because of the impossibility of distinguishing between 1900 and 2000, precipitating a global domino effect over twenty-four hours as each successive time zone moved from 1999 to 2000, and 'entered', or failed to enter, the twenty-first century. Planes dependent on computers might fall from the sky once their systems failed, or global banking would go into freefall, activating a planetary economic crisis. The BBC website contained a 'Y2K: The Millennium Bug' page that allowed readers the opportunity to click on countries around the world in order to get national predictions of the repercussions. The site noted that 'Estimates of the damage that could be caused ranged from global meltdown to mild irritation.'[2] Typical of the fears was a 15 March 1999 report in the American journal *The Nation*:

Most worrisome, because of their vast potential for destruction, are the world's nuclear weapons and nuclear power plants. For if the interconnected system collapses and cascades into systemic infrastructure failures, power and communications could be lost worldwide. Restoration may be delayed or even impossible in a world where everything else has snapped to a halt. In the chaos and confusion that would follow no one knows what would happen to nuclear bombs and nuclear reactors. In the truly worst-case scenario, accidental nuclear war and/or reactor meltdowns could release enough deadly radioactivity to return the planet to the insects.[3]

Time, literally, would prove wrong any projections of the death of humanity, and the Millennium Bug – like the Millennium Dome – had far less impact than had been predicted. Blair's optimism on New Year's Eve, even if excessive, was not entirely erroneous. If the end of the nineties was not the last day before disaster, it was also, in many ways, an obvious advance on the beginning of the nineties.

How to summarise what had happened in Britain over the decade that preceded the national and global non-event of the Millennium Bug? George Orwell, the author quoted fondly by John Major, had argued the critical importance of nationalism; that while Britain as a nation is changing, it is always coherent. One of the key developments the decade activated was rethinking about the United Kingdom as a united nation. The change was made manifest in the devolution of political power in the late 1990s through independent assemblies in Scotland, Wales and Northern Ireland, even if relationships between these bodies and a still-dominant Westminster were sometimes tense and mutually suspicious. But this political devolution lagged behind a cultural devolution that was already under way at the start of the decade. The most obvious expression of this independence occurred in Scotland, where the literary renaissance of the 1980s developed confidently and variously in the 1990s, writers as expansive and revelatory as Irvine Welsh, A. L. Kennedy, Alan Warner, Jackie Kay and Iain Banks adding to a swelling Scottish chorus that could include James Kelman's defiant challenge to Standard English orthodoxy at the Booker Prize. The changes in Wales were less widespread or dynamic, admittedly, but examples such as the flourishing of Gwyneth Lewis's bilingual poetry, the international success of the Welsh-language film *Hed Wyn*, and the establishment of the Welsh Book of the Year award were signs of a revived cultural confidence. Given the dire state of affairs in Northern Ireland at the start of 1990, the advances in the political circumstances were astonishing. Substantive problems and animosities were still in play by the decade's end, but novels such as *Eureka Street* and *Fat Lad*, and films such as *The Crying Game*, explored with clear and generous eyes the complex human dimensions of an evolving, but discernibly improving, situation, one almost unimaginable at the start of the decade. Britain, then, was demonstrably a less 'united' kingdom in 1999, but only in the superficial and stifling sense of united as something uniform. Power was not diminished, merely dispersed.

A key element of the nation's increasing heterogeneity was the slow, but continuing, improvement in circumstances politically, economically and especially culturally of first, second and third generation Britons, whose presence and engagement in British society was helping to transform it. As with, say, the case of Northern Ireland, it is important not to fall for an idealised take on reality, to believe that problems and prejudices evaporated. The Rushdie Affair alone was proof of contentious and ongoing complexities. But if fish and chips had been supplanted as the national dish; if young writers originally from St Kitts and Guyana could be elected Fellows of the Royal Society of Literature; if a television series mocking racial and ethnic stereotypes from all angles could be a hit; and if the fiftieth anniversary of the arrival of a ship carrying migrants from the West Indies could be celebrated by the Prince of Wales, something substantial was changing in terms of the makeup and outlook of British identity. And despite John Major's despairing call for a move 'back to basics', the decade was also one of more liberal and liberating attitudes to gender and sexuality. The nineties was a more liberated decade than the eighties, so that 'girls who are boys who like boys to be girls' could be celebrated, and films on the conflict in Northern Ireland could simultaneously explore the hidden complications of desire. The popular phenomena of Chick Lit and Lad Lit presented the ordinary comedy of sex, along with the hardiness of traditional sexual roles. The decade also witnessed an increased willingness to explore the darker sides of sexuality, where money, power and passion might create disturbed and disturbing scenarios that playwrights, novelists and poets confronted with a bold, unrelenting honesty that challenged rather than comforted or entertained.

The myth of socio-economic equality, of a 'classless society' put forward by both main political parties and achieved by neither, was one of the more intriguing aspects of a Britain that had in part been reshaped forcefully by overt class conflict under Margaret Thatcher. Notions of class proved far more resilient than might have been assumed in a country won over to a vision of New Britain in which, to borrow from New Labour's 1997 campaign song, 'Things Can Only Get Better'. For many, of course, despite the gloss, things stayed much the same, or got worse, while for others the allure of 'Megabucks. Wages. Interest. Wealth' proved illusory. Entrenched class antagonisms did not vanish, as the speaker of Simon Armitage's 'Great Sporting Moments' announced with passion and wit. For less eloquent characters such as Kelman's Sammy Samuels, resistant self-preservation to the prevailing class structure is success enough, requiring ingenuity and courage and dogged persistence. The largely empty and disingenuous rhetoric of classlessness masked the ongoing dominance of the few, a dominance at times encoded into the celebrated culture that also marked the nineties. A Britain in which a princess killed in a car crash and a tiger shark in a tank of formaldehyde could be iconic was in thrall to thrills and surfaces and the pervasive commodification of culture. Writers as different as Salman Rushdie and J. K. Rowling experienced the sometimes-brutal allure celebrity fosters, while the rise of literary prizes marked the perceived need to ensure public and media interest in a crowded and noisy cultural market. It seemed to work, and in a decade when the competition included Princess Di, the Spice Girls and David Beckham, that was no small success.

As the decade hurtled towards its conclusion, with consumerism, individualism and the attendant always-in-the-moment narcissism to the fore, literature offered an important and accepted counterblast by reviewing and representing the past; or, in an age of postmodern scepticism, the 'pasts'. If Britain as a geographical and political entity was more devolved at the end of the decade than at the beginning, the awareness of history was in many ways more complex and deep. Some of the acknowledged interest in history (real and fictionalised) derived from the almost unprecedented coincidence of the end of the decade, century and millennium. The past mattered, but what also was clear was that, rather than the more univocal histories of yore, historical writing in the nineties reflected and reinforced an awareness of the polyphonous nature of the past, and of the ways in which certain voices had been silenced, or had gone unheard. History writing in the 1990s could attend to facticity of history while also employing an array of aesthetic tools to complicate any simple reading of the past. Readers were encouraged and perhaps required not simply to read about the past, but also to reflect on their own understanding of history, and the potential deficiencies and blind spots of that understanding. Novels such as Martin Amis's *Time's Arrow*, Adam Thorpe's *Ulverton* or A. S. Byatt's *Possession* revealed and explored the constructed nature of historical thinking and writing, while more realistic works such as Pat Barker's *Regeneration* trilogy and Sebastian Faulks's *Birdsong* endeavoured to place readers within an historical setting without immersing them so deeply that readers failed to engage with the informed contemplation of the lessons history might teach. This intricate mix of reality and fiction that historical works produced in the 1990s was amply complemented by the acknowledged diversity and quality of speculative writing, in the broad sense. Such work encompassed the science fiction of Iain M. Banks and the fictional science of Jeanette Winterson or Tom Stoppard. Other forms of fantasy such as Harry Potter and the works of Philip Pullman offered alternative realms of being and existing especially but not exclusively for the young, or the young at heart. Ebooks, increasingly accessible over the equally fantastic social media network, initiated new forms of reading and access to available material. Despite the jeremiads about the death of the book in an age of shrinking attention spans, literature retained its significance as public utterance.

Literature produced in the 1990s itself was distinctive, energetic and stimulating, registering the explosion of creative talent and a healthy, active group of readers and viewers celebrating the imaginative zest that in part came from the vivid and vital place of the fantastic in the public imagination. Hindsight's 20/20 vision teaches us that the fears imagined by the prospect of the Millennium Bug and the hopes manufactured by the Millennium Dome would prove illusory. This book has tried to argue that the 1990s was a decade of substantive literary, social and political invention and transformation, and that while certain established forces remained, emerging energies propelled the long cultural devolution that was such an important dynamic of the decade – a dynamic that continued, slowly, perhaps, but inexorably. For all that dynamism, it seems appropriate in a conclusion about beginnings and endings, or endings and beginnings, that potentially the future of the planet, let alone of Britain, appeared to hang in very precarious balance. Would the Millennium Dome get to open? And, if it did, would its ultimate success or failure reveal something substantive and true about the state of contemporary Britain? Far more importantly for Britain and the world beyond, would the Millennium Bug begin the process that would return the planet to the insects, with planes falling from the sky and nuclear missiles being launched automatically on a helpless humanity? As the last seconds of the 1990s ticked away, it was impossible for anyone in Britain to know for certain.

Notes

1. https://www.theguardian.com/world/2000/jan/02/millennium.uk6 (Accessed May 15, 2017)
2. http://news.bbc.co.uk/hi/english/static/millennium_bug/countries/us.stm (Accessed September 10, 2016)
3. https://www.thenation.com/article/nightmare-scenario/ (Accessed September 10, 2016)

Bibliography

Adonis, Andrew and Stephen Pollard (1997), *A Class Act: The Myth of Britain's Classless Society*, London: Penguin.
Alvi, Moniza (2000), *Carrying My Wife*, Newcastle: Bloodaxe.
Amis, Martin (1991a), *Time's Arrow, or the Nature of the Offence*, London: Jonathan Cape.
Amis, Martin (1991b), 'Return of the Male', *London Review of Books*, 5 December, pp. 3–5.
Amis, Martin (2000), *Experience*, London: Jonathan Cape.
Anderson, Benedict (1983), *Imagined Communities: Reflections on the Origin and Spread of Nationalism*, Cambridge: Verso.
Appignanesi, Lisa and Sara Maitland (eds) (1990), *The Rushdie File*, Syracuse: Syracuse University Press.
Armitage, Simon (2001), *Selected Poems*, London: Faber & Faber.
Ashcroft, Bill, Gareth Griffiths and Helen Tiffen (1989), *The Empire Writes Back: Theory and Practice in Post-colonial Literatures*, London: Routledge.
Aston, Elaine (2013), 'Feeling the Loss of Feminism: Sarah Kane's *Blasted* and an Experiential Genealogy of Contemporary Women's Playwriting', in Penny Farfan and Lesley Ferris (eds), *Contemporary Women Playwrights: Into the Twenty-First Century*, London: Palgrave Macmillan.
Auden, W. H. (1950), *Collected Shorter Poems 1930–1944*, London: Faber & Faber.
Baker, Kenneth (1993), *The Turbulent Years: My Life in Politics*, London: Faber & Faber.
Banks, Iain M. (1996), *Excession*, London: Orbit.
Barker, Pat (1991), *Regeneration*, London: Viking Press.
Bassnett, Susan (ed.) (2003), *Studying British Cultures: An Introduction*, second edition, London: Routledge.
Bell, Eleanor and Gavin Miller (eds) (2006), *Scotland in Theory: Reflections in Culture and Literature*, Amsterdam: Rodopi.
Bentley, Nick (ed.) (2005), *British Fiction of the 1990s*, Abingdon, Oxon: Routledge.
Bhabha, Homi (1994), *The Location of Culture*, New York: Routledge.
Bhaskar, Sanjeev, Meera Syal and Anil Gupta (1998–2001), 'Goodness Gracious Me', BBC.

Birkerts, Sven (1994), *The Gutenberg Elegies: The Fate of Reading in an Electronic Age*, London: Penguin.
Blur (1995), 'Girls and Boys', from Parklife.
Boyle, Danny (dir.) (1996), *Trainspotting*, Channel Four Films et al.
Brooker, Joseph (2010), *Literature of the 1980s: After the Watershed*, Edinburgh: Edinburgh University Press.
Button, Virginia (1997), *The Turner Prize*, London: Tate Gallery Publishing.
Byatt, A. S. (1990), *Possession: A Romance*, London: Chatto and Windus.
Cannadine, David (1983), 'The Context, Performance and Meaning of Ritual: The British Monarch and the "Invention of Tradition", c.1820–1977', in Eric Hobsbawm and Terence Ranger (eds), *The Invention of Tradition*, Cambridge: Cambridge University Press.
Cannadine, David (1999), *The Rise and Fall of Class in Britain*, New York: Columbia University Press.
Cattaneo, Peter (dir.) (1997), *The Full Monty*, Red Wave Films et al.
Chomsky, Noam (1992), *Deterring Democracy*, London: Vintage.
Choy, Jung Min (1997), 'Racist Ontology, Inferiorization, and Assimilation', in Eric Mark Kramer (ed.), *Postmodernism and Race*, Westport: Preager, pp. 115–28.
Craig, Cairns (1999), *The Modern Scottish Novel: Narrative and the National Imagination*, Edinburgh: Edinburgh University Press.
Craig, Cairns (2006), 'Devolving the Scottish Novel', in James P. English (ed.), *A Concise Companion to Contemporary British Fiction*, Oxford: Blackwell Publishing, pp. 121–40.
Crawford, Robert (1996), *Masculinity*, London: Cape.
Dabydeen, David (1990), 'On Not Being Milton: Nigger Talk in England Today', in Christopher Ricks and Leonard Michaels (eds), *The State of the Language*, Berkeley: University of California Press, pp. 3–14.
Dabydeen, David (1995), Interview with Felicity Head, *Links and Letters*, 2, pp. 79–86.
De Groot, Jerome (2010), *The Historical Novel*, Oxford: Routledge.
Duffy, Carol Ann (1994), *Selected Poems*, London: Penguin.
Duffy, Carol Ann (1999), *The World's Wife*, London: Picador.
English, James P. (2005), *The Economy of Prestige: Prizes, Awards and the Circulation of Cultural Value*, Cambridge, MA: Harvard University Press.
English, James P. (2006), 'Introduction: British Fiction in a Global Frame', in James P. English (ed.), *A Concise Companion to Contemporary British Fiction*, Oxford: Blackwell Publishing, pp. 1–18.
English, James P. and John Frow, (2006), 'Literary Authorship and Celebrity Culture', in James P. English (ed.), *A Concise Companion to Contemporary British Fiction*, Oxford: Blackwell Publishing, pp. 39–57.
English, Richard (2003), *Armed Struggle: The History of the IRA*, London: Macmillan.
Evans, Richard J. (1997), *In Defence of History*, London: Granta.
Faludi, Susan (1991), *Backlash: The Undeclared War against American Women*, New York: Crown.
Faulks, Sebastian [1993] (1997), *Birdsong*, London: Vintage.
Ferguson, Neil (1998), *The Pity of War: Explaining World War One*, London: Allen Lane.

Fielding, Helen (1996), *Bridget Jones's Diary*, London: Picador.
Fukuyama, Francis (1989), 'The End of History?', *National Interest*, 16 (Summer), pp. 3–18.
Fukuyama, Francis (1992), *The End of History and the Last Man*, New York: Avon Books.
Gibson, Mel (dir.) (1995), *Braveheart*, Icon Entertainment International et al.
Gilroy, Paul (2000), 'Cruciality and the Frog's Perspective', in James Procter (ed.), *Writing Black Britain, 1948–1998: An Interdisciplinary Anthology*, Manchester: Manchester University Press, pp. 307–19.
Gilroy, Paul (2002), *There Ain't No Black in the Union Jack: The Cultural Politics of Race and Nation*, Routledge Classic edition, New York: Routledge.
Gleick, James (1987), *Chaos: Making a New Science*, London: William Heinemann.
Godber, John (1995), *Lucky Sods and Passion Killers*, London: Bloomsbury.
Gramich, Katie (2003), 'Cymru or Wales: Explorations in a Divided Sensibility', in Susan Bassnett (ed.), *Studying English Cultures*, London: Routledge, pp. 97–112.
Hall, Stuart (1990), 'Cultural Identity and Diaspora', in Jonathan Rutherford (ed.), *Identity: Community, Culture, Difference*, London: Lawrence and Wishart, pp. 222–38.
Hall, Stuart (1996), 'New Ethnicities', in David Morley and Kuan-Hsing Chen (eds), *Stuart Hall: Critical Dialogues in Cultural Studies*, London: Routledge, pp. 442–9.
Harris, Anita (ed.) (2004), *All about the Girl: Culture, Power and Identity*, New York: Routledge.
Head, Dominic (2002), *The Cambridge Introduction to Modern British Fiction, 1950–2000*, Cambridge: Cambridge University Press.
Heaney, Seamus (2000), *Beowulf: A New Verse Translation*, New York: W. W. Norton.
Heidemann, Birte (2016), *Post-Agreement Northern Irish Literature: Lost in a Liminal Space?*, London: Palgrave Macmillan.
Hitchens, Christopher (2002), *Why Orwell Matters*, New York: Basic Books.
Hollinghurst, Alan (1994), *The Folding Star*, London, Vintage.
Hornby, Nick (1995), *High Fidelity*, London: Victor Gollancz.
Huggan, Graham (1997), 'Prizing Otherness: A Short History of the Booker', *Studies in the Novel: Postcolonialism, History and the Novel*, 29: 3 (Fall), pp. 412–33.
Hughes, Ted (1997), *Tales from Ovid: Twenty-Four Passages from the Metamorphoses*, London: Faber & Faber.
Hulse Michael, David Kennedy and David Morley (eds) (1993), *The New Poetry*, Newcastle: Bloodaxe.
Hutcheon, Linda (1988), *A Poetics of Postmodernism: History, Theory, Fiction*, London: Routledge.
Hutton, Will (1996), *The State We're In*, revised edition, London: Vintage.
Jackson, Ben and Robert Saunders (eds) (2012), *Making Thatcher's Britain*, Cambridge: Cambridge University Press.
Janik, Del Ivan (1995), 'No End of History: Evidence from the Contemporary English Novel', *Twentieth Century Literature*, 42: 1 (Summer), pp. 160–89.
Jones, Gwyneth (1991), *White Queen*, London: Victor Gollancz.

Jones, Owen (2011), *Chavs: The Demonization of the Working Class*, Cambridge: Verso.
Jones, Tudor (1996), *Remaking the Labour Party: From Gaitskell to Blair*, London: Routledge.
Jordan, Neil (dir.) (1992), *The Crying Game*, Palace Pictures and Channel Four Films.
Kane, Sarah (2011), *Blasted*, London: Bloomsbury.
Kay, Jackie (1993), *Other Lovers*, Newcastle: Bloodaxe.
Kelman, James (1994), *How Late it Was, How Late*, London: Martin Secker and Warburg.
Kennedy, A. L. (1993), *Looking for the Possible Dance*, London: Vintage.
Kennedy-Andrews, Elmer (2008), *Writing Home: Poetry and Place in Northern Ireland, 1968–2008*, Suffolk: Boydell and Brewer.
King, Bruce (2004), *The Oxford English Literary History, Vol. 13, 1948–2000: The Internationalization of English Literature*, Oxford: Oxford University Press.
Korte, Barbara and Eva Ulrike Pirker (2011), *Black History White History: Britain's Cultural Programme between Windrush and Wilberforce*, Bielefeld, Germany: Transcript Verlag.
Kravitz, Peter (1997), 'Introduction', *The Picador Book of Contemporary Scottish Fiction*, London: Picador, pp. xi–xxxvi.
Kureishi, Hanif (1990), *The Buddha of Suburbia*, London: Faber & Faber.
Lawton, David (1993), *Blasphemy*, Philadelphia: University of Pennsylvania Press.
Ledent, Bénédicte (1995), 'Overlapping Territories, Intertwined Histories: Cross-Culturality in Caryl Philips's *Crossing the River*', *Journal of Commonwealth Literature*, 30: 1, pp. 55–62.
Leigh, Mike (dir.) (1993), *Naked*, Thin Man Films et al.
Levi, Primo (1995), *The Reawakening*, New York: Touchstone.
Lewis, Gwyneth (1995), *Parables & Faxes*, Newcastle: Bloodaxe.
Lewis, Gwyneth (1998), *Zero Gravity*, Newcastle: Bloodaxe.
Loach, Ken (dir.) (1998), *My Name is Joe*, Alta Films et al.
Longley, Michael (1999), *Selected Poems*, Winston-Salem: Wake Forest University Press.
Luckhurst, Roger (2005), 'British Science Fiction in the 1990s: Politics and Genre', in Nick Bentley (ed.), *British Fiction of the 1990s*, Abingdon, Oxon: Routledge, pp. 78–91.
McArthur, Brian (1998), *Requiem: Princess of Wales 1961–1997 – Memories and Tributes*, New York: Arcade.
McEwan, Ian (1997), *Enduring Love*, London: Vintage.
McEwan, Ian (2005), *Saturday*, London: Vintage.
McLean, Iain (2007), 'The National Question', in Anthony Seldon (ed.), *Blair's Britain 1997–2007*, Cambridge: Cambridge University Press, pp. 487–508.
McRobbie, Angela (2009), *The Aftermath of Feminism: Gender, Culture and Social Change*, London: Sage.
Madden, John (dir.) (1998), *Shakespeare in Love*, Universal Pictures, et al.
Malik, Kenan (2013), 'Foreword', in Robert Eaglestone and Martin McQuillian (eds), *Salman Rushdie: Contemporary Critical Perspectives*, London: Bloomsbury, pp. vii–x.

Marber, Patrick (1997), *Closer*, London: Methuen Drama.
Marwick, Arthur (1995), 'Two Approaches to Historical Study: The Metaphysical (Including "Postmodernism") and the Historical', *Journal of Contemporary History*, 30: 1, pp. 5–35.
Marwick, Arthur (2000), *A History of the Modern British Isles, 1914–1999: Circumstances, Events, Outcomes*, Oxford: Oxford University Press.
Marwick, Arthur (2007), 'Class', in Paul Addison and Harriet Jones (eds), *A Companion to Contemporary Britain 1939–2000*, Oxford: Blackwell Publishing, pp. 76–92.
Millar, Frank (2007). 'Ireland: The Peace Process', in Anthony Seldon (ed.), *Blair's Britain 1997–2007*, Cambridge: Cambridge University Press, pp. 509–28.
Mitchell, James (2009), *Devolution in the UK*, Manchester: Manchester University Press.
Montague, John (1993), *Time in Armagh*, Loughcrew, County Meath: Gallery Books.
Nairn, Tom (1977), *The Break-up of Britain: Crisis and Neo-nationalism*, London: NLB.
Nairn, Tom (2006), 'Break-up: Twenty Five Years On', in Eleanor Bell and Gavin Miller (eds), *Scotland in Theory: Reflections in Culture and Literature*, Amsterdam: Rodopi, pp. 17–34.
Newbolt, Sir Henry (2014), 'Vitaï Lampada', in Jon Stallworthy (ed.), *The New Oxford Book of War Poetry*, Oxford: Oxford University Press, p. 151.
Newell, Mike (dir.) (1994), *Four Weddings and a Funeral*, Polygram Filmed Entertainment et al.
O'Brien, Sean (1998), *The Deregulated Muse*, Newcastle: Bloodaxe.
Orwell, George (1998), 'The Lion and the Unicorn: Socialism and the English Genius', in Peter Davison (ed.), *The Complete Works of George Orwell, Vol 12, A Patriot After All, 1940–1941*, London: Secker and Warburg, pp. 391–434.
Paterson, Don (1993), *Nil Nil*, London: Faber & Faber.
Patterson, Glenn (1992), *Fat Lad*, London: Chatto and Windus.
Paxman, Jeremy (1998), *The English: A Portrait of a People*, London: Penguin.
Philips, Caryl (1993), *Crossing the River*, London: Bloomsbury.
Pipes, Daniel (1999), *The Rushdie Affair: The Novel, The Ayatollah, and The West*, New Brunswick, NJ: Transaction Publishers.
Poole, Richard (1995), 'Gwyneth Lewis talks to Richard Poole', *Poetry Wales*, 31: 2, pp. 24–9.
Powell, Enoch (2001), 'Rivers of Blood', *The Occidental Quarterly: Western Perspectives on Man, Culture and Politics*, 1: 1 (Fall), pp. 13–18.
Procter, James (ed.) (2000), *Writing Black Britain, 1948–1998: An Interdisciplinary Anthology*, Manchester: Manchester University Press.
Pullman, Philip (1995), *The Northern Lights*, London: Scholastic Point.
Ranger, Terence and Eric Hobsbawm (eds) (1983), *The Invention of Tradition*, Cambridge: Cambridge University Press.
Ravenhill, Mark (2001), *Plays: 1*, London: Bloomsbury Methuen Drama.
Rebellato, Dan (2001), 'Introduction', in Mark Ravenhill, *Plays: 1*, London: Bloomsbury Methuen Drama.
Robbins, Keith (1988), *Nineteenth-century Britain: Integration and Diversity*, Oxford: Clarendon Press.

Rojek, Chris (2007), *Britmyth: Who Do the British Think They Are?*, London: Reaktion.
Rushdie, Salman (1991), *Imaginary Homelands: Essays and Criticism, 1981–1991*, New York: Granta Books.
Rushdie, Salman (2012), *Joseph Anton: A Memoir*, New York: Random House.
Rushdie, Salman (1995), *The Moor's Last Sigh*, London: Jonathan Cape.
Scruton, Roger (2000), *England: An Elegy*, London: Chatto and Windus.
Sheridan, Jim (dir.) (1993), *In the Name of the Father*, Hell's Kitchen Pictures and Universal Studios.
Sierz, Aleks (2001), *In-Yer-Face Theatre: British Drama Today*, London: Faber & Faber.
Sinclair, Iain (1999), 'All Change. This Train is Cancelled', *London Review of Books*, 21: 10, pp. 14–18.
Spice Girls (1997), *Girl Power: The Official Book by the 'Spice Girls'*, London: Andre Deutsch.
Stephenson, Heidi and Natasha Langridge (1997), *Rage and Reason: Women Playwrights on Playwriting*, London: Methuen.
Stevenson, Randall (2004), *The Oxford English Literary History, Volume 12. 1960–2000, The Last of England?*, Oxford: Oxford University Press.
Stone, Oliver (dir.) (1987), *Wall Street*, Twentieth Century Fox Film Corporation et al.
Stoppard, Tom (2000), *Plays 5: Arcadia, The Real Thing, Night & Day, Indian Ink, Hapgood*, London: Faber & Faber.
Suaerberg, Lars Ole (2001), *Intercultural Voices in Contemporary British Literature*, London: Palgrave.
Taft, Jessica K. (2004), 'Girl Power Politics: Pop Culture Barriers and Organizational Resistance', in Anita Harris (ed.), *All about the Girl: Culture, Power and Identity*, London: Routledge, pp. 69–78.
Thorpe, Adam (1992), *Ulverton*, London: Minerva.
Thorpe, Adam (2015), 'History with the Shatter-Marks: Adam Thorpe in Conversation with Natasha Alden', in Alexander McFie (ed.), *The Fiction of History*, Abingdon: Routledge, pp. 193–205.
Todd, Richard (1996), *Consuming Fictions: The Booker Prize and British Literature Today*, London: Bloomsbury.
Turner, Alwyn W. (2013), *A Classless Society: Britain in the 1990s*, London: Aurum Press.
Turner, Paul (dir.) (1992), *Hedd Wyn*, Pendeifg Ty Cefn and SC4.
Upshal, David (Producer) (1998), *Windrush*, Episode 1, 'Arrival', BBC 2. Broadcast 30 May.
Urban, Ken (2011), 'Commentary', in Sarah Kane, *Blasted*, London: Bloomsbury, pp. 63–113.
Wallace, Gavin and Randall Stevenson (eds) (1993), *The Scottish Novel since the Seventies: New Visions, Old Dreams*, Edinburgh: Edinburgh University Press.
Walters, Wendy (2005), *At Home in Diaspora: Black International Writing*, Minneapolis: University of Minnesota Press.
Warner, Alan [1995] (2015), *Morvern Callar*, London: Vintage.
Waugh, Patricia (2005), 'Science and Fiction in the 1990s', in Nick Bentley (ed.), *British Fiction of the 1990s*, Abingdon, Oxon: Routledge, pp. 57–77.

Wells, H. G. (1938), *World Brain*, London: Methuen.
Welsh, Irvine (1993), *Trainspotting*, London: Minerva.
White, Hayden [1995] (2002), 'The Historical Text as Literary Fact', in Brian Richardson (ed.), *Narrative Dynamics: Essays on Time, Plot, Closure and Frames*, Columbus: Ohio State University Press, pp. 191–210.
Williams, Nerys (2003), 'Gwyneth Lewis: Blasphemy, Taboo and Testing Bilingualism', *Poetry Wales*, 38: 3, pp. 1–12.
Williams, Patrick and Laura Chrisman (eds) (1994), 'Preface', in Patrick Williams and Laura Chrisman (eds), *Colonial Discourse and Post-Colonial Theory: A Reader*, New York: Columbia University Press, pp. ix–x.
Wilson, Robert McLiam [1996] (2015), *Eureka Street: A Novel of Ireland Like No Other*, New York: Arcade Publishing.
Winterson, Jeanette (1991), *Written on the Body*, London: Vintage.
Winterson, Jeanette (1995), *Art & Lies: A Piece for Three Voices and a Bawd*, London: Vintage.
Winterson, Jeanette (1997), *Gut Symmetries*, London: Granta Books.
Woolf, Virginia (1967), 'The Leaning Tower', in Leonard Woolf (ed.), *Virginia Woolf: Collected Essays, Vol. 2*, London: Chatto and Windus, pp. 162–81.
Worpole, Ken (2001), 'Cartels and Lotteries: Heritage and Cultural Policy in Britain', in David Morley and Keith Robbins (eds), *British Cultural Studies: Geography, Nationality, Identity*, Oxford: Oxford University Press, pp. 235–48.
Zangen, Britta (2003), 'Women as Readers, Writers and Judges: The Controversy About the Booker Prize for Fiction', *Women's Studies*, 32: 3, pp. 281–99.

Index

Academy Awards, 30, 34
Acheson, Dean, 21
Adonis, Andrew and Stephen Pollard, 14, 97, 111–13, 204
   A Class Act: The Myth of Britain's Classless Society, 97
Affleck, Ben, 195
Albarn, Damon, 132, 145
Alvi, Moniza, 12, 50, 59, 60–1, 129
   A Bowl of Warm Air, 60
   Carrying My Wife, 59–60
   The Country on My Shoulder, 59
   'The Double City', 60
   'I Would Like to Be A Dot In A Painting by Miró', 59
Amis, Kingsley, 16, 131, 146–7
Amis, Martin, 7, 16–17, 19, 69, 88–9, 125, 129, 131–2, 145–8, 158–61, 175, 179, 197, 202
   Experience, 146
   The Information, 16, 145
   London Fields, 132
   Money: A Suicide Note, 145
   The Rachel Papers, 145
   Times Arrow: Or the Nature of the Offence, 17, 145, 158–61, 175, 179, 202
Anderson, Benedict, 12, 50
Angry Young Men, 75
Ankersmit, Frank, 157
Armitage, Simon, 7, 118, 129, 198, 201
   'Great Sporting Moments: The Treble', 118, 121, 201

Ashcroft, Bill, Gareth Griffith and Helen Tiffen, 51–2
   The Empire Writes Back: Theory and Practice in Post-Colonial Literatures, 51–2
   The Post-Colonial Studies Reader, 52
Aston, Elaine, 73–4
Auden, W. H., 'Funeral Blues', 93
Austen, Jane, 85, 173
   Pride and Prejudice, 85

BAFTA, 34
Baker, Kenneth, 3
Ballard, J. G., *Crash*, 123
Balsom, Denis, 26–7
Banks, Iain M., 10, 18, 182–3, 200, 203
   Consider Phlebas, 182–3
   Culture series, 182–3
   Excession, 18–19, 183
Barddas Press, *Counting One and One as Three*, 28
Barings Bank, 126
Barker, Pat, 17, 69, 129, 150, 158, 161–4, 166–7, 170, 202
   Regeneration, 150, 161–4, 170
   The Regeneration Trilogy, 17, 139, 158, 161, 166–7, 202
Barnes, Julian, 42–5, 125, 129, 145
   England, England, 43–5
   A History of the World in 10½ Chapters, 158–9
Barthes, Roland, 161
Battle of Passchendaele, 30

Battle of Stirling Bridge, 155
BBC, 139
Beatles, The, 55, 90, 131–2, 148
Beckham, Victoria, 117–18
Berlin Wall, 5, 156
Berners-Lee, Tim, 174
Betjeman, John, 147
Bhabha, Homi, *The Location of Culture*, 51
Birkerts, Sven, 15, 179
   The Gutenberg Elegies: The Fate of Reading in an Electronic Age, 15
Blair, Leo, 3
Blair, Tony, 3–4, 6, 8, 14, 19, 22–3, 25, 50, 95, 97–8, 117–18, 123–4, 129–30, 154, 182, 197–8, 200
Bloodaxe Press, 28, 58
Bloomsbury Publishing, 179
Blur, 134
   'Country House', 132
   'Girls and Boys', 12, 71, 81, 201
   The Great Escape, 132
   Parklife, 132
Bly, Robert, *Iron John: A Book About Men*, 87–9
Bond, James, 88–9
Book Sellers Association, The, 125
Booker Prize, 8, 16, 61, 93, 107–9, 137–46, 161, 200
Bourdieu, Pierre, *The Field of Cultural Production*, 137–8
Boyle, Danny, 39, 40, 134
Bragg, Melvin, *The South Bank Show*, 129
Brassed Off, 112
Britain's Book Awards Children's Book of the Year, 179
British Gas, 97
British Nationality Act of 1948, 46
British Telecom, 97
Britpop, 6, 9, 12, 44, 129, 131–2, 134, 148
Brooke, Peter, 198
Brooker, Joseph, *Literature of the 1980s: After the Watershed*, 5
Brookner, Anita, 143
Brosnan, Pierce, *Goldeneye*, 89

Brown, Cedric, 97
Brown, Gordon, 3–4, 6, 8
Brown, Melanie, 134
BSkyB, 125
Button, Virginia, 137
Byatt, A. S., 146
   Possession: A Romance, 18, 139–40, 146, 152, 159, 170–3, 192, 202

Cairns, Craig, 34–5
   History of Scottish Literature, 35
Callaghan, James, 2, 23, 98
Cambridge University, 7, 28, 62–3, 99
Campaign, 135
Cannadine, David, 150, 155
   The Rise and Fall of Class in Britain, 96–8
Canterbury Tales, The, 141
Cape, Jonathan, 145
Carey, Peter, 138
Carron, Owen, 24
Channel 4, 49, 139,
Chaos theory, 18–19, 76, 176–7, 189, 190–1
Chekhov, Anton, 4
   Three Sisters, 104
Chick Lit, 6, 72, 85, 201
Chicken tikka masala, 11, 48, 197
China, 11, 45
Chomsky, Noam, *Deterring Democracy*, 197
Choy, Jung Min, 56
Christie, Linford, 48
Churchill, Winston, 21, 113, 154, 160
Class, 2–3, 8, 12, 14–15, 30–1, 379, 41, 43, 50, 53, 66, 69, 76, 79, 90, 93, 95–101, 103, 105–21, 126, 131–2, 139, 141–2, 152, 158, 162–4, 186, 201–2
Clause IV, 6, 154
CNN, 124
Cocker, Jarvis, 131
Coetzee, J. M., 138
   Disgrace, 138–9
Cold War, 5, 21, 23, 151, 154, 156

Computers in Crisis: How to Avert the Coming Worldwide Computer Systems Meltdown, 199
Condon, Paul, 49, 61
Connery, Sean, *Thunderball*, 89
Connolly, Cressida, 175–6, 186
Conrad, Joseph, 4, 64
  Heart of Darkness, 64
Conservative Group for Europe, 5
Conservative Party, 1–4, 6, 14, 23, 26, 34, 45, 73, 96, 154
Cook, Robin, 11, 48
Cool Britannia, 9, 19, 129–33, 148, 154, 197, 198
Crawford, Robert, 'Male Infertility', 88–9
  Masculinity, 88
Cronenberg, David, *Crash*, 123
Cunningham, Valentine, 141
Curtis, Richard
  Four Weddings and a Funeral, 14, 93
  Notting Hill, 93

Dabydeen, David, 12, 50, 63–5, 69, 142
  The Black Presence in English Literature, 63
  Black Writers in Britain 1760–1890, 63
  Disappearance, 65
  The Intended, 64
  'On Not Being Milton: Nigger Talk in England Today', 64
  Slave Song, 64
  'Song of the Creole Gang Women', 142
Daily Mail, The, 4, 7
Daily Telegraph, The, 124
Daniels, Phil, 132
Davidson, Jaye, 34
Dawes, Kwame, *Progeny of Air*, 144
Dawkins, Richard, *The Blind Watchmaker*, 176
Day-Lewis, Daniel, 33
De Groot, Jerome, 150
De Man, Paul, 161

Del Amitri, 134
Derrida, Jacques, 161
Devolution, 6, 9, 11, 23, 25, 45
Dimbleby, David, *Charles: The Private Man, The Public Role*, 128
Downing Street Declaration, 25
Doyle, Roddy, *Paddy Clarke Ha Ha Ha*, 138
Duffy, Carol Ann, 7, 13–14, 36–7, 74, 95–6, 100, 129, 144
  'Making Money', 14, 96, 100
  Mean Times, 144
  'Originally', 36
  The World's Wife, 74
Dunmore, Helen, *A Spell for Winter*, 143
Duran, Jane, *Breathe Now, Breathe*, 144

Eagleton, Terry, 147
Eastwood, Clint, 33
Eckhart, Aaron, 172
Economist, The, 130
Edinburgh, 38–9, 41, 58, 108, 134, 162, 179
Edwards, Paul, 63
Einstein, Albert, 176, 186–9, 191
Eliot, T. S., *The Wasteland*, 191
Emin, Tracey, 6, 131, 135
Enfield, Harry, 126
English, James, 22, 34, 126, 137–9
Enitharmon Press, 144–5
Eno, Brian, 134
Estuary English, 118–19
European Union, 22, 44
Evans, Ellis, 29–30
Evans, Richard J., *In Defence of History*, 157
Exchange Rate Mechanism, 1

Faber & Faber, 144
Facebook, 80
Faludi, Susan, *Backlash: The Undeclared War against American Women*, 86
Faulkner, William, *As I Lay Dying*, 141

Faulks, Sebastian, 17, 158, 164–7, 202
  Birdsong, 17, 152, 158, 164–7, 172, 202
Feminism, 8, 72, 74–5, 86–7, 89
Ferguson, Niall
  The Pity of War, 166–7
  Virtual History: Alternatives and Counterfactuals, 160, 167
Fermat's Last Theorem, 176
Fettes College, 3, 118
Fielding, Helen, *Bridget Jones's Diary*, 72, 75, 85–7
Fleming, Ian, 89, 137
Forster, E. M., 138, 173
Forward Poetry Prize, 16, 28, 119, 144, 148
Frow, John, 126, 141
Fukuyama, Francis, 5, 7, 17, 157
  The End of History and the Last Man, 5
Full Monty, The, 112

Gallagher, Liam, 133
Gallagher, Noel, 131–2
Galloway, Janice, 34
Gee, Maggie, 145
Gibson, Mel, 10, 36, 155
  Braveheart, 10, 36, 38–40, 154–5, 194
Gilroy, Paul, 11, 49
  There Ain't No Black in the Union Jack, 69–70
Ginger Spice, 133
Gleick, James, *Chaos: Making a New Science*, 176–7, 189, 192
Godber, John, *Lucky Sods*, 15, 113–17
Gomer Press, 27–8
Good Friday Agreement, 23, 25, 156
Goodness Gracious Me!, 12, 56–8
Gould, Stephen J., *Bully for Brontosaurus*, 176
Gow, Ian, 25
Gramich, Katie, 25–6
Granta, 7, 69, 129
Graves, Robert, 162, 163

Gray, Alasdair, 10, 34–5
  Lanark: A Book in Four Lives, 10, 34
Greer, Germaine, 139, 143
Guildford Four, 33
Guinness Peat Aviation Book Award, 33
Gunn, Neil, 34–5
Gunn, Thom, *Man with Night Sweats, The*, 144

Hall, Stuart, 12, 26, 49, 51, 56, 67
Halliwell, Geri, 133–4
Hare, David, 76
Harper Collins, 124, 145
Harris, Robert, *Fatherland*, 160
Harrison, George, 55
Harrison, Tony, 99
Harvey, Marcus, 'Myra', 136
Hawking, Stephen, 186
  A Brief History of Time: From the Big Bang to Black Holes, 176
Hawthorn, Geoffrey, *Plausible Worlds: Possibility and Understanding in History and the Social Sciences*, 160
Hawthornden Prize, 144
Head, Dominic, 14, 91
Heaney, Seamus, 173
  Beowulf, 153, 155–6
Heath, Edward, 2
Hedd Wyn, 29–30, 155
Heidemann, Birte, 32
Hell's Kitchen Films, 33
Heseltine, Michael, 3
Highlands, 22, 36, 38–9
Hirst, Damian, 6, 16, 131–2
  'The Acquired Ability to Escape', 135
  'Freeze', 135
  'Mother and Child Divided', 135–6
  'The Physical Impossibility of Death in the Mind of Someone Living', 135
  'Thousand Years', 135
Hitchens, Christopher, 6, 180
HIV/AIDS, 13, 93, 128
Hobsbawm, Eric, 155

Hodge, John, 40
Hollinghurst, Alan, *The Folding Star*, 13, 92–3, 144
Homer, 141, 156
  Illiad, 156
Hong Kong, 11, 45, 152
Hornby, Nick, 129
  Fever Pitch, 87
  High Fidelity, 13, 72, 87
Howe, Geoffrey, 1–2, 4
Huggan, Graham, 137–8, 142
Hughes, Ted, 147–8, 153
  Birthday Letters, 16, 17, 144, 148
  Tales of Ovid, 153
Hull Truck Theatre, 113–14
Hulme, Kerry, 138
Hulse, Michael, David Kennedy and David Morley, *The New Poetry*, 98
Hurd, Douglas, 3–4, 141
Hutcheon, Linda, *A Poetics of Postmodernism: History, Theory, Fiction*, 158
Hutton, Will, 104
  The State We're In, 101

Iggy Pop, 134
  'Lust for Life', 39
Independent, The, 22, 85, 99, 129, 141
'Invention of Tradition', 155
In-Yer-Face Theatre, 7, 72, 75–6, 80, 94, 130
IRA, 24–5, 32–3, 34
Irish Free State, 152
Ishiguro, Kazuo, 129
Izzard, Eddie, 131

Jacobsen, Howard, 139
James Tait Black Memorial Prize, 69, 92, 144
Jameson, Fredric, 161
Janik, Ivan Del, 161
Jardine, Lisa, 147
Jenkins, Simon, 108
Jones, Gwyneth, *White Queen*, 19–20, 179, 183–4
Jones, Owen, 14
Jones, Tudor, 6

Jordan, Neil
  The Crying Game, 14, 33–4, 93, 200
  Mona Lisa, 33
Joyce, James, *Ulysses*, 153–4

Kane, Sarah, 13, 19, 90, 152, 198
  Blasted, 7, 13, 72–7, 79, 85, 105
Kavanagh, Pat, 125, 145
Kay, Jackie, 12, 58–9, 198, 200
  The Adoption Papers, 58
  'In My Country', 58
  Other Lovers, 58
Kelman, James, 19, 34–5, 38, 42, 148, 200, 202
  A Disaffection, 144
  How Late It Was, How Late, 8, 10, 15–16, 107–9, 138, 140–2, 144
Keneally, Thomas, 138
Kennedy, A. L., 8, 10, 20, 34, 58, 89, 129, 141, 200
  Looking for the Possible Dance, 40–1
Kennedy-Andrews, Elmer, 31
Khomeini, Ayatollah, 4
King, Bruce, 12, 47, 50
King, Sir Bernard, 1
King, Stephen, 180
Kinnock, Neil, 3, 6
Kipling, Rudyard, *The Jungle Book*, 54
Kravitz, Peter, 35–6, 41, 45
Kristol, Irving, *National Interest, The*, 5
Kureishi, Hanif, 12, 52–4, 58, 129
  My Beautiful Laundrette, 53
  The Buddha of Suburbia, 12, 53–6
Kyd, Thomas, *Spanish Tragedy, The*, 152

Labour Party, 3–4, 6, 9, 14, 23, 25, 34, 76, 96, 101, 124, 132, 135, 154, 182, 207
LaButte, Neil, *Possession*, 172–3
Lad Lit, 72, 87, 201
Larkin, Philip, 16, 131, 146–8
  Selected Letters of Philip Larkin 1940-1985, 147

Lawrence, Stephen, 12, 49, 61, 136
Lawson, Nigella, 141
Lawton, David, *Blasphemy*, 62–3
Ledent, Bénédicte, 69
Leeson, Nick, 126
Leigh, Mike, 111–12
  Naked, 112
Levi, Primo
  If This Is a Man, 159
  The Reawakening, 159
Lewis, C. S., *Chronicles of Narnia*, 177, 178, 180
Lewis, Gwyneth, 10, 35, 64, 200
  Parables & Faxes, 28
  Sonedua Redsa, 28
  'Welsh Espionage', 29, 37
  Zero Gravity, 28
Lezard, Nicholas, 141
Loach, Ken
  Ladybird, Ladybird, 111
  My Name is Joe, 15, 111
  Raining Stones, 15, 111
  Riff-Raff, 111
Loaded, 8, 87
Lodge, David, *Thinks*, 175
London Review of Books, 198
Longley, Michael, 'Ceasefire', 156
Loren, Sophia and Peter Sellers, *The Millionairess*, 56
Luckhurst, Roger, 175, 178
  'British Science Fiction in the 1990s: Politics and Genre', 175

MacDiarmid, Hugh, 34
McDonald, Trevor, 48
McEwan, Ian, 145, 148,
  Amsterdam, 16, 141–2
  Atonement, 142
  Enduring Love, 141–2, 175–6, 187
  Saturday, 20, 198
McGregor, Ewan, *The Phantom Menace*, 126
McLean, Iain, 25
McNeil, Helen, 145
McRobbie, Angela, 74–5, 85
Madden, John, *Shakespeare In Love*, 18, 152, 193–5

Major, John, 1–3, 6–9, 13–14, 21–6, 42, 45, 48, 56, 73, 93, 95–8, 112, 115, 130, 154, 182, 198, 200–1
Major-Ball, Thomas, 2
Malik, Kenan, 62
Marber, Patrick, 91
  Closer, 13, 75, 80–5
Marlowe, Christopher, 195
Marwick, Arthur, 97, 121, 157
Maxim, 8, 87
Men Behaving Badly, 13
Mengele, Josef, 159
Metafictional, 17, 90, 158
Millar, Frank, 25
Millennium Bug (Y2K Bug), 20, 199–200, 203
Millennium Commission, 198
Millennium Dome, 20, 198–200, 203
Milton, John, 64
  Paradise Lost, 181
Mitchell, James, 22, 27
Montague, John
  Time in Armagh, 168
  'A Welcoming Party', 168
Monty Python's Life of Brian, 62
Morton, Andrew, *Diana: Her True Story*, 128
Motion, Andrew, 147–8
  Larkin: A Writer's Life, 147
Murdoch, Iris, 131
Murdoch, Rupert, 124–5
My Left Foot, 33

Nairn, Tom, *The Break-up of Britain: Crisis and Neo-nationalism*, 9
Nation, The, 199–200
National Eisteddfod, 27, 30, 155
  Urdd National Eisteddfod, 28
National Lottery, 15, 95, 112–17, 198
Nationalism, 9, 11, 22, 36, 154, 200
Net Book Agreement, 125
Neuberger, Rabbi Julia, 108–9, 141
New Brutalism, 13, 72
New Generation Poets, 7, 60, 119, 129, 148, 197
New Labour, 4, 6, 8, 11, 19, 22–3, 44, 97, 124, 130–1, 154, 178, 182, 197, 201

New Labour, New Life for Britain, 4
'Things Can Only Get Better', 201
New Lad, 7
New Man, 7–8, 72, 87–9
New York Review of Books, 180
New York Times, The, 86, 108, 130, 145, 146, 179
New Yorker, 123
Newbolt, Henry, *Vitaï Lampada*, 2
Newell, Mike, *Four Weddings and a Funeral*, 14, 93
News Corporation, 124
Norman, Mark, 193–4

Oasis, 131–2
O'Brien, Sean, 36
  'Cousin Coat', 99–100
Ofili, Chris
  'The Holy Virgin Mary', 136
  'No Woman No Cry', 136
Okri, Ben, *The Famished Road*, 138, 145
Oldman, Gary, *Nil By Mouth*, 112
Ondaatje, Michael, *The English Patient*, 138–9
Orange Network, 143
Orange Prize, 16, 27, 142–4
Orton, Joe, 131
Orwell, George, 6, 9, 22, 55, 138, 154, 200
  'The Lion and the Unicorn: Socialism and the English Genius', 23, 42, 98
Ovid, *Metamorphoses*, 153
Owen, Agnes, 10
Owen, Wilfred, 158, 162, 166
Oxford University, 2–3, 7, 26, 28, 65, 118, 130, 141, 167, 181–2
  Christ Church College, 181
Oxford University Press, 144

Paltrow, Gwyneth, 140, 173, 193, 195
Parker, Charlie, 33
Parker Bowles, Camilla, 128
Parris, Matthew, 73

Paterson, Don, 129
  'An Elliptical Stylus', 119–20
  Nil Nil, 119
Patterson, Glenn, *Fat Lad*, 32–3, 200
Paulin, Tom, 139, 147
Paxman, Jeremy, *The English: A Portrait of a People*, 42
Peepal Tree, 144–5
Phillips, Caryl, 12, 50
  Cambridge, 66
  Crossing the River, 66–9, 158
  The Final Passage, 66
  Higher Ground, 66
Picador, 144
  The Picador Book of Contemporary Scottish Fiction, 35
Pinter, Harold, 131
Pipes, Daniel, 62–3
Pirker, Eva Ulrike, 47–8, 150
Plath, Sylvia, 16, 147–8
  The Bell Jar, 148
  Collected Poems, 148
Plutarch, 191
Poetry Book Society, 119, 148
Poetry Society, The, 7, 98, 129
  'New Generation', 60
  The Poetry Review, 7, 60, 129
Poll Tax, 23–4
Posh and Becks, 15, 134
Post-colonialism, 51–2
Post-feminism, 72, 74, 75, 83, 85, 86, 90
Postlethwaite, Pete, 33
Postmodern history, 17, 157–8, 177
Potter, Harry, 6, 15, 18, 130, 177–82, 203
Powell, Anthony, *A Dance to the Music of Time*, 182
Powell, Enoch, 69
  'Rivers of Blood', 47
Prescott, John, 6, 14, 96, 114
Primal Scream, 134
Prince Charles, 47, 123, 127–8, 201
Princess Diana, 15–16, 95, 123–4, 127–8
Private Eye, 124
Prix Goncourt, 137, 139–40
Proust, Marcel, 137

Pullman, Philip, 178, 203
  The Amber Spyglass, 181
  Northern Lights, 178, 181–2
  The Subtle Knife, 181
Pulp, 131, 134
  'Common People' 131
  'Mile End', 131
  'Sorted out for E's & Wizz', 131

Queen Elizabeth I, 129

Ravenhill, Mark, 152, 198
  Shopping and Fucking, 7, 13, 72, 79–80, 82, 85, 91, 101–6, 111, 126
Rea, Stephen, 34
Reagan, Ronald, 21
Redwood, John, 26
Reed, Lou, 134
Reynolds, Albert, 25
Richardson, Miranda, 34
Rivers, W. H. R., 158, 161–3
Robbins, Keith, 27
Rogue Trader, 126
Rojek, Chris, 22, 131
Rolling Stones, The, 132
Rosenthal, Norman, 136
Rowling, J. K., 15, 126, 129, 130, 178–82, 202
Roy, Arundhati, *The God of Small Things*, 138
Royal Academy of Art, 136
Royal Opera House, 113
Royal Society of Literature, 69
Rushdie, Salman, 4–5, 7, 12, 18–19, 49–52, 61–3, 69, 123, 127, 129, 131, 138, 145–6, 158, 175, 179, 184–5, 197, 202, 204, 207–9
  The Ground Beneath Her Feet, 127
  Midnight's Children, 49, 61, 138, 158, 185
  The Moor's Last Sigh, 18, 127, 175, 184
  The Satanic Verses, 4–5, 49, 61–3, 127
  'Why I have Embraced Islam', 5
Rushdie Affair, 5, 11, 15, 49, 52, 61, 201

Russell, Bertrand, 162
Ryland, Mark, 152

Saatchi, Charles, 131, 135
Saatchi Gallery, 135
Said, Edward, *Orientalism*, 51
Saltire Society Scottish First Book Award, 58
Sands, Bobby, 24
Sassoon, Siegfried, 158, 162–4, 170
  'Finished With the War: A Soldier's Declaration', 162
Schabowski, Günter, 156
Science fiction, 18–19, 174–5, 179, 181–3, 203
Scott, Paul, 138
Scott, Ridley, *Blade Runner*, 133
Scott, Walter, 34
Scottish Arts Council Book Award, 58
Scottish National Party, 34, 36, 155
Scruton, Roger, *England: An Elegy*, 42–3, 45
Section 28 of the Local Government Act of 1988, 13, 71, 73
Self, Will, 141
September 11, 2001, 157
Seren Press, 27
Shakespeare, William, 6, 173, 180, 191, 193–5
  Antony and Cleopatra, 191
  Hamlet, 152, 194
  Macbeth, 141
  The Merchant of Venice, 194
  Titus Andronicus, 78, 152
  Twelfth Night, 195
Shakespeare's Globe Theatre, 152, 173
Sheridan, Jim, *In the Name of the Father*, 33
Sieghart, William, 144
Sierz, Aleks, 72, 80
Sinclair, Iain, 197–8
Sky TV, 125
Smarties Book Prize Gold Medal, 179
Smith, Chris, 48
Smith, John, 3

Spice Girls, 6, 13, 71, 74, 89–90, 132–4, 202
   Forever, 134
   'Girl Power', 6, 71–2, 74, 89, 90, 133
   Spice, 134
   Spice Girls, 90
   'Spice up Your Life', 133
   Spiceworld, 133
   'Wannabee', 71
Spivak, Gayatri Chakravorty, 'Can the Subaltern Speak?', 51
SS Empire Windrush, 11, 47–8
Standard English, 10, 39, 41, 200
Stevenson, Randall, 125
Stirling University, 58
Stoker, Bram, 175
Stone, Oliver, *Wall Street*, 16, 125–6
Stoppard, Tom, 174, 179, 203
   Arcadia, 19, 76, 175–7, 188–93
   The Invention of Love, 76
   Rosencrantz and Guildenstern Are Dead, 193
   Shakespeare In Love, 18, 152, 193–5
Suede, 131, 134
Suez Crisis, The, 21
Sun, The, 124
Sunday Times, The, 128
Sunday Times Young Writer of the Year Award, 69
Swift, Graham, 148
   Last Orders, 16, 139–41

T. S. Eliot Prize for Poetry, 148
Taft, Jessica, 89
Tan, Amy, 143
Tate Gallery, 113
Texas, 134
Thatcher, Dennis, 2
Thatcher, Margaret, 1–4, 21–4, 95–7, 101, 118, 123, 126, 134, 147, 154, 182, 197, 201
Thatcherism, 2, 6, 96, 121
Thomas, R. S., 25–6
Thompson, Emma, 33
Thorpe, Adam, *Ulverton*, 18, 152–3, 168–70, 172–3, 202
'Three Wales Model', 26

Todd, Richard, *Consuming Fictions: The Booker Prize and British Literature Today*, 35, 140, 145–6
Trevor-Roper, Hugh, 155
Troubles, The, 9, 24, 31–2, 34, 156, 168
Turk, Gavin, 135
Turner, Alwyn, *A Classless Society: Britain in the 1990s*, 73, 95–6, 117
Turner, Ted, CNN, 124
Turner Prize, 136–7, 139
Twentieth Century Fox, 124
Tyler, Anne, 143

U2, 131
Universal Pictures, 33
University of Edinburgh, 144
University of Wales Press, 27

Virgil, *Aeneid*, 47
Vogue, 7, 129

Wales Book of the Year, 8, 27, 144–5
Wallace, Gavin, 36, 39
Walters, Wendy, 68
Wanamaker, Sam, 152
Warner, Alan, 10, 14, 34, 41–2, 200
Waterstones, 125, 106, 125
Waugh, Auberon, 143
Waugh, Patricia, 175
Weevil, Assia, 147
Wells, H. G., 174, 175–7, 180, 183, 189
   The Time Machine, 174–5, 177, 189
Welsh, Irvine, 6–10, 20–1, 32, 35, 105–8, 134, 198, 200
   Trainspotting, 6, 10, 15, 22, 25, 37–42, 106, 126, 134
Welsh British Academy Film Awards, 30
Welsh Language Act, 10, 27
Westwood, Vivian, 131
Whitbread Best Novel, 4
Whitbread Book of the Year, 153
White, Hayden, 151, 157
White, Michael, 154

Whiteread, Rachel, 6, 135–6
  'House', 136
Whittaker, Forrest, 33–4
'Whose Heritage? The Impact of Cultural Diversity on Britain's Living Heritage', 48, 50
Wiggins, Marianne, 4, 143
William Hill Sports Book of the Year, 87
Williams, Patrick and Laura Chrisman, *Colonial Discourse and Post-Colonial Theory: A Reader*, 52
Williams, Raymond, 5, 29
Wilson, A. N., 141
Wilson, Robert McLiam, *Eureka Street: A Novel of Ireland Like No Other*, 15, 24–5, 31–2, 109–11, 200
Winstone, Ray, 112
Winterson, Jeanette
  Art & Lies: A Piece for Three Voices and a Bawd, 91
  Gut Symmetries, 19, 175, 185–6, 188, 192
  Oranges Are Not the Only Fruit, 90, 185
  The Passion, 90, 185
  Sexing the Cherry, 90, 185
  Written on the Body, 13, 90–1, 93
Woolf, Virginia, 98–9, 173
  'The Leaning Tower', 98
World Wide Web, 18, 80, 174–5, 178
Worpole, Ken, 113
Wright, Ian, 48
Wylie, Andrew, 125, 145–6

Year 2000 Computing Crisis, 199
Young British Artists, 6, 9, 16, 44, 76, 129, 134
  'Sensation', 135

Zephaniah, Benjamin, 'What Stephen Lawrence Has Taught Us', 49–50, 61

EU representative:
Easy Access System Europe
Mustamäe tee 50, 10621 Tallinn, Estonia
Gpsr.requests@easproject.com

www.ingramcontent.com/pod-product-compliance
Lightning Source LLC
Chambersburg PA
CBHW071840230426
43671CB00012B/2013